ECONOMICS

A Comprehensive Approach for GCSE

BELL & HYMAN

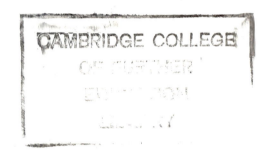
Published by
BELL & HYMAN
an imprint of Unwin Hyman Limited
Denmark House
37–39 Queen Elizabeth Street
London SE1 2QB

British Library Cataloguing in Publication Data
Curry, Paul
  GCSE economics.
  1. Economics
  I. Title
  330   HB171.5

ISBN 0–7135–2697–1

Designed and edited by Impression

Typeset in Great Britain by August Filmsetting,
Haydock, St Helens

Printed in Great Britain by
R. J. Acford Limited, Chichester

CONTENTS

PART 1

PART 2

PREFACE

This book has been written as a result of the experience gained through fourteen years teaching experience and also involvement in devising the GCSE Economics syllabus and specimen exam. paper with the London and East Anglia Group.

It has been compiled in two parts. The first covers largely descriptive topics and lays down the foundations of the subject. The second covers the more advanced analytical topics. The language used in both parts is designed to be simple enough to provide access for a wide range of abilities. The text coverage is comprehensive and written with reference to all regional examination board syllabi in GCSE Economics.

There are a number of Case Studies in the text which can provide the basis for GCSE assignments. The 'Things to Do' sections test a variety of skills relating to comprehension, application, manipulation of data, investigation and evaluation. The examination questions largely refer to the regional GCSE sample papers approved by the Secondary Examinations Council.

Paul Curry

ACKNOWLEDGEMENTS

The author and the publishers wish to thank the following for permission to reproduce illustrations:

Mick Gowar 1.1a, 1.1b, 14.20
Michael Sones 1.2a, 1.5b, 1.6, 1.7, 3.10a, 3.10b, 5.12, 5.13, 5.14, 5.16, 6.1, 6.3, 6.8a, 8.2a, 8.10, 10.5a, 10.12a, 10.12b, 10.12c, 12.10, 14.19, 15.9, 16.9
OXFAM 2.2d (Mick Rogers), 2.3 (M. Almond), 2.9b (Bill Wise), 2.10a (Karen Twining), 2.10b, 2.10c, 2.10d (Jeremy Hartley), 2.12 (Bridie Russell)
Panos Pictures 2.7 (Sean Sprague), 7.16a (Mark Edwards), 7.16b (Mark Edwards), 7.16c (Sean Sprague)
Ford Motor Company Limited 3.1, 10.14a
The Mary Evans Picture Library 5.5, 7.6b, 9.1, 9.2, 14.13a
Lloyds Bank Limited 5.6, 5.7, 5.15
George Williams 5.11
Asda 6.2b
Brent Cross Shopping Centre 6.4b (Dennis Bunn)
The Health Education Council 6.8b, 7.3
The Family Planning Association 7.1b
Stefano Cagnoni (Report, London) 9.5
F. R. Curry 10.4a, 10.4b, 10.13
The Cambridge Committee for Aerial Photography © Crown Copyright 10.11
London Docklands Development Corporation 10.16
The BBC Hulton Picture Library 14.3b, 14.3c
Shell Photographic Centre 15.5
The EC Commission 15.13, 15.14
The London Stock Exchange 16.4, 16.6
The Bank of England 16.11

Cover photo from the Art Directors Photo Library
Acknowledgements are also due to the following sources from which illustrations have been adapted:

Massachusetts Institute of Technology 1.3
The Sunday Times 3.3
Regional Trends 1982, Regional Profiles 7.2, 7.8, 7.12, 10.8a, 10.8b
1981 Census 7.9
New Earnings Survey 1985 9.17
Independent Chartered Surveyors 10.16e
The Treasury (© Crown copyright) 12.3, 12.9
Customs and Excise Department 12.8
Inland Revenue 12.9
OECD 12.9, 15.10
© Crown Copyright 1983 *Economic Progress Report* 14.4b
Department of Employment 14.6, 14.10
Employment Gazette 14.16
The Financial Times 15.12
The Stock Exchange 16.5

The following examination boards are thanked for permission to reproduce questions:

The Northern Examining Group; The London and East Anglian Examining Group; The Midland Group; The Southern Group; The Welsh Group.

We also wish to thank all the newspapers and companies who courteously allowed us to reproduce articles and information. We have failed to trace the copyright holders for some illustrations despite every effort.

PART 1

1

WHAT IS ECONOMICS ALL ABOUT?

INTRODUCTION – SATISFYING OUR WANTS

Imagine someone said to you that they would give you three wishes for the possessions you would most like to have and money was no object. It would not take long to think of some desirable possessions: perhaps a sports car, a large house in the country with a swimming pool, a video recorder, a holiday abroad, and so on. But would you always be content with your three items? Probably not. Some would wear out sooner or later (a holiday abroad would wear out very quickly!) and it would not take you long to think of at least three more items you would like to own. In addition, new goods would probably come onto the market to continually whet your appetite. The fact is that our **wants** are almost unlimited and we never seem to be totally satisfied with what we have got. There is always something more we would like. For people in rich countries it may mean wanting a bigger house or car; for people in poor countries it may mean wanting more food in order to stay alive, or a better shelter.

Can our wants be satisfied? If you go back to your original list of three wishes, how many of them do you really think you will obtain? The sad fact is that we cannot all have as much as we want and this is not just a question of money. The government could print more money for everyone but if there were no more goods in the shops all that would happen would be prices would rise. The real problem is that there are a limited number of goods available to buy and this is in turn because there are strictly limited resources available in the world from which goods can be produced.

THE FACTORS OF PRODUCTION

The resources we have available are called the **factors of production** in Economics. They comprise land, labour, capital and enterprise.

Land includes all the natural resources of the world which can be found on and below the ground, and in and beneath seas and rivers. Land is very much fixed in quantity and the raw materials extracted from it, unless recycled, will eventually run out. Examples of this factor might be iron ore, North Sea oil, fish and agricultural products.

Labour comprises all the work performed by human beings whether skilled, unskilled, manual or 'white collar' (Fig. 1.1a). People who are unemployed are still counted as being part of the labour force since they could work if required to do so.

Capital (often referred to as **capital goods**), is perhaps the most difficult factor to explain but nevertheless probably the most important. Capital goods are anything which makes the production of other goods easier. For example, the production of agricultural goods is made much easier by the use of tractors and other farm machinery which are referred to as capital goods. In manufacturing, capital goods are vital for production. They might cover anything from factory buildings to plant, machinery, computers and word processors (Fig. 1.1b overleaf). Without capital, producing any goods would be very difficult, if not impossible, and often the more capital goods a country has the richer it becomes.

To make goods the above factors need to be combined together and the person who does this is known as the **entrepreneur**. Such a person is more than just a businessperson since the entrepreneur is a risk taker. The business he or she may set up could fail, involving considerable personal financial loss. Certainly the entrepreneur has to be able to organise the production process and establish a market for the product. Without such risk takers, the production of goods would be hard to imagine. Sometimes this fourth factor is simply called **enterprise**.

Fig. 1.1a (left)   Skilled labour at work in a printing firm – negatives being checked.
Fig. 1.1b (overleaf)   An example of a capital good – machine being set up for volume binding of documents

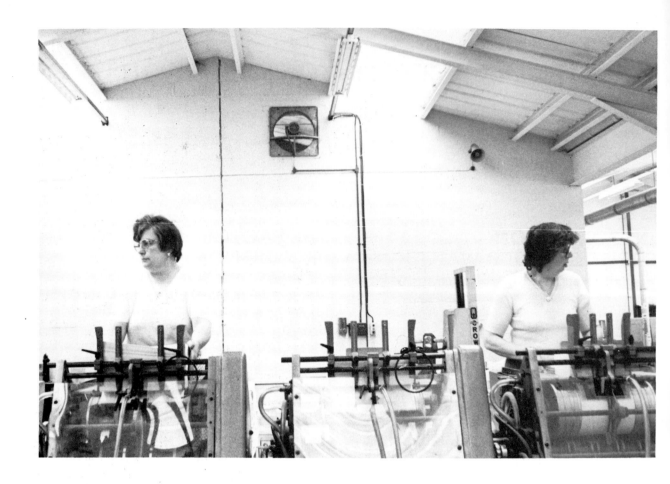

CONSUMER AND CAPITAL GOODS

Combining the factors of production can lead to two types of goods which are very important to distinguish. The goods which directly satisfy our wants and give us pleasure are called **consumer** goods. They would certainly appear on your list of three desirable items and could also include clothes, records, food, drink, etc.

Capital goods, however, do not by themselves give a lot of pleasure but are vital in the process of producing consumer goods and, indeed, other capital goods (Fig. 1.1b). It is hard to imagine for example anyone wanting a cement mixer as a present but such a machine is vital to the production of cement which in turn may be used to build houses which are consumer goods. Thus without capital goods it is very difficult to produce consumer goods.

Some goods can act as both consumer and capital goods. A computer used at home to play games is very much a consumer good but when used at work, for example in stock control, functions as a capital good. Similarly a fiction book will give pleasure and acts as a consumer good, whilst a repair manual book aids in the mending of items and is regarded as a capital good.

THE ECONOMIC PROBLEM

The factors of production are strictly limited in quantity compared to our wants. Even the factor labour, which may appear abundant because of increasing world population, is limited in quality (a healthy diet, education, skills, etc.) if not quantity. In any case additional labour creates additional sets of wants simply adding to the problem of satisfying them via the limited factors of production.

Economics therefore, is about a problem: the problem of matching a limited supply of capital and consumer goods to unlimited wants (Fig. 1.2a and b overleaf).

This has led to Economics being called the 'science of scarcity', the factors of production being scarce in relation to our unlimited wants. If all our wants could be satisfied then we would not have to 'economise' in our purchases and Economics as a subject would have no real meaning. In reality however the economic problem is always likely to exist, not least because our natural resources in a number of cases are running out.

Fig. 1.2a Our unlimited wants as expressed by the desire to always own and enjoy more expensive consumer goods and services

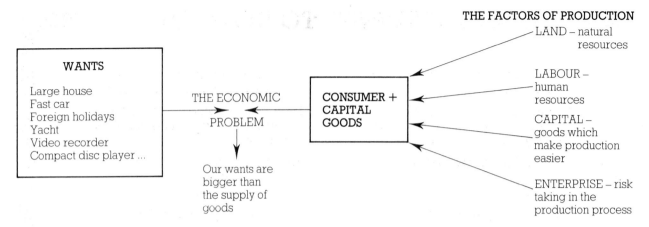

Fig. 1.2b A summary of the economic problem expressed by the imbalance between wants and goods

For instance, the world supply of oil may only last another 40–50 years with a similar supply life for minerals such as copper and tin. The imbalance between our resources and wants prompted a far reaching study to be carried out by the Massachusetts Institute of Technology in 1970. It aimed to find out how long the world could survive with an ever rising population but ever diminishing resources. The results of the study are shown in Fig. 1.3: the limits to world growth will be reached before the year 2000 unless something is done to control population, pollution and the depletion of natural resources. The study may be rather pessimistic in its predictions but it certainly shows the scale of the economic problem!

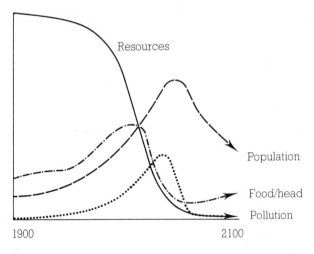

Fig. 1.3 The limits to economic growth showing wants as expressed by population overtaking natural resources

The economic problem also varies in degree *between* different countries and even *within* countries. For people in parts of Africa the economic problem is one of simple subsistence – staying alive in the face of failing harvests. In California, by contrast, the problem may be finding a house with grounds big enough to build a swimming pool! Californians may have an economic problem but it is clearly of a different intensity to that of children starving in Ethiopia (Fig. 1.4).

It is because the factors of production are scarce that they must not be wasted. Questions such as which goods to produce and in what quantities, which methods of production to use and how the goods should be distributed, all have to be answered. These problems are common to all countries regardless of their stage of development. The approaches to solving these questions do differ, however, between countries. A government may, for example, organise production (a **command** economy), or individuals may be left free to make their own production decisions (a **free market** economy). In many countries a combination of these two systems is favoured (a **mixed** economy).

The later chapters in this book all relate to the economic problem because Economics is about using the factors of production in the best available way to satisfy as many wants as possible. Thus *3 Specialising in what we are best at* looks at how production might be increased by operating on a large scale. *4 Exchanging goods – money and banking* arises as a topic because once goods are made, they have to be exchanged and money is used to do this. International trade covered in *14 Why we trade with other countries* is an important topic because we cannot produce certain types of goods in Britain so we exchange some of our goods with those we require from abroad. It is important to understand how all the chapters in this book relate to solving the economic problem.

THINGS TO DO

1 Why do our **wants** appear to be unlimited?

2 Why is simply printing more money for everyone unlikely to satisfy more wants?

3 Why might **capital** be regarded as the most important factor of production?

4 The following are a list of products that can be divided into **capital** and **consumer** goods. Make a heading for each type of good, then list the products under the appropriate headings. Some could go under both headings, so justify your answers.
telephone, clock, fish and chips, lorry, typewriter, flowers, spoon, ruler, casssette player, screwdriver, newspaper, dictionary, painting, garage, piano

5 In what way are the **factors of production** limited in quantity?

6 Describe in a sentence what you understand by the **economic problem**.

7 Why is Economics sometimes called the 'science of scarcity'?

8 Fill in the missing words in the passage below from the list which follows:

*wastage   limited   unlimited
wants   scarcity
factors of production*

We all want many things. For some people it may be a new computer for Christmas, for others food to survive. Our wants are _____. The resources available to satisfy our wants are called the _____. They are strictly _____ in quantity. The economic problem relates to the _____ of the factors in relation to our _____. Solving this problem involves combining the factors in the best way possible to ensure no ____.

Fig. 1.4   The imbalance between wants in different parts of the world

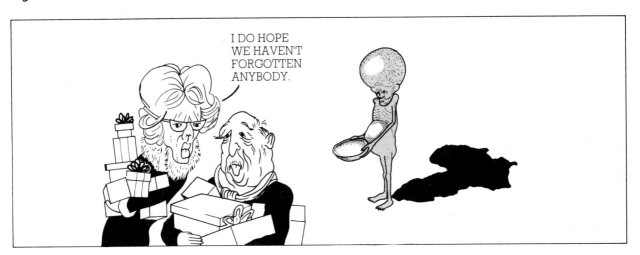

I DO HOPE WE HAVEN'T FORGOTTEN ANYBODY.

CHOICE AND OPPORTUNITY COST

The economic problem of being unable to satisfy all of our wants means that a **choice** has to be made between buying one good and another. You may have to choose between buying a new record and a shirt, or between a camera and a cassette player. Even in a food supermarket, shopping on a limited budget may mean that buying more steak may only be possible at the expense of some vegetables or cereals. The problem of choice relates to the idea of scarcity. The factors of production are scarce so choice has to be exercised in the satisfaction of our wants. The alternative choice which is not taken up is known as the **opportunity cost** in Economics. It is the cost of the foregone alternative. The opportunity cost of buying a new car may be the foreign holiday that is then not possible. The foregone alternative is again an illustration of the economic problem. It represents the wants that are *not* satisfied (Fig. 1.5b).

Opportunity cost is well illustrated in the choice involved between the production of capital and consumer goods. Clearly the importance of capital goods cannot be underestimated, but how are more of them to be obtained? The choice of

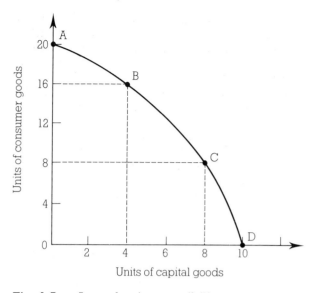

Fig. 1.5a A production possibility curve
Fig. 1.5b (below) The problem of choice can be difficult when many different makes and models exist

producing more capital goods can only be achieved at the expense of foregoing some consumer goods now. This sacrifice is worthwhile in

the long run because the additional capital goods can be used to produce more consumer goods eventually. However for some countries the initial sacrifice of consumer goods may be difficult if this condemns some people to starvation. Undoubtedly though the most industrialised countries (those with most capital goods) are those with the highest living standards.

The problem of choice can be illustrated graphically (Fig. 1.5a). The two goods from which a choice has to be made are put on each axis of the graph. If the example of capital and consumer goods is used, then the axes might look like those in Fig. 1.5a.

With a given quantity of factors of production several choice combinations of capital and consumer goods may be possible. At the extremes all consumer and no capital goods could be produced (point A on the graph), or all capital and no consumer goods (point D on the graph). Thus 20 units of consumer goods would have to be sacrificed to produce 10 units of capital goods. Other combinations may be possible as the graph shows. A combination of 16 consumer goods and 4 capital goods might be chosen (B) or 8 consumer and 8 capital goods (C). It is important to realise that the opportunity cost of producing more capital goods will be fewer consumer goods so that moving from point B to C on the graph means giving up 8 units of consumer goods to gain 4 units of capital goods. Producing more capital *and* consumer goods is not possible unless some factors are lying idle. Joining up all possible choice combinations produces what is called a **production possibility curve** in Economics.

ECONOMICS AS A SCIENCE

Economics deals with the behaviour of human beings and for this reason it is known as a social science. A 'social' science differs from a 'natural' science like Physics because people do not always behave in a consistent way, unlike a liquid such as water which will *always* freeze at 0°C. To say 'our wants are unlimited' will be true for most people but there will be some who are content with existing goods. People are assumed to be rational in their behaviour however, and where rational behaviour produces consistent results an economic 'law' may be put together. For example if the price of a good in the shops falls, it is probable that more people will buy that good. Because this is true for most types of good and most groups of people, this observation can be stated as an economic law – as the price of a good falls, more of it will be bought. What has to be appreciated is that such laws are generalisations and do not *always* hold true. Economic laws however are useful predictors of human behaviour.

Economics is also often called a 'positive science'. This means it concentrates on factual observations concerning economic decisions such as how industry *is* organised or what taxes *are* paid. This can be contrasted with a 'normative science' where opinions are often given. Normative statements may state 'rich people *should* be taxed more heavily' or 'more companies *ought* to be de-nationalised'. Such 'value judgements' do not fall within the scope of Economics and are better left to politicians.

ECONOMIC SYSTEMS

As we saw earlier, in order to solve the problem of satisfying wants, alternative economic systems exist in the world: free market, command, and mixed economies.

1 FREE MARKET ECONOMIES

In the **free market economy** (also known as *laissez-faire*) wants are expressed by individual consumers traditionally in the 'market place' (Fig. 1.6 overleaf). Individual producers are left free to try and satisfy these wants. The mechanism by which this operates is called 'the price system'. If a consumer wants a particular good a producer will supply it for a price. If the good is easy to make and the raw materials abundant, the price will be fairly low, but a good involving skilled labour and scarce raw materials will carry a high price to reflect its value. The point is that no government intervention takes place in this system and the consumer is 'sovereign' in deciding which wants to satisfy. Other key features of the market economy are the freedom of individuals to own and inherit property, competition amongst producers to ensure prices are kept to a minimum, and profit being the principal motive to keep producers in business.

There are, however, problems associated with the market economy. The distribution of wealth may be uneven since some producers will be successful and others not. Also one producer may take over others, creating a monopoly or single seller which may result in higher prices. Pollution may be a bi-product of production which could adversely affect the environment because its control could not be adequately enforced. Some goods not required by individuals but wanted by the community as a whole, e.g. defence, may not be produced. Finally without some governmental control, such an economy could become unstable creating unemployment and inflation (rising prices).

2 COMMAND ECONOMIES

A **command** or 'planned' **economy** arises when a central authority 'commands' the use of the factors of production. Countries such as the USSR or China are good examples of command economies though such economies are not peculiar to communism. In South America, for example, there are

Fig. 1.6 (above)   A fruit and vegetable market where consumers and suppliers meet directly.   **Fig. 1.7** (right)   The National Health Service, an example of a 'public good'

military dictatorships in some countries that 'command' the use of many resources.

The main logic behind command economies is the achievement of a more equal distribution of income and wealth in an economy, in contrast to a market economy where there are winners and losers in production, and inherited wealth on the one hand and unemployment on the other, which means great inequalities can develop.

Planning an economy involves the government or central authority estimating wants and organising the factors of production through large numbers of administrators known as 'bureaucrats'. Production is designed for 'use' rather than for profit, and distribution is organised on the basis of 'needs' rather than 'wealth'.

The problems associated with command economies largely stem from the difficulties involved in planning the use of so many resources. Shortages can and often do develop. Also individual consumers lose their freedom of choice in satisfying wants: the state decides their priorities for them.

3   MIXED ECONOMIES

There is no good example of a 'pure' market economy in the world today since governments play an important part in the running of most countries. Countries such as the USA and Britain, however, still have a large part of their economic activities run by the market and individual freedom of choice is valued highly. Market economies with government intervention are known as 'mixed'; in Scandinavian countries the government plays a significant role in the organisation of resources, but in the USA this activity is kept to a minimum.

The role of the government is to try and correct some of the unfairnesses of the market economy, for example, by making the distribution of wealth more equal. This is normally achieved by taxing the rich more heavily and redistributing the money to the poor. It is also unfair that some goods like health and education should only be available to people who can afford to pay for them. Through taxation the government may provide a free education and health service (Fig. 1.7). The government may also intervene in the economy to try and prevent excessive unemployment and inflation which can cause great hardship to large numbers of people.

THINGS TO DO

1 Use the terms **choice**, **opportunity cost**, and **scarcity** in a sentence to show how they are related to the economic problem of satisfying wants.

2 The following table shows the possible combinations of two products, X and Y, which can be attained in an economy.

$$X \quad 8 \quad 6 \quad 5 \quad 3 \quad 0$$
$$Y \quad 0 \quad 5 \quad 7 \quad 10 \quad 12$$

(a) Plot these choice combinations on a graph and join together the points to form a **production possibility curve**.

(b) What is the **opportunity cost** in terms of X of increasing the production of Y from 7 to 10 units?

(c) What is the opportunity cost in terms of X of increasing the production of Y from 5 to 7 units?

(d) How do production possibility curves illustrate the basic economic concepts of **scarcity** and **choice**?

3 Distinguish between the following **positive** and **normative** statements:
   'Britain is a mixed economy.'
   'Trades Unions are the cause of unemployment in Britain.'
   'Taxation can redistribute wealth.'
   'The government should do more to help small businesses.'
   'Lower taxes can provide an incentive to work harder.'

4 Summarise the main advantages and disadvantages of (a) **market** (b) **command economies**. How far do **mixed economies** overcome the problems associated with market and command economies?

2

THE ECONOMIC PROBLEM IN LESS DEVELOPED COUNTRIES

INTRODUCTION

In the last chapter the economic problem was seen to be all about satisfying wants. Since our wants are much greater than the output which can be produced from the factors of production – land, labour, capital (and enterprise) – Economics is concerned with using the factors in the best possible way to ensure that as far as possible there is no wastage.

The economic problem is clearly illustrated by the plight of the poor or less developed countries (LDCs). Their problem is not about people choosing a new record or dress but about having to sacrifice food for clothing or shelter. The factors of production in LDCs are often of very poor quality so that satisfying even basic wants is frequently very difficult.

WHAT IS A LESS DEVELOPED COUNTRY?

Figure 2.1 shows those parts of the world regarded as less developed countries (LDCs) and since many of them lie in the southern part of the hemisphere with the richer countries in the north, we talk about the North–South divide in the world's wealth. The wealth of a nation can be determined in two main ways:

1 by looking at the size of the nation's income in relation to its population

i.e. $\dfrac{\text{national income}}{\text{population}}$

This gives a figure for income per head and clearly if a country has a low figure it is labelled

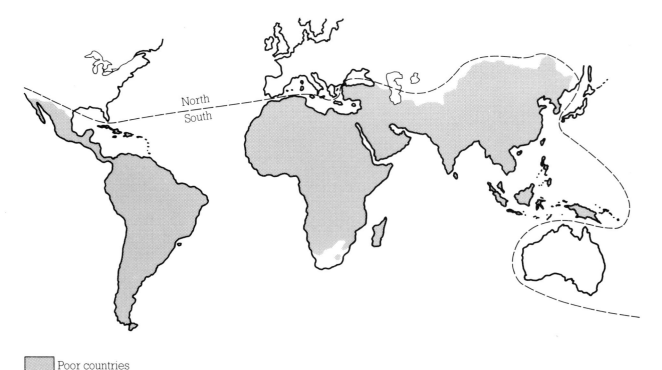

☐ Poor countries

Fig. 2.1　The North-South divide

less developed, while a high figure would mean the country is **developed**. There is no sharp dividing line between the above labels but countries such as India with incomes per head of population under £100 are amongst the poorest and West Germany with an income per head of over £1000 is one of the richest;

2 by the amount of industry in a country – it was clear from Chapter 1 that capital goods were an important factor of production and countries with a large amount of industrial capital are labelled developed because their potential for the future production of consumer goods is obviously high. Thus although South Africa has a non-white population that suffers much malnutrition and poverty, its large level of industrialisation allows it to be included in the group of developed countries.

THINGS TO DO

1 Draw or trace a map outline of the world similar to Fig. 2.1. Shade in the poor countries of the world and, using an atlas, mark the position of Ethiopia and India – two of the poorest. Label also the North–South divide and two developed countries (DCs).

2 Why does a high income per head figure for a country not always mean that the people living in that country are rich?

3 From the following table, draw a bar graph of population in one colour and alongside, in a different colour, a similar graph for the national income of each area.

Area	National income (000m US $)	Population (m)
North America	1200	275
Western Europe	750	400
China	170	850
Africa	100	450
India	75	600

Which is the richest area in the world and which is the poorest? Calculate the income per head of population figure for China.

THE PROBLEMS LESS DEVELOPED COUNTRIES FACE

Any nation's success at solving the economic problem depends on being able to use its factors of production to the best advantage. The problems poor countries face reflect their poor quality factors.

1 LAND

Land refers to all natural resources and one aspect of this factor which particularly concerns LDCs is the fertility of the soil and its ability to support nutritious crops. Similarly the climate in LDCs will very often not support cattle or the growth of the right crops essential for a healthy diet (Fig. 2.2). A balanced diet, particularly for children, relies on a good supply of protein foods. Unfortunately

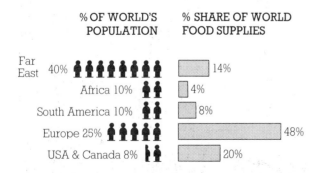

Fig. 2.2a The imbalance of food consumption and population

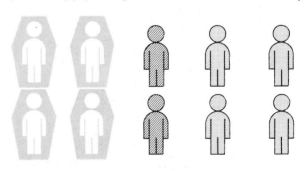

Fig. 2.2b The probable mortality rate for children under 5 years old in LDCs: 4 out of 10 will die and a further 2 will suffer serious malnutrition

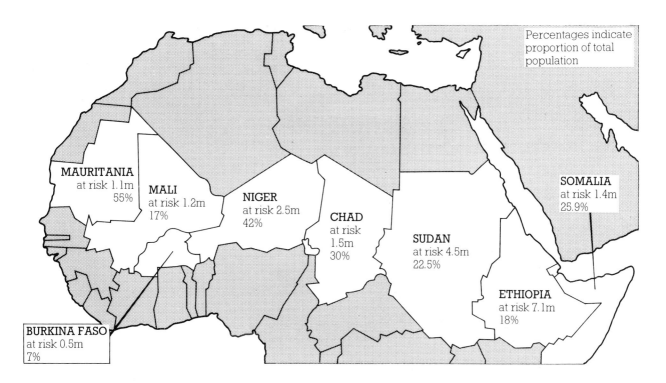

MAURITANIA
at risk 1.1m
55%

MALI
at risk 1.2m
17%

NIGER
at risk 2.5m
42%

CHAD
at risk
1.5m
30%

SUDAN
at risk 4.5m
22.5%

SOMALIA
at risk 1.4m
25.9%

ETHIOPIA
at risk 7.1m
18%

BURKINA FASO
at risk 0.5m
7%

Percentages indicate proportion of total population

starchy foods such as yams, sweet potatoes and rice can be produced more easily in many hot dry climates than protein foods such as meat and fish.

Too much starch in the diet can lead to a disease known as kwashiorkor. The symptoms of this form of malnutrition curiously enlarge a child's body producing a pot-belly swollen with fluid, puffy limbs and sores. Without protein-rich food, the child will eventually die (Fig. 2.3).

Fig. 2.2c (above) The drought in the Sahara region of Africa means a large proportion of affected countries risk hunger and starvation (1985 estimates)

Fig. 2.2d (bottom left) Famine means families are constantly on the move in search of food and water

Fig. 2.3 (bottom right) A child suffering from kwashiorkor

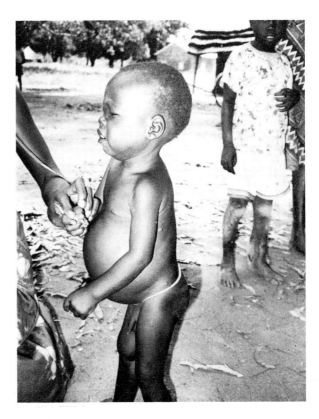

THINGS TO DO

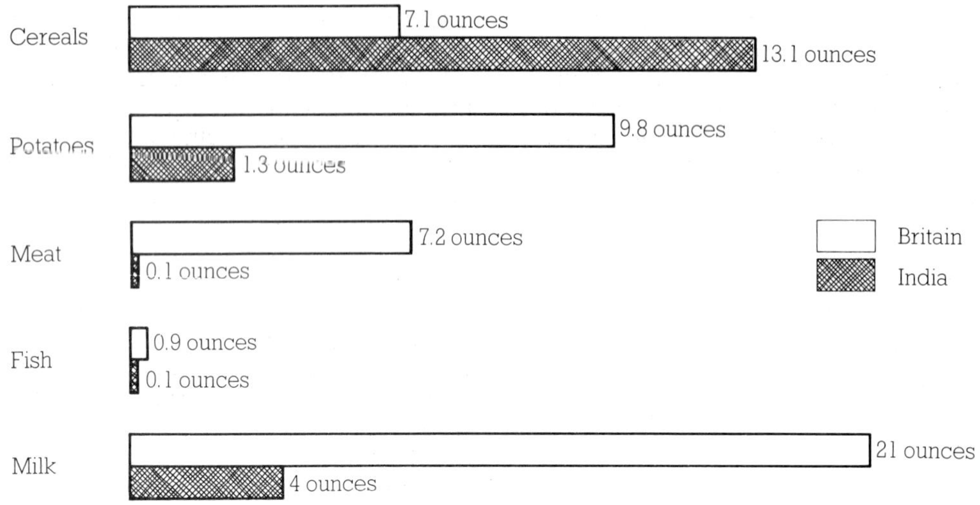

Cereals	7.1 ounces (Britain) / 13.1 ounces (India)
Potatoes	9.8 ounces (Britain) / 1.3 ounces (India)
Meat	7.2 ounces (Britain) / 0.1 ounces (India)
Fish	0.9 ounces (Britain) / 0.1 ounces (India)
Milk	21 ounces (Britain) / 4 ounces (India)

Legend:
- ☐ Britain
- ▨ India

Fig. 2.4

1 Study Fig. 2.4 and say if you think the average Indian has a balanced diet.

2 Figure 2.5 shows what is often called 'the vicious circle of poverty'. Try to explain in your own words what it means and suggest any ways that it can be broken.

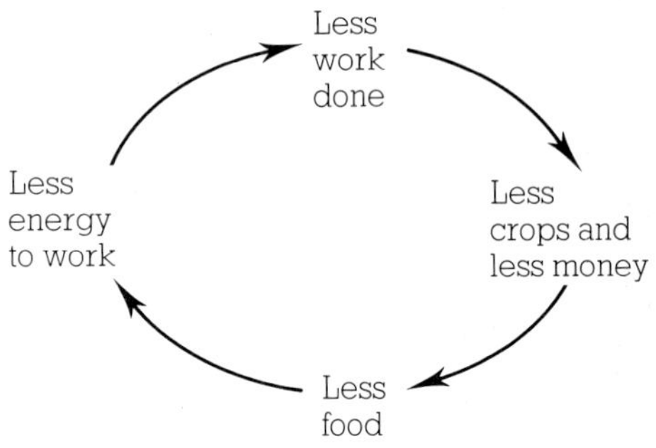

Less work done → Less crops and less money → Less food → Less energy to work → Less work done

Fig. 2.5   The vicious circle of poverty

2   LABOUR

Since LDCs have large populations, it may be thought that this factor is relatively abundant in supply. However it is not the *quantity* but the *quality* of the labour force which is important and quality in turn depends on diet, education, a good health service and mobility. Also remember that every new birth creates a new set of wants further widening the gap between wants and resources. Some of the differences between the populations of rich and poor countries can be seen by comparing (a) life expectancy figures (how long the average male/female can expect to live); (b) infant mortality figures (the number of babies that die before reaching the age of one year, per 1000 live births); (c) adult literacy figures (the % of adults in the total population that can read and write); and (d) age distribution figures (which show the % total population that are below 16 years, the % aged between 16–65 years, and those over 65).

The population problem in LDCs is becoming worse rather than better. The evidence shows that the **birth rate** (number of live births per 1000 population) only begins to fall when countries reach a certain level of affluence. By then, the fall in the death rate has led to a greater confidence that babies will survive and so families want fewer children. Nowhere is the population explosion better illustrated than Mexico City which has now become the world's largest city with over 18m inhabitants. The city produces 6000 more tons of rubbish daily than it can collect. It is so polluted that the effect of breathing its air for a day is as bad as smoking 40 cigarettes!

Another common feature of LDCs is the high proportion of the workforce either self-employed or working, unpaid, for the head of the family, usually in agriculture. By contrast only about 7% of the workforce in industrialised countries work on the land, the majority being engaged in service occupations (banking, insurance, civil service, education, etc.) with a significant number in industry. Figure 2.6 compares occupational distributions in Pakistan and the USA.

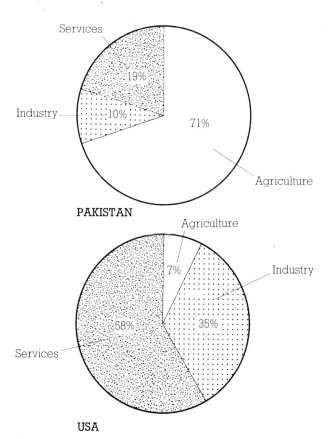

PAKISTAN

USA

Fig. 2.6 Occupational distributions of population in Pakistan and the USA – what are the major differences?

3 CAPITAL

In Chapter 1 the significance of capital was discussed in some detail. In many ways it is the most important factor of production because it provides the means for securing more consumer goods in the future. Without capital goods the growth prospects for an economy are very poor and the world's richest nations are those with the largest stock of capital. What is also important to understand is the notion of opportunity cost applied to capital and consumer goods. Acquiring additional capital goods means sacrificing more consumer goods now, or in other words sacrificing current living standards for improved ones tomorrow. Thus the opportunity cost of more capital goods becomes the consumer goods that cannot now be produced.

For LDCs this choice can be very severe since many cannot provide sufficient consumer goods to satisfy even basic wants (Fig. 2.7). In some cases it may be a choice between more machinery and less food: clearly a difficult one when widespread malnutrition may exist already.

One further problem related to capital goods is the fact that they often replace people in the tasks they perform and in countries with massive populations, creating large pools of unemployment is obviously very undesirable.

Many of the poorest countries therefore have only the simplest of capital goods (called **simple technology**) and to develop need to find new machines that are simple to construct and do not put people out of work. In the next part of this chapter we will be looking at how improvements in technology can best be brought about and this certainly does not imply that the best or most sophisticated machines are appropriate for such countries.

Fig. 2.7 An illustration of how one of the most basic wants – shelter – cannot be satisfied in an LDC

THINGS TO DO

1 Study Fig. 2.8 then answer the questions that follow which are designed to test your interpretation of the information.

    (a) Which country has the lowest life expectancy figures? What is the cause of the low figures?

    (b) For what age group is there the largest difference in figures between Europe and Africa? Why is this the case? How could Africa's age distribution be made to look more like that of Europe?

    (c) Why do you think advanced capital machinery would be inappropriate for Ethiopia's economy?

    (d) In Fig. 2.8 (a), explain what the figure of 63 means for Mexico.

    (e) In Fig. 2.8 (d) what helps to sustain people over 65 in Europe that is almost non-existent in Africa?

2 Below is a table of the projected top 10 most populated countries in the year 2050 with 1982 figures shown in brackets. Work out the % increase between the two dates and construct a bar graph to show the figures.

Country	2050	(1982)
India	1513m	(717m)
China	1450m	(1008m)
Nigeria	471m	(91m)
USSR	358m	(265m)
Bangladesh	357m	(93m)
Indonesia	332m	(153m)
Pakistan	302m	(87m)
USA	228m	(226m)
Brazil	279m	(127m)
Mexico	182m	(73m)

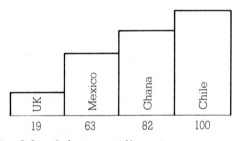

Fig. 2.8a Infant mortality rates

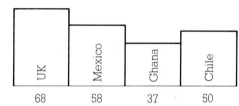

Fig. 2.8b Male life expectancy (years)

	%
UK	95
Chad	7
Ethiopia	5
Guinea	5
Niger	1

Fig. 2.8c Adult literacy as a % of the population able to read

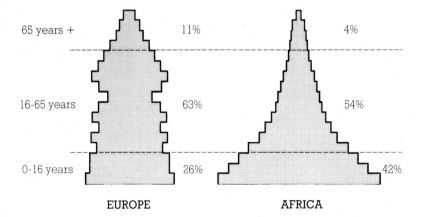

Fig. 2.8d Age distribution

IMPROVING THE FACTORS OF PRODUCTION

1 LAND

Obviously climatic conditions in LDCs cannot be changed but there are two significant improvements which can be made to raise productivity on the land. Firstly the addition of fertilisers to crops can dramatically increase yields, sometimes by as much as 300%. Such improvements have given rise to the term **green revolution** and perhaps nowhere is this more true than in Japan, which for such a small group of islands is nearly self-sufficient in food. But how are the fertilisers paid for? If farmers are producing at near subsistence level surely they will not be able to afford to buy fertilisers? The answer lies in the fact that since fertilisers are bound to increase yields (if properly applied) farmers can pay for them by committing part of the expected future yield to the fertiliser company – a practice which is commonly applied. Thus the sacrifice involved in obtaining more capital goods can be made from *future* consumer goods – a very important step forward towards economic growth.

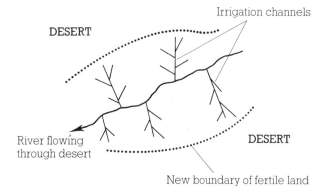

Fig. 2.9a   Making the desert fertile

The second improvement that can be applied to land is irrigation. In particular, desert land can be turned into highly productive farmland providing some water is available which can be directed through irrigation channels (Fig. 2.9). In Israel parts of the Sinai desert have been transformed into rich orange groves through irrigation.

Fig. 2.9b   Cabbages growing in Ethiopia with the help of irrigation – the pump for the borehole is in the tent

Fig. 2.10a Simple technology. One of the simplest forms of capital good is a wooden hoe but whilst it is very cheap, it hardly makes a dramatic improvement to production. A wooden plough used with an animal is the first advancement

Fig. 2.10b (Below left) Intermediate technology is designed to make maximum use of a country's existing resources – usually people rather than capital goods. Here specifically designed intermediate technology is being used to remove maize from cobs

Fig. 2.10c (below right) Intermediate technology and semi-skilled labour are used to make sandals

STAGES IN TECHNOLOGY

President Nyerere of Tanzania:

". . . . I've been telling my own people, 'We've got to change, we must mechanize, we must have better tools. But what are better tools? Not the combine harvester. If I were given enough combine harvesters for every family in Tanzania, what would I do with them? No mechanics, no spare parts . . ." A shudder at the thought, "It would be a very serious problem – unless, of course, I sell them for hard cash. But we still have to give the people better tools, tools they can handle, and can pay for. Americans, when they speak of better tools, are talking about something quite different. We are using hoes. If two million farmers in Tanzania could jump from the hoe to the oxen plough, it would be a revolution. It would double our living standard, triple our product! This is the kind of thing China is doing. An ancient people, dealing with the difficulties of feeding seven hundred million people. The stage of their development is relevant to us. I wish I could state this as true, observed fact, and nothing more. But when I say 'From China we can learn,' they say we are going Red."

Fig. 2.10d
(right) Advanced technology must be introduced carefully if it is not to upset the delicate economic balance in LDCs. Advanced technology usually needs large amounts of capital (which LDCs often cannot afford) and does away with the need for labour (of which LDCs often have an overabundance). Here a well is being deepened in Mali with the help of advanced technology

2 LABOUR

To improve the labour factor, both the quantity and quality need to be altered. The simple solution to overpopulation may appear to lie in the development of widespread family planning programmes to reduce the birth rate but such programmes have been tried and after only initial short-term success have failed. Why? The answer lies in the fact that people in LDCs actually want large families. This is because children in many of these countries cost little to bring up – they do not require lots of new clothes, toy train sets or computer games and from an early age can actually play a positive role in the production process by helping in the fields since they will not be required to go to school. Perhaps more importantly, people want large families to provide them with their security in old age. Don't forget for most poor countries no state pensions exist and without their children to keep them, individuals could not survive into old age. Family planning programmes therefore can probably only work when a higher level of development has been reached which allows some form of state support for the old.

Improving the quality of the labour force is easy enough to achieve in principle but much harder in practice. Perhaps the biggest single gain could come from offering a more comprehensive education service so that any new technology introduced could be understood by more people. The table below shows how difficult this has been to achieve and a heavy reliance on human assistance from the rich countries has been necessary to set up schools, colleges and universities.

The gap in educational opportunities

Country	% children educated 5–19 years old
USA	100
UK	94
India	41
Kenya	39
Ethiopia	8

Source: UN, 1979 figures

Similarly a better health service would help prevent some of the widespread diseases that occur in LDCs. The table below, which shows the gap in the health service between rich and poor countries, implies that again much human aid in the form of doctors and nurses from the rich countries will be required if significant improvements are to take place.

The gap in the health service

Country	Number of people per doctor
USSR	267
USA	549
UK	711
Nigeria	9 591
Indonesia	11 740
Ethiopia	72 582

Source: UN, 1982 figures

3 CAPITAL

Improving this factor involves the constraints that any machinery has to be simple to make, inexpensive and not put people out of work. Figure 2.10 identifies stages in technology –
   (a) Simple technology
   (b) Intermediate technology
   (c) Advanced technology
and shows what is appropriate for LDCs.

As you will probably realise, agriculture in DCs uses **advanced technology** and this accounts for the small 7% figure (USA) of working people in this industry. Many LDCs still use only **simple technology** in farming and for them a major agricultural revolution would take place if every farmer were able to implement the use of **intermediate technology** in production. Advanced technology would not solve the problem because it would replace too many people and, given education standards, be very difficult to service and maintain. This is what is meant by appropriate technology and intermediate technology is the most appropriate for the needs of LDCs (2.10).

THINGS TO DO

1 How and why does **development** lead to a sacrifice?

2 Why is the **occupational distribution** of population different between DCs and LDCs?

3 In what way are children an economic asset in LDCs?

4 Why is **intermediate technology** the 'appropriate' technology in LDCs?

AID TO LESS DEVELOPED COUNTRIES

In order to improve their factors of production, LDCs rely on the richer nations to provide aid which comes in a variety of different forms. The distinctions are between bilateral and multilateral aid which show where the aid comes from, and grants and loans which show the terms under which the aid is given.

Bilateral literally means two-sided and represents aid arranged solely between a rich country and a poor one. The UK, for example, has special links with Commonwealth countries and the majority of our foreign aid is given on a bilateral basis to countries such as India, Pakistan and Kenya. **Multilateral** means many-sided, and represents aid coming from a variety of the richer countries which is channelled through agencies such as the United Nations or World Bank. Multilateral aid can provide a much larger pool of finance than single bilateral agreements can and important projects requiring a large amount of finance may only be possible through multilateral payments. The Kariba Dam, for example, built on the River Zambesi in Africa with a large World Bank loan, provides nearly 80% of Mozambique's electricity.

The distinction between grants and loans is fairly simple. **Grants** represent gifts of money which do not have to be repaid and about two thirds of all aid is in grant form. **Loans** do have to be repaid but usually the interest charged on the loan is very low and the time allowed for repaying the loan can be as long as 50 years.

One other piece of terminology worth noting comes with the terms tied and untied aid. **Tied aid** accounts for over half of bilateral aid and means that the recipient has to spend the money on things made in the donor country, not something all LDCs want to do as similar goods could be bought more cheaply on the open market. **Untied aid** does not have the same strings attached to it.

A large proportion of all bilateral aid goes to providing 'technical assistance' to LDCs and pays for the salaries of doctors, engineers, teachers, etc. who are 'imported' from the richer countries to train and improve the quality of the workforce. The proportions of these different types of aid given are shown in Fig. 2.11.

There are a number of problems associated with aid, perhaps the most serious being that the countries in most need are certainly not those receiving the most funds. In fact the largest aid recipient is Egypt, probably because both the Russians and Americans have regarded it as being strategically important. This suggests that at least some aid is governed by political considerations – especially as Israel is the third largest aid recipient. The table below gives some examples of income per head received in aid which takes into account the total aid in relation to population and shows clearly that some of the poorest countries receive trivial amounts of aid per head. India, for instance, although receiving the second highest amount of total aid comes at the bottom of the aid per head table.

Country	Aid per head in dollars
Israel	247.4
Jordan	60.5
Egypt	34.9
Syria	24.1
Bangladesh	12.9
Pakistan	8.9
Indonesia	7.9
India	2.9

Source: UN, 1981 figures

What is also true is that the richest countries are not always the most generous givers of aid to poor countries. The USA for example has probably the highest national income figure in the world and gives the highest amount of aid. But this aid only represents about 0.2% of US income (equivalent to a fifth of a penny in every pound earned), far less than the percentages given by Sweden (0.9% of national income), the Netherlands (0.8%) and Australia (0.5%). Britain gives less than 0.4% of its national income to poor countries, a percentage that has been declining throughout the 1970s and 1980s.

Some mention should be made of the various agencies involved in providing aid to LDCs. Oxfam was founded in 1942 initially to help refugees from World War II. By 1961 Oxfam was helping over 400 projects in 50 countries mostly in Asia, Africa and the Middle East. Oxfam today aims to respond in a practical way to human need, working mainly in the areas of agriculture, health

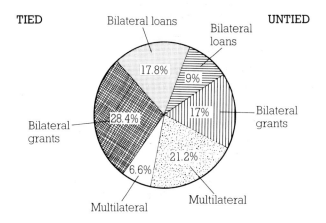

Fig. 2.11 Aid to LDCs

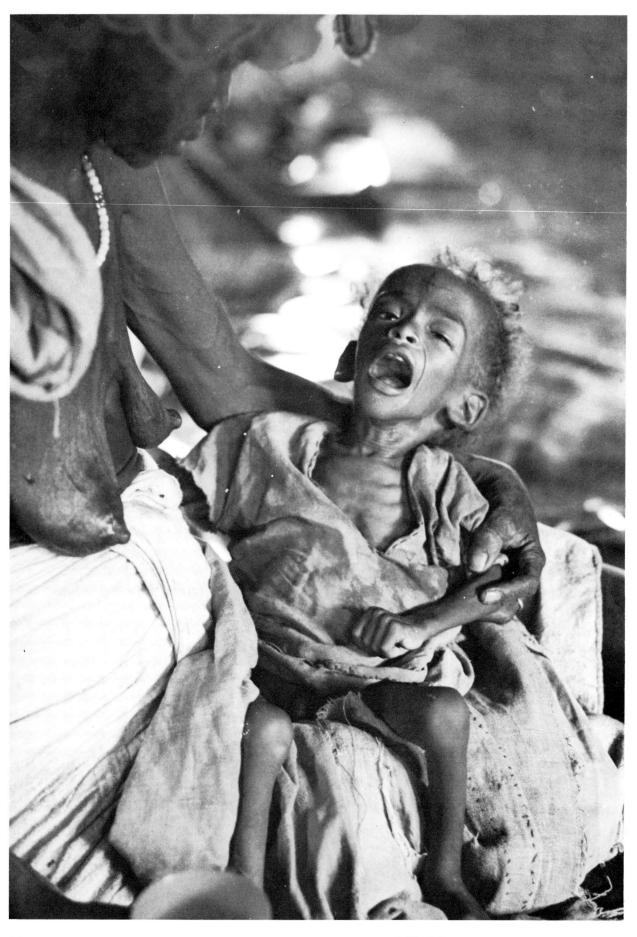

and social development (Fig. 2.12). In 1982 it provided aid totalling nearly £13m. The United Nations Children's Fund (UNICEF) is another agency specialising in help for children from LDCs. In 1985 it promoted child health programmes in 109 countries and supplied £125m worth of medicines and vaccines against TB, diptheria, tetanus and other diseases. Band Aid has now become recognised as a major relief agency after the impact of the 'Feed the World' record and other fundraising events, inspired by Bob Geldorf. In 1985 alone over £50m was raised by the Band Aid Trust.

One final point about aid is that in total it is still very small in relation to the money earned by LDCs from exports. This has given rise to the slogan 'trade not aid' where the poor countries feel that their best chance of development comes from an expansion of trading links with the rich countries rather than charity donations of aid. This seems to be an important point especially when recently the USA imposed a 'morality' constraint on its own aid funds whereby it will cut off all funds to voluntary organisations which carry out abortion, or even merely encourage it, as part of family planning programmes.

THE WORLD BANK

The World Bank is worth mentioning in some detail since nearly all its capital is directed towards LDCs. It was set up in 1946 and is based in Washington, sharing the same premises as another important institution, the International Monetary Fund. The full title of the World Bank is the International Bank for Reconstruction and Development or IBRD.

The World Bank's capital comes from three sources: subscriptions come from the rich countries in proportion to the size of their national incomes; bonds are issued in world financial markets; and finally income is received from some of the Bank's trading activities.

The Bank's funds are normally loaned to countries with national income per head figures of less than £700, though more recently, to help the poorest nations, the International Development Association has been set up to channel loans to countries with less than £150 income per head. Credit is often given for 50 years, interest free, with no capital repayments expected before the first ten years of the loan. Examples of projects financed by the Bank include agriculture, education, transport and electric power schemes.

The main limitation on the effectiveness of the World Bank comes from the size of its budget which although around £6000m is still only equivalent to about 3% of the UK's national income.

THINGS TO DO

1 Distinguish between (*a*) **bilateral** and **multilateral** aid; (*b*) **tied** and **untied** aid.

2 'Aid to LDCs is governed by the politics of the rich countries'. Discuss.

3 Why is more aid to LDCs not the most appropriate solution to their problems?

4 What is the role of the World Bank in the economic development of poor countries?

3

SPECIALISING IN WHAT WE ARE BEST AT

INTRODUCTION

In Chapter 1 it was clear that the factors of production were scarce in relation to our wants and that 'solving' the economic problem implies using the factors in the best way possible to maximise output. For the factor labour this means deciding what tasks people should perform in the economy and on a broader level deciding what size of business is appropriate for optimum production. In the UK over the last 30 years there has been a consistent movement towards producing in larger units with many mergers between smaller firms taking place, the advantages of large-scale production being known as **economies of scale**. To achieve the best possible allocation of resources it is also important to have labour mobility.

In an economy where there will be declining and expanding industries, labour will ideally move geographically, from one region to another, and occupationally, learning new skills appropriate to growth industries. In practice, however, labour is not highly mobile in either respect and the reasons for this need to be understood, so that some possible ways in which mobility can be improved can be suggested.

This chapter looks at all these aspects of production as it is necessary to understand them if the maximum number of wants are to be satisfied.

THE DIVISION OF LABOUR – SPECIALISING IN WHAT WE ARE BEST AT

In early civilisations the idea of specialisation did not really arise. People tended to live in isolated communities, undertaking a variety of tasks aimed at survival and subsistence. Nowadays the picture is very different indeed. Even at school most people specialise in certain subjects and in the sixth form only two or three 'A' levels may be chosen. School leavers may learn just one specialised skill in their first job, for instance in the commercial sphere they learn to operate a word processor. In the administrative organisation of a school there are subject specialists, laboratory technicians, secretaries, caretakers, all with a particular job. In fact in today's economy it is difficult to find examples of people who are *not* specialists.

The **division of labour** is the economic term used to describe human specialisation. Why has it become so highly developed?

Suppose Tom and Jane work in an electrical repair shop each servicing television and radios. On average Tom, who has an interest in televisions, can repair four of these a day and four radios in a day dividing half his time on each. Jane, who has an interest in radios, can service two televisions and six radios in a day, similarly dividing her time. How could their output increase without either having to work harder? The answer lies in allowing each to specialise in what they are best at. If Tom specialises in televisions he could repair eight in a day and if Jane specialises in radios she could repair twelve in a day. Thus before specialisation only six televisions in total were repaired and now eight. Similarly only ten radios were repaired and now twelve. Clearly specialisation can increase output. The following table summarises the situation:

	Television repairs	Radio repairs
	BEFORE SPECIALISATION	
Tom	4	4
Jane	2	6
	—	—
TOTAL	6	10
	AFTER SPECIALISATION	
Tom	8	–
Jane	–	12
	—	—
TOTAL	8	12

So far this seems fairly straightforward but what if Jane is better than Tom at repairing both televisions and radios? Is specialisation appropriate and is there a role in the economy for the person who is not as good at tasks compared to other people? Consider the example below:

	Television repairs		Radio repairs
Tom	3	and	2 in a day
Jane	4	and	6 in a day
	—		—
TOTAL	7		8

Can output be increased? The answer is yes if Jane, who has an absolute advantage in both types of repair, specialises in the one where she has the greater **comparative advantage**. Clearly this is in radio repairs. If Tom specialises in television repairs and Jane divides her time 75% to radio repairs and 25% to television repairs then the results will be as shown:

	Television repairs	Radio repairs
Tom	6	—
Jane	2	9
	—	—
TOTAL	8	9

In other words, if Jane can repair four televisions with half her time then 2 can be repaired with 25% of her time. Similarly if six radios can be repaired with half her time and three with 25% of her time, nine can be finished with 75% of her time. Thus output can be increased, even where one person has an absolute advantage in both tasks, if they specialise in the area where they have the greater comparative advantage. This is a very important principle which can be applied to the theory of international trade. It shows that even where one country has an absolute advantage over another country in the production of a range of goods, trade can still benefit *both* countries. Thus there is a close link between the advantages of human specialisation and international specialisation (see Chapter 15).

Apart from the demonstrated advantages of increasing output, the division of labour has other advantages which can be summarised as follows:

1 'Practice makes perfect'
The more a particular task is performed the more skilled a person becomes resulting in not only more production but better quality production too.

2 A saving on tools
Performing one task rather than a number requires only one set of tools rather than a whole range. This could mean an improvement in the quality and output of machines and tools used.

3 Little time wasted moving between jobs
From the company's point of view the division of labour means less movement as a person performs one task in one place. This advantage is the reverse for the worker who may find doing one job all day without many breaks rather monotonous.

4 A saving on training costs
Breaking down a complex production plan into simple tasks means that workers can be trained quickly and inexpensively. In motor car manufacturing, for instance, many of the production line jobs require only unskilled labour.

5 The increased use of machines
Because the division of labour often requires a series of simple tasks it becomes possible to introduce machines which can replace human beings (Fig. 3.1). Robots are well established in

Fig. 3.1 Robots in the Ford Motor Company's Dagenham assembly plant

27

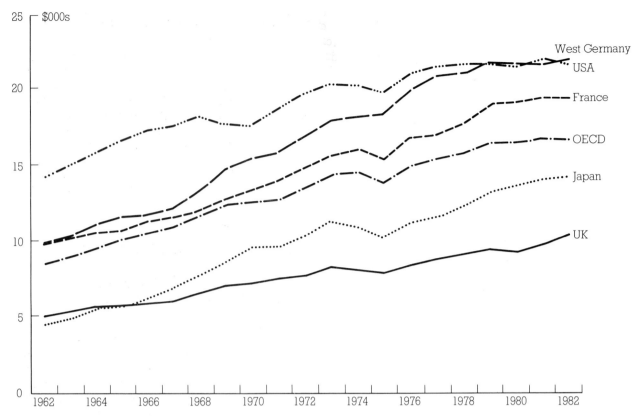

Fig. 3.2 Productivity: industrial production per head in common currency ($s) during the period 1962–82

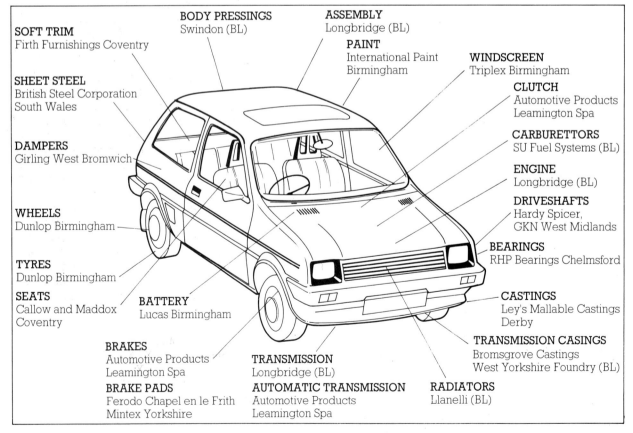

Fig. 3.3 The firms supplying component parts for the BL Metro – any disruption in supply by any one firm and up to 250 000 workers are vulnerable

the motor industry and can be programmed to perform an increasingly complex set of routines, particularly where the welding of a car is concerned. Figure 3.1 shows two welding robots used at the Ford Motor Company's Dagenham Plant for the Sierra Body construction. For this car a total of 54 robots are used on the assembly line. It may be worth noting at this point that the increased use of machines can improve labour productivity but in turn create unemployment. **Labour productivity** measures the output which results from a given quantity of labour and replacing labour with capital often means more output with less labour, an improvement in productivity. Increased productivity does not usually mean working harder, merely having better equipment to work with as a means of boosting output. Figure 3.2 shows UK productivity in comparison to other industrial countries. The fact that it is below the other countries does not necessarily mean the labour force in Britain works any less hard. It may reflect the inferior equipment available, its design and efficiency, the managerial skill exercised in co-ordinating all factors of production, or the training qualifications and efficiency of all employees.

The division of labour, whilst bringing many advantages for the company, gives rise to some important disadvantages for the workers concerned. The point about monotony has already been mentioned and work can be de-humanising if all initiatives and responsibility are taken away from the worker. The use of the division of labour also increases the risk of workers being made redundant when new machines are invented. Having such a narrow skill base it will then be more difficult to find another job, increasing the risk of longterm unemployment. Finally one serious problem for both workers and the company alike arises from the 'interdependence' of workers in a large assembly plant. This means that one group of workers very much depend on another group for the finished product to emerge at the end of the production line. If one small group of workers were to go on strike then the whole factory could be laid off. Equally since many outside components are used in assembly plants, particularly in the motor industry, any breakdown in supply could adversely affect production. Figure 3.3 shows the variety of companies supplying components for the British Leyland Metro, and if supply of any one is disrupted for any length of time the car could not be completed and thousands of workers might be laid off.

Balanced against these disadvantages has to be the fact that without this specialisation goods could not be made cheaply enough to bring them within reach of the mass consumer and the price paid for a variety of experiences at work would be a more highly priced product.

ECONOMIES OF SCALE

The division of labour is normally most effectively practised in companies operating on a large scale. There are other advantages attached to producing on a large scale which are collectively known as **economies of scale**. There are two types of economies: **internal** which apply to the individual firm or producer and **external** which apply to the whole industry of which the firm is a part. (It is not always the case that a large industry is made up of large firms. The woollen industry, for example, has many small producers so that external but not internal economies exist.)

INTERNAL ECONOMIES

There are five principal internal economies of scale which are known as **technical**, **marketing**, **managerial**, **risk-bearing** and **financial**.

1   TECHNICAL ECONOMIES

The larger the firm the easier it is to employ specialist machines and the division of labour. Machines can help improve labour productivity and usually reduce the unit cost of output because they can work faster than human beings and do not require a wage, only electricity to work. Some machines such as robots are only profitable if used on a large scale so that small firms may find many types of machinery beyond their financial reach. In most companies a variety of machines will be required, each working at a different rate, and only large companies will be able to achieve a balanced team of machines. Suppose a firm employs three different types of machine: machine X producing 20 components per hour; machine Y producing 30 components per hour; and machine Z producing 15 components per hour. Each component is combined to make the finished product but if only one of each type of machine is employed, the maximum output will be 15 components per hour, proceeding only as quickly as the slowest machine. What is required is a team of machines to ensure all machines work at full capacity. The lowest common denominator of the machines' output is 60 so that if three of X are bought, two of Y, and four of Z, output can be 60 per hour with all machines being fully used. Only large firms can afford to buy balanced teams of machines to optimise their use.

	MACHINE X	
20 components per hour	X X X	= 60
	MACHINE Y	
30 components per hour	Y Y	= 60
	MACHINE Z	
15 components per hour	Z Z Z Z	= 60

2 MARKETING ECONOMIES

Large firms can afford to buy their raw materials in bulk and for this a discount is obtained, thus lowering the costs of production. At the other end of the production process the large firm can afford to market its product in a big way, perhaps adopting a national advertising campaign using television commercials and newspapers. Since a full page advert in the Daily Mirror can cost £28 000 only large firms can afford this kind of promotion.

3 MANAGERIAL ECONOMIES

Large firms can achieve some division of labour in their managerial functions. All large companies have a Personnel and Training Department responsible for recruiting and staff development, a Sales and Marketing Section, and a Research and Development Department. Managers who specialise in these roles will develop expertise and perform their jobs better. In the small firm some of these areas will have to be shared between managers; in the sole trader type of business, the owner will have to perform all managerial functions. Clearly the large firm will be more managerially efficient if people can develop expertise.

4 RISK-BEARING ECONOMIES

In order to achieve security and continuity the large company will probably diversify its operations to provide a variety of products in a variety of geographical markets. ICI, one of the UK's largest companies, is discussed in more detail later (see Chapter 8) and is a good example of a company achieving risk-bearing economies. Figure 3.4 summarises the diversity of ICI's activities.

Small firms do not have the resources and diversity and are therefore more vulnerable to changes in demand for their product. It is interesting to note that tobacco companies, seeing the demand for cigarettes falling, are diversifying into a wide range of products. BAT, for example (producing brands like 'Embassy') is now a holding company for the large range of products and services shown in Fig. 3.5.

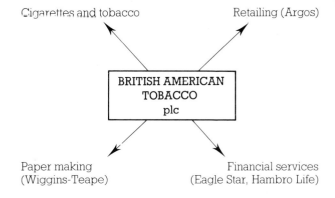

Fig. 3.5 How BAT achieves risk bearing economies

5 FINANCIAL ECONOMIES

Large companies often find it cheaper and easier to raise capital than small companies because they are nationally known with a proven track record. Much of the capital raised by large companies comes in the form of share issues. Shares have the advantage of being transferable, the Stock Exchange providing a huge market place where secondhand shares can be bought and sold. Because shares can be easily exchanged for money and because they allow the owner to 'share' in the profits of the company, they are an attractive proposition for investors. Small firms find it difficult and more expensive to raise large amounts of capital because often they are not well known, and in the case of sole traders and partnerships cannot actually issue shares.

Fig. 3.4 ICI's diversity of products and markets – a multi-national company

6 DISECONOMIES

Economies of scale imply that 'bigger is better', and in many large firms this holds true, but are there limits to just how far economies of scale can be achieved? Figure 3.6 shows that there are limits to economies of scale because problems can arise when a company gets too large. The morale of the workforce may deteriorate when people feel insignificant as part of a large organisation; communicating with all the various departments becomes

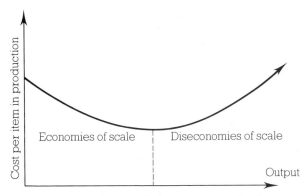

Optimum size of output for lowest cost production

Fig. 3.6   The limits to the economies of scale

more difficult; and co-ordinating all parts of the business is less easy when production sites may be spread around the country.

Evidence of diseconomies occurring has come from mergers between firms which have resulted in a worse financial performance. The motor industry is a good example where British Leyland, having been created out of a merger between Rover, Austin Morris, Jaguar and Leyland Buses, went bankrupt in 1975 and was then nationalised by the government.

SMALL IS BEAUTIFUL

This phrase was coined by an economist called Schumacher in a book of the same name about the virtues of producing on a small scale. Small firms still far outnumber large firms and there are good reasons why so many small firms exist. (In Chapter 6 this is discussed in more detail with reference to the retail trade.)

1 **The demand for variety** – over many product areas consumers do not want standardisation which allows small firms to predominate. In the clothing industry, for example, there is a demand for individuality in looks so that most companies at the fashion end of the market are small.

2 **Capital** – is important to enable growth and small firms find sources of capital limited which may prohibit large-scale expansion.

3 **Personal service** – where this is important a firm may have to remain small. Service industries are often characterised by small firms, for instance, hairdressers, solicitors and accountants.

4 **Geographical position** – if a business is isolated geographically it may be remote from major markets and thus have to stay small. The village shop will not have the potential to become a large supermarket because of its limited number of customers.

5 **Luxury goods** – highly priced goods will have a limited market and this may necessitate them being produced on a small scale, for example, building firms producing exclusive properties.

6 **Infancy** – many firms will be small because they are just in their infancy and establishing a market. All large companies had small beginnings.

EXTERNAL ECONOMIES

Large industries can gain certain advantages because of their size. External economies can be grouped into three types: **concentration**, **information** and **disintegration**.

1 CONCENTRATION

Where a large industry is concentrated in one area certain external advantages may arise. The woollen industry in West Yorkshire is a good example of a concentrated industry and Fig. 3.7 (overleaf) shows some of the benefits the industry as a whole gains.

These advantages help to attract other firms connected with woollen products into the area, further reinforcing the external economies. It should be noted though that the advantages of concentration can turn into external diseconomies if demand for the region's product falls. In the case of the woollen industry, the development of man-made fibres and cheaper foreign products has created unemployment in West Yorkshire. Thus there has to be a balance between diversity and concentration to secure a longterm economic future for a region.

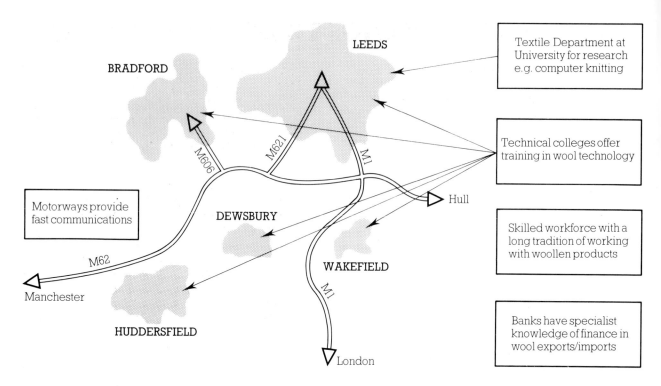

Fig. 3.7 The economies of concentration – the woollen industry in West Yorkshire

2 INFORMATION

Large industries can usually keep member firms better informed about new technological developments, employment opportunities, export markets and so on. The Textile Institute, for example, is a body where representatives from the industry can meet and exchange ideas for the benefit of all firms. Similar bodies exist in most large industries.

3 DISINTEGRATION

Figure 3.3 showed the sizeable number of firms involved in the production of a Mini Metro. In a large industry specialist firms concentrate on a particular part of the final product, developing expertise which can be used to improve specifications and performance. The advantages of this 'disintegration' can be illustrated using the car industry: Triplex have developed special safety glass for car windows which if shattered breaks into small round, not sharp, pieces; and Dunlop have developed 'anti-blowout tyres' to improve road holding and safety. An external diseconomy might arise, however, if a specialist component firm supplying the whole industry goes bankrupt.

INTEGRATION

The process of **integration** or mergers between firms can best be understood by looking at the stages involved in the production process.

The first or **primary** stage in production, involves the extraction of raw materials from land (or sea) and includes agriculture which uses the land for crop and animal produce. The raw materials are then used in the **secondary** stage of production where manufacturing takes place. The final stage in production, the **tertiary** stage, is concerned with the distribution of the product to the consumer and service industries which largely support the manufacturing process. Figure 3.8 shows that these three stages in production can be seen as a vertical process.

Fig. 3.8 The stages in the production process

Vertical integration occurs when two firms at different stages in this production process merge together. It may be for example that a brewery engaged at the secondary stage in the manufactur-

THINGS TO DO

1 Using the following example, show how the application of the division of labour principle can help to improve production:

	Gardening (sq. metres of land)	Selling computers (abroad)
John	10	8
Lisa	9	0

[John and Lisa each spend half a day on each activity.]

If computer exports are much more valuable than a tidy garden what does this imply about the division of labour principle?

2 Explain clearly the meaning of **interdependence** and why it creates problems for large firms.

3 Describe the various influences which help to determine labour productivity.

4 Why is 'big' not always 'beautiful' in large firms?

5 For each of the following products or services explain why you think a small or large size business is appropriate:
hairdressing; steel; banking; accountancy; railways.

6 State whether the following are internal or external economies:
(a) the Ford Motor Company increases its number of robots;
(b) Lucas develops a long-life battery suitable for all motor cars.

7 Study the table below.
Graphically plotting cost/unit on the vertical axis and number of units on the horizontal axis show how economies and diseconomies of scale occur. What is the optimum or lowest cost output? Plot a graph of total costs against number of units. Explain why the gradient of the curve changes and at what output gradient is zero. What is the significance of this output?

Total costs	Units	Cost per unit
£10 000	2 000	
£12 000	3 000	
£15 000	5 000	
£20 000	10 000	
£36 000	12 000	
£65 000	13 000	

ing of beer, merges with a public house at the tertiary stage to ensure effective retailing of its product. Such a move is known as vertical integration **forwards**. Equally vertical integration **backwards** can arise when a manufacturer takes over its raw material source, for example a sugar refiner taking over sugar beet plantations. Where a manufacturer takes over the whole industry's source of raw material, the move may be anti-competitive if rival manufacturers are charged a higher price to obtain the raw materials.

Horizontal integration occurs when two firms at the same stage of production making the same or similar products, merge together. Such integration can occur at any of the three stages of production. The Thorn–EMI merger is an example of two manufacturers in the electronics industry horizontally integrating. Habitat and Heals is an example of two furniture retailers at the tertiary stage merging. Horizontal integration can be anti-competitive because it narrows consumer choice. Where two firms, both with a large share of the market, merge, the Monopolies Commission may be called in to investigate whether or not such a merger is in the public interest. The role of the Monopolies Commission is explained in more detail in Chapter 8.

Conglomerate mergers are separated from vertical and horizontal because they involve firms which join together with unrelated products or services. The reasons for such mergers taking place are not always clear though achieving financial or managerial economies of scale could be a possible motive. Cadbury–Schweppes is a good example of a conglomerate merger which took place because Cadbury felt the market for chocolates had limited potential growth, partly because of the falling birth rate in the 1970s. The company did feel that there was scope for expansion in the soft drinks market and so took over Schweppes,

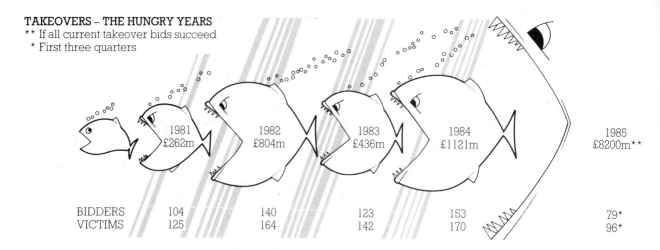

TAKEOVERS – THE HUNGRY YEARS
** If all current takeover bids succeed
* First three quarters

Fig. 3.9 The growing number of takeovers in the early 1980s

starting the 'Sch ... You know who' advertising campaign bringing in vastly increased sales. If economies of scale are the main economic benefit from mergers the evidence which exists does not seem to show many public gains from recent merger activity. Moreover since competition may be reduced it seems important to closely regulate merger activity. This again does not seem to have been the case in practice (see Chapter 8). Figure 3.9 shows the increasing number of mergers in recent years.

THE MOBILITY OF LABOUR

Just as the division of labour and economies of scale are featured in an economy organising its factors to achieve optimum output to satisfy as many wants as possible, so having a mobile labour force is equally important as declining industries shed labour and expanding industries demand more labour.

There are two main types of **mobility**: **geographical** which is connected with the movement of people from one part of the country to another; and **occupational** which is connected with the movement of people from one job to another. There are a number of factors which influence each type of mobility.

1 GEOGRAPHICAL

One of the most important factors affecting geographical mobility is the social ties people may have in a particular area. Anyone born and brought up in one area with an extended family close by and who has worked in the locality for a prolonged period will find uprooting to a new area difficult. The most geographically mobile of the population are in the 18–25 age group. Young people generally attach less importance to social ties and tend to adapt quickly to new surroundings. By contrast people over 50 are relatively immobile.

A further barrier to geographical mobility comes in the wide variation of housing costs around the country. In London and the South-East housing costs are nearly double those in parts of the North-East so that anyone living in the North and offered a job in London will find it very difficult to afford the move. The same is true for people living in London. They may well be tempted to stay in London even if suitable employment came up elsewhere, because it could prove too expensive to move back to the capital later on in their career.

Finally people with a family may find moving from one area to another disruptive in terms of their children's education. This is particularly important where secondary education is concerned since examination courses can differ widely between schools in different parts of the country. Parents may be unwilling to risk their children's chances of exam success by moving from one area to another.

2 OCCUPATIONAL

The degree to which a person is occupationally mobile can be affected by a large number of sometimes inter-connected factors. Age can significantly affect mobility since a young person tends to be adaptable to new skills and ideas whereas older people become more set in their ways. Older people too tend to be earning higher salaries than younger people and may be less attractive to a new employer who may need to retrain them. The educational qualifications a person has obtained can affect the range of jobs open to them. Some careers require degrees as entry qualifications so drastically limiting the number of people able to apply. The skill and training a person possesses can affect mobility. If it is a transferable skill, such

WHO HAS THE BETTER SENSE OF DIRECTION?

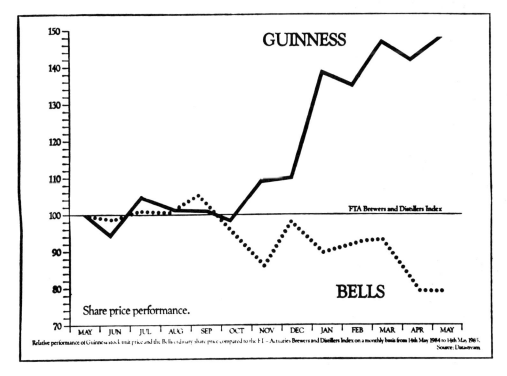

Since 1980 Bells' share of the UK Scotch Whisky market has declined by 20%.

Overseas, Bells has also failed to achieve its promised inroads into the crucial US market.

By contrast, the Guinness Group has not only revitalised its core brewing business and established a second major profit source, Retailing, it has also developed a strategy of "Growth for Tomorrow" by investment in Healthcare and Publishing.

Both Bells' predicament and Guinness' revitalisation have been recognised by the Stock Market as the graph, for May 1984 to May 1985, so vividly demonstrates.

Guinness' record justifies the claim that it can steer Bells in the right direction. The market confidence in the considerable abilities of the Guinness management team should further enhance Bells' shareholders' confidence.

On 14th May 1985, before rumours of the Guinness bid, Bells' shares languished at 143p.

Bells' shareholders are not only being offered a substantial premium over this price, they are being offered shares in an exciting, enlarged Guinness Group.

The growth prospects of this Group can only lead Bells' shareholders in one direction.

Towards accepting the very full offers made by Guinness.

GUINNESS PLC

DRAUGHT AND BOTTLED GUINNESS HARP KALIBER. DRUMMONDS MARTIN THE NEWSAGENT, LAVELLS. 7-ELEVEN STORES, CHAMPNEYS AND STORO CASTLE HEALTH RESORTS NATURE'S BEST VITAMINS GUINNESS PUBLISHING.

Bells has lost its way. Guinness is good for Bells.

Fig. 3.10a

BELL'S ESTIMATE ANOTHER YEAR OF RECORD PRE-TAX PROFITS IN 1985

Bell's confirm that Pre-Tax Profits for the year ended 30th June 1985 will be ahead of those for the year ended 30th June 1984.

1983
The Queen's Award
for Export Achievement

STAY WITH THE WINNING TEAM — REJECT THE GUINNESS BID

PROFIT BEFORE TAX £m	1974	1975	1976		1978	1979	1980	1981	1982	1983	1984
	3.02	4.18	7.53		13.61	16.82	16.84	20.02	27.60	31.27	35.17

Note: Years 1974 to 1976 inclusive are the twelve month periods to 31st December. Years 1978 onwards are the twelve months period to 30th June.

This advertisement is published by Arthur Bell & Sons plc whose directors (including those who have delegated detailed supervision of this advertisement) have taken all reasonable care to ensure that the facts stated and opinions expressed herein are fair and accurate and each of the directors accepts responsibility accordingly.

Fig. 3.10b

as typing or word processing, then mobility may be increased; a narrow, quickly-learned skill may be less transferable. Personality and motivation have a lot to do with occupational mobility. Employers base most appointments on an interview. The person that can communicate ideas well and shows the motivation to succeed is likely to be more mobile than someone who lacks self-confidence. Finally government training schemes make some impact on mobility; the Youth Training Scheme in particular aims to give young people the transferable skills required by industry and commerce.

3 HOW CAN MOBILITY BE IMPROVED?

As far as geographical mobility is concerned there are no easy answers. The development of new towns such as Milton Keynes and Telford, with high technology industries and low cost housing, will help to attract people, but not always those who are unskilled and in need of work. It is highly skilled people who are in most demand and usually those who are young and recently trained in new technologies. Companies do provide removal expenses as an incentive for employees to move and the government in the past has provided lodgings allowances for people who are unemployed in an area and who move out to look for work. This measure however has proved only marginally successful and in a significant number of cases people who have moved to new areas to look for work have after a short period of time moved back to their original location. Occupational mobility can be improved through retraining schemes and the acquisition of transferable skills. New initiatives in education such as the Technical and Educational Vocational Initiative and the Certificate of Pre-vocational Education aim to provide transferable skills. Government retraining centres play a role in improving occupational mobility though compared to some other European countries such as Sweden, the UK lags behind in the amount of money set aside for this purpose.

THINGS TO DO

1 Classify the following into **primary**, **secondary** and **tertiary** industries: banking, steel, mining, transport, hairdressing, construction, textiles, electronics, education, chemicals.

2 Say whether the following mergers are **vertical**, **horizontal** or **conglomerate**.

   (a) A newspaper takes over a printing firm.

   (b) A firm making sewing machines creates its own retail outlets.

   (c) ASDA and Harris–Queensway merge.

   (d) Nationwide and Woolwich building societies merge.

   (e) Nestlé takes over Findus frozen foods.

   (f) An oil company merges with a computer manufacturer.

3 Which type of merger (horizontal, vertical, conglomerate) most threatens competition?

4 How can mergers benefit the public?

5 Why is the immobility of labour a difficult problem to solve?

6 Use the two advertisements relating to the proposed takeover of Bells by Guinness (Fig. 3.10) to answer the following questions.

   (a) How would this proposed merger be classified?

   (b) What evidence do Guinness use to show their takeover is justified?

   (c) What evidence do Bell's use to reject the Guinness bid?

   (d) How might a merger affect competition in the drinks market?

   (e) What reasons might Guinness have for wanting to take over Bells?

   (Guinness successfully acquired Bells in August 1985.)

7 Figure 3.11 shows regional
unemployment in different parts of
the country. Where are the main
spare pools of labour and what
barriers exist to prevent people
moving from high to low
unemployment regions?

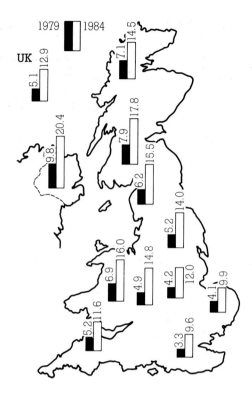

Fig. 3.11 UK regional
unemployment as a % of total
workforce

4
AN INTRODUCTION TO THE PRICE MECHANISM

INTRODUCTION

In Chapter 1 the economic problem of how to satisfy unlimited wants with strictly limited factors of production, was discussed together with some alternative approaches that have been developed to solve the problem. One important approach mentioned was that of the market economy where it was suggested that consumers would express their wants in the market place, demanding goods and services. Producers would then respond to these wants by supplying goods and services to the market at a price which would reflect costs and competition.

The process of how the market economy works is shown in Fig. 4.1. Wants are expressed by consumers who turn to the market place to contact producers/retailers supplying the good or service. The price paid for the good reflects the strength of consumer demand and the quantity supplied for sale.

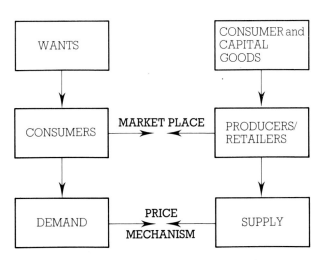

Fig. 4.1 How the market economy satisfies wants

The **price mechanism** is the term used to describe how resources are allocated according to the forces of demand and supply. This chapter provides an introduction to the factors influencing demand and supply and shows how the price of goods and services are determined by the interaction of these two forces.

DEMAND

If someone wants to buy something new, what factors influence their decisions to go ahead with the purchase? Suppose a new pair of shoes is being considered: probably the most important influence will be price. Also important will be the colour, styling and quality of materials used. A wise shopper will also compare prices of preferred styles in different shops to find which pair offer best value. Finally a constraint on the ability to purchase the most desirable shoes comes in the limitation of the income of the purchaser. Someone on a high income may be quite prepared to pay over £50 for a pair of shoes whereas someone on a low income may consider £25 expensive.

Thus in general terms four main influences on demand can be identified:
1 the price of the good being considered (Pn);
2 the tastes of the purchaser – colour, style, quality, etc. (T);
3 the price of other goods related to the one being considered (P1 . . . Pn–1);
4 The income of the purchaser (Y).
[n = good being considered for purchase]

Sometimes these influences are expressed in the form of a functional relationship:

$$Dn = f(Pn, T, P1 \ldots Pn{-}1, Y)$$

This is simply saying that the demand for a good is influenced by all of the above factors. Unfortunately such a relationship is difficult to work with because there are so many variables. Ideally there should be just one variable that can be plotted against demand. This being the case the simplest solution is to isolate one of the above influences on demand, then assess at a later stage how the other three variables might affect this relationship. The influence the price of the good has on quantity demanded is seen as being most important and this will now be examined in some detail.

Imagine an individual's demand for shoes over the period of a year in relation to the price of shoes. If shoes had an average price of £40 a pair, perhaps only 2 pairs would be bought. If, however, they were only £5 a pair perhaps as many as 9 pairs would be demanded. In fact a hypothetical table can be drawn up showing the possible quantity of shoes demanded in a year at different prices. It might look like this:

Price of shoes (pair) £	Quantity demanded in a year
40	2
30	4
20	6
15	7
10	8
5	9

Such a table is known as a **demand schedule**. The demand schedule can be simply translated onto a graph by plotting the price of shoes on the vertical axis and the quantity demanded on the horizontal axis (Fig. 4.2). It is important to recognise that the *shape* of the demand curve is determined by the relationship between the price of the good and the quantity demanded. Nearly all demand curves have a similar shape sloping down to the right. This gives rise to the **law of demand** which states that more of a good will be demanded at a lower price and less will be demanded at a higher price. This law is an economic law and relates to human behaviour. In this sense it assumes people behave rationally and whilst this is the case in most situations, there may be instances when the law does not hold. Goods like Rolls Royces and fur coats which have 'snob' appeal may only be bought because their prices are high, thus making them exclusive. At the other end of the scale, some goods are bought only because nothing better can

be afforded. They are sometimes labelled 'inferior' goods and if their price fell but incomes in general rose, fewer of them might actually be bought. Examples of inferior goods might include spam and black and white televisions. An economic law thus differs from a law in mathematics or science because it is a *general conclusion* about human behaviour. A law in a natural science always holds true.

Having considered the relationship between price and quantity demanded, it is important to return to the other factors which influence demand, namely tastes, the price of other related goods and income. These three other influences are together known as the **conditions of demand**. They can affect the *position* of the demand curve but not its shape. Consider the example of an individual's demand for records. The demand schedule for albums over a year might look as follows:

Price of records (£)	Quantity of records demanded
14	4
12	6
10	8
8	10
6	12
4	14
2	16

Now suppose that the price of cassettes goes down as mass production methods in Japan lower unit costs. Because cassettes are substitutes for records, the demand pattern for records might change as follows:

Price of records (£)	New quantity of records demanded
14	2
12	4
10	6
8	8
6	10
4	12
2	14

Plotting the two demand schedules on the same graph produces the result shown in Fig. 4.3.

It is clear that the position of the demand curve has changed in response to one of the conditions of demand changing. In this case cassettes represent the 'price of other related goods'. If their price had actually risen instead then the demand curve would have shifted to the right as records were substituted for cassettes. The 'price of other related goods' also includes those which are

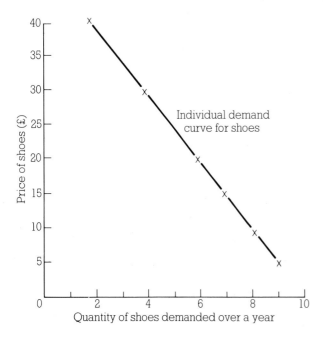

Fig. 4.2 An individual demand curve for shoes

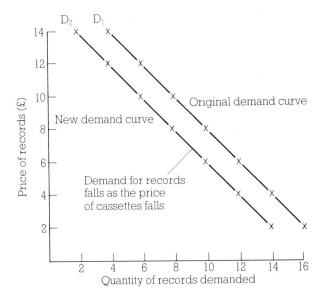

Fig. 4.3 The effect a change in the conditions of demand has on the demand curve position

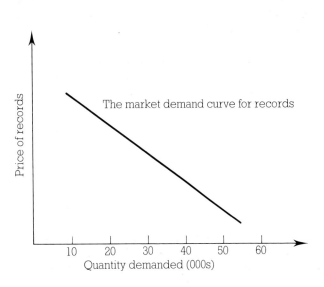

Fig. 4.5 A market demand curve

complementary to the good in question. If their price falls then demand for the original good will rise. If, for example, the price of video recorders falls significantly, this will increase the demand for video tapes as the tapes are complementary to the recorder. In general if any of the conditions of demand change, then the demand curve will move position left or right parallel to the original curve. The main possibilities are summarised in Fig. 4.4.

So far demand has been talked about with reference to an individual. What is more important is not just one person's individual preferences but all purchasers of a particular product or service. The activities of all the consumers in the market can be recorded in the form of a **market demand curve** (or schedule). It has a similar shape to an individual's curve but the quantity axis will record a much larger amount (Fig. 4.5).

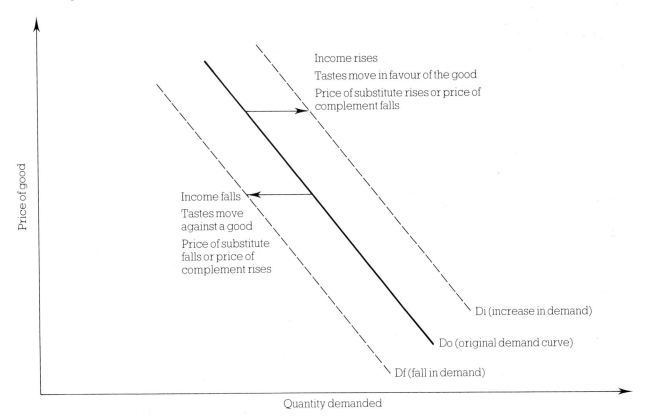

Fig. 4.4 How changes in the conditions of demand affect the position of the demand curve in general

SUPPLY

Just as there are various factors that influence demand, so a list of factors that affect the supply of a good or service can be compiled. Obviously the price at which the product will sell is an important influence affecting supply: the higher the selling price the greater the potential profit for the producer. Production also depends on the cost and availability of the factors of production, especially labour. Technical progress will also affect supply: in particular factory robots have helped to increase productivity. In industries like agriculture, changes in the weather can significantly affect output, a wet summer reducing the number of crops which ripen. This unpredictability in supply has led to farmers in the European Community (EC) being given financial support to protect their incomes. A further significant influence on the cost of supply comes when taxes are imposed on producers by the government, raising the cost of supply or, in the opposite case, when a subsidy is provided which lowers the cost of supply.

The factors affecting supply can thus be summarised:
1 the price of the good;
2 the cost and availability of the factors of production;
3 technical progress;
4 the weather;
5 taxes and subsidies.

As with demand, only one variable can be plotted against supply so the relationship between the price of the good and quantity supplied is isolated, the other influences (2) to (5) being called the **conditions of supply**.

A producer is usually in business to make a profit and will therefore be more willing to supply a large quantity of a good if he receives a high price for it. Equally a low price provides a small return and will probably result in a lower output. Thus a supply schedule for records might look like this:

Price of records (£)	Quantity of records supplied (000s)
14	13
12	12
10	11
8	10
6	9
4	8
2	7

If this schedule is plotted on a graph then a supply curve like that in Fig. 4.6 results.

The shape of the supply curve nearly always slopes down to the left reflecting the **law of supply**. This states that more of a good will be supplied at a higher price and less at a lower price. As with demand, the shape of the curve is determined by

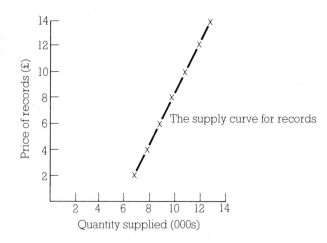

Fig. 4.6 A supply curve for records

the relation of price and quantity supplied. The conditions of supply can now be considered as they affect the *position* of the supply curve. Suppose, for example, a pay rise is awarded to the labour force at the record pressing plant. This might add £2 to the cost of producing a record. Thus the new supply schedule would look as follows:

Price with increased labour costs (£)	Quantity of records supplied (000s)
16	13
14	12
12	11
10	10
8	9
6	8
4	7

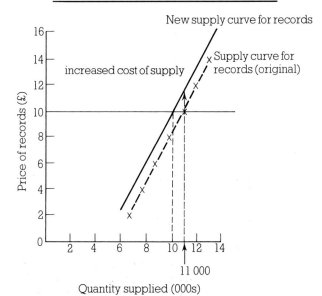

Fig. 4.7 The effect a change in the conditions of supply has on the supply curve position

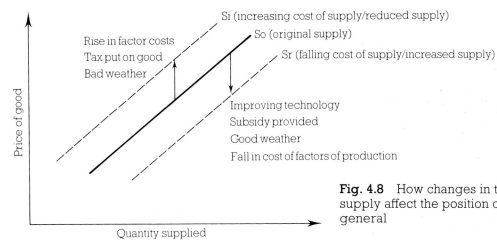

Fig. 4.8 How changes in the conditions of supply affect the position of the supply curve in general

Plotting the new schedule onto a graph produces the result in Fig 4.7.

The new supply curve is above the original reflecting the increased cost of supply. Looked at another way *less* is now supplied at the original set of prices. As the graph shows, when records were £10, 11 000 were supplied to the market. After the wage rise only 10 000 are supplied at a price of £10.

Figure 4.8 summarises how the other conditions of supply would affect the *position* of the supply curve if they altered.

One special type of supply curve that applies particularly to agriculture arises when the quantity supplied to the market is fixed. In farming, for instance, a fixed acreage of a certain crop will be planted at the start of the growing season which cannot then be altered. A fixed supply curve is shown in Fig. 4.9.

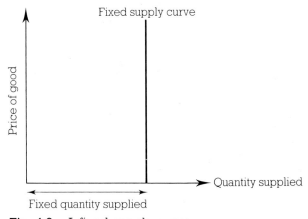

Fig. 4.9 A fixed supply curve

Normally supply will only be fixed for a short period: in farming this would mean a growing season. In the longer run the fixed factor (land in the case of farming) causing the fixed supply may be more variable, allowing supply to better respond to price changes.

COMBINING DEMAND AND SUPPLY

The useful thing about plotting demand and supply graphically is that they can be combined together on the same graph since they use the same axes. A hypothetical market demand and supply schedule for video recorders is shown below:

Price of video recorders (£)	Quantity of video recorders demanded (000s)	Quantity of video recorders supplied (000s)
500	10	90
450	20	80
400	30	70
350	40	60
300	50	50
250	60	40
200	70	30

Plotting this schedule graphically produces the result in Fig. 4.10.

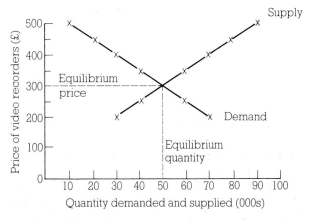

Fig. 4.10 The equilibrium position of the market mechanism

The price where demand and supply intersect is known as the **equilibrium price** and similarly on the horizontal axis the **equilibrium quantity** can be found. In this case supply equals demand at a price of £300 with 50 000 video recorders being bought and sold. The importance of this equilibrium cannot be emphasised enough. It shows the price where the quantity consumers want to buy is matched exactly by the quantity producers offer for sale. In this case there are no unsold video recorders and no shortage of them at the equilibrium price. If producers tried to charge more, say £350, then, as the schedule shows, 60 000 would be offered for sale but only 40 000 demanded leading to a 20 000 surplus. Equally if video recorders were underpriced, at say £200, only 30 000 would be supplied but 70 000 demanded creating a shortage of 40 000 recorders. Thus the equilibrium price is the mechanism for ensuring that wants are matched to consumer or capital goods. Goods that involve using scarce factors will tend to have a high price; those which are easy to mass produce in large quantities will have a lower price. The price mechanism ensures no wastage of resources because the price will move up or down to the equilibrium to ensure supply and demand match. When shops have sales they may do so because at the original price a surplus of certain items arose. The sale price represents their estimation of the equilibrium price and it usually ensures that all remaining items are sold.

How might the equilibrium price change? If any of the conditions of demand or supply alter then this will have an effect on equilibrium price and quantity. Suppose that technical improvements in the factory making video recorders allow them to be produced at a lower cost. The supply curve will move down as shown in Fig. 4.11 creating a new equilibrium price, P_1. Notice that the quantity demanded responds to the change in supply, moving from X to Y. Demand in this sense has *extended* along the curve.

To say that demand has increased might imply that the demand curve shifted *position*, something that could only happen if the conditions of demand changed. If, for example, the demand for video records did actually increase due to rising incomes then the curve would change position as shown in Fig. 4.12. In this case the equilibrium price would rise from Po to P_1 and the quantity supplied would *extend* from X to Y. If producers expect demand to carry on increasing they may invest in more productive machinery in the long-term, perhaps increasing supply to Sx and reducing the price below the original equilibrium to Px.

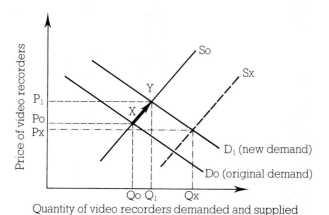

Fig. 4.12

In general if any of the conditions of demand or supply change, the position of one curve will always alter whilst movements along the other will occur in response causing an **extension** or **contraction**. A **fall** in demand for example will lead to a **contraction** in supply.

This introduction to the price mechanism shows how the economic problem can be solved in an automatic way without any government intervention taking place. Price is the mechanism which matches wants to resources. The system is fast acting and efficient because there is no wastage at the equilibrium price. It can be unfair, however,

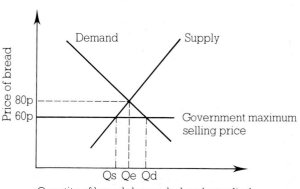

Quantity of video recorders demanded and supplied

Fig. 4.11

Quantity of bread demanded and supplied

Fig. 4.13

because if the consumer cannot afford the equilibrium price then that particular want is not satisfied. If the government decide to intervene in the price mechanism to keep prices low in essential goods then problems can arise if they set a maximum price below the equilibrium. Figure 4.13 shows that if the equilibrium price for bread is 80p per loaf and the government maximum price is 60p, at this price Qs will be supplied and Qd demanded.

Thus a shortage of Qd – Qs results. The only fair solution would be to *ration* bread but administering this would be costly, queues might develop outside bakers and some under counter sales might take place for favoured customers. Thus although government intervention seems well intentioned, it can still lead to a situation where a large number of wants go unsatisfied.

THINGS TO DO

1 What is meant by the **law of demand**? For which types of good does the law *not* always hold true?

2 Suggest three reasons why the **conditions of demand** for records might alter.

3 Study Fig. 4.14. If Do is the original

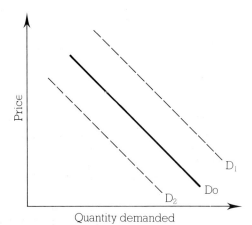

Fig. 4.14

demand curve for the stated products say whether the following changes in the conditions of demand would move it to D_1 or D_2:
  (a) 'Fabergé' aftershave is heavily advertised;
  (b) Contamination is suspected in Austrian wines;
  (c) British Rail improve catering facilities on Inter-City trains.

4 Plot the following demand and supply schedules (shown for houses) on a graph with clearly labelled axes:

  (a) What is the equilibrium price?
  (b) If the government tries to limit the price of houses to £20 000 what will be the result?
  (c) If the sellers of houses decide

to charge £50 000 per house, how large will the surplus be?
  (d) If building societies lower the cost of mortgages, how will this affect the position of the demand curve?
  (e) If the government abolish the stamp duty sellers pay when a house is sold, how might this affect the position of the supply curve?

Price of houses (£000s)	Quantity demanded (000s)	Quantity supplied (000s)
50	2	5
40	4	4
30	6	3
20	8	2
10	10	1

5 A wine bar finds that its demand schedule for wine is as follows:

Price of wine (£)	Bottles of wine demanded/night
10	50
8	70
6	90
4	110

On average one person drinks a bottle of wine each night and the capacity of the wine bar is 70 people. What price should it charge for wine? If only 30 people arrive before 9pm what should it do to the price of wine to achieve full capacity before 9pm?

6 In Fig. 4.15, if So is the original
supply curve, state whether the
following changes in conditions of
supply would move it to S_1 or S_2 for
the related products:

(a) Productivity at the Ford Motor
Company improves (Ford
Cars);

(b) The rent goes up at Esso's
Head Office in Victoria (Esso
Petrol);

(c) The government puts a tax on
soft drinks (Pepsi-Cola);

(d) British Rail announce an
increase in freight charges
(Coal).

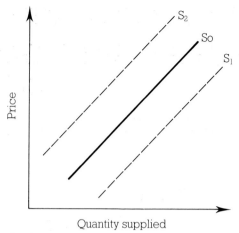

Fig. 4.15

5

EXCHANGING GOODS – MONEY AND BANKING

INTRODUCTION

In the last chapter it was clear that economies of scale and the division of labour enabled more goods to be produced at a lower unit cost than if small-scale production with little or no specialisation existed. Thus large-scale production can satisfy more wants and better solve the economic problem. But how can the large volume of goods produced be sold and exchanged for other goods? Today it is taken for granted that money will be used for buying and selling goods. A company manufacturing goods receives a money income from sales which is partly passed on to employees who can decide what to buy with their money. Money, however, had to be invented and before it existed a rather clumsy system of exchange took place called **barter**. Barter is said to take place when goods are exchanged directly. In primitive societies barter still exists but it does create a number of problems. Imagine, for example, a shoe maker who might want to swap his shoes for some flour. Not only has he got to find someone who wants shoes for the surplus flour he has produced, but also the shoes have to be the appropriate size for the miller's feet. Barter therefore became very time consuming and required this **double coincidence of wants** to take place at all. Deciding how much one good was worth in terms of another also created arguments and bad feeling. How much would a pair of shoes be worth in terms of spears and meat? Figure 5.1 shows the confusion!

THE ORIGINS AND FUNCTIONS OF MONEY

Money developed essentially to overcome the problem of the double coincidence of wants. Money can be defined as anything which is generally acceptable as a means of exchanging goods or settling debts. If the shoemaker could receive money in exchange for his shoes and then use the money to buy flour, the process of exchange becomes much quicker and avoids the double coincidence of wants because shoes can be exchanged with anyone who has money. Equally the miller may not want shoes but will be happy to exchange flour for money.

What makes money generally acceptable? Whatever is used as money needs to be fairly *durable* since it will be used a large number of times in the process of exchange. It also needs to be *portable* since it will be carried around a great deal. Also essential is for money to be *divisible* since goods will be exchanged in varying quantities, requiring different denominations of money. It also helps if money is quickly *recognisable* and its *value* should not change too much or too often!

The list of items that have been used as money in the past is a long one (Fig. 5.2). In New York there is a collection of over 70 000 different specimens which have been used, including jade, tea, mats, coconuts, beads, silk and stone rings. The most

Not surprisingly a better system of exchange soon came along!

Fig. 5.1

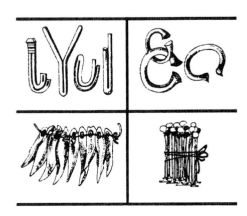

Fig. 5.2 Some of the early forms of money

widely used forms of money in the past have been grain, cattle, salt, shells and metals. Even today in rural parts of the less developed world a person's wealth is measured in terms of cattle and the Roman word for money *pecunia* comes from *pecus*, their name for cattle.

Today money is often defined in terms of legal and non-legal tender money. **Legal tender** has to be accepted by law and in England and Wales it comprises notes and coins issued by the Bank of England. **Non-legal tender** money is principally made up of cheques and credit cards which do not have to be accepted by law but are extremely convenient methods of payment. In fact when talking about the total amount of money in circulation in Britain today, non-legal tender money makes up about 85% of all money used, the remainder being legal tender.

Whilst the issue of legal tender money can be carefully controlled by the Bank of England, the amount of non-legal tender issued is mainly determined by the banking sector which prints its own cheques and credit cards. The banks, being profit-making institutions, do not always share the same view as the government about controlling the amount of money in circulation!

Money is an indispensable commodity in the modern economy to allow the efficient exchange of goods. It performs four vital functions without which economic development could not take place:

1 It acts as a **medium of exchange**. Because money comes in the middle of the exchange, the whole process can be speeded up. With a credit card many transactions can be completed with just one piece of plastic, making the whole process of exchange extremely simple (Fig. 5.3). (A credit card is of course a form of money, just like notes, coins and cheques.)

Barter = direct exchange: double coincidence of wants required

Money comes in the middle of exchange: *no* double coincidence of wants required

Fig. 5.3 How money acts as a medium of exchange

2 Money also acts as a **store of value** because it can be saved to be spent at a later date. While keeping money in a piggy bank is one option, money to be saved over long periods can earn interest in a bank or building society increasing the value of the amount saved. One problem connected with saving money comes in a period of rising prices (called **inflation**). If prices in the shops are going up by 10% a year, then a stereo cassette player costing £100 in January will rise to about £110 by the end of December. If the interest paid on savings is 5% a year then £100 saved in January will only be worth £105 by the end of December. Thus the purchasing power of savings tends to fall when inflation is high, making money a rather poor store of value.

3 Money acts as a **unit of account**. Because our currency is divisible into £ and pence every good can be given a value which reflects its scarcity. Thus a loaf of bread which is fairly readily available, might cost around 60p, whereas a Rolls Royce car can cost over £30 000, reflecting its very high value and scarcity. Units of a currency can also be compared internationally so that the value of the £ abroad can be measured in terms of the American dollar.

4 Finally money is a **standard for deferred payments**. This is one of the most important functions of money because it means money can be loaned out to be repaid at a later date. Banks accept deposits of money and are able to use these deposits to provide loans for business development. The loans can then be repaid from the future profits of the business (Fig. 5.4). Because money is measured in standard units, the value of the repayment will be the same as the value of the loan, with interest added on for the use of the money. If money did not perform this function it would be very difficult for an economy to develop. New enterprises have to borrow money to start and later expand. When money acts as a standard for deferred payments then equality in the value of loan and repayment is guaranteed.

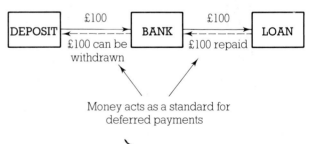

Money acts as a standard for deferred payments

Fig. 5.4

The four functions of money are often taken for granted in our economy today because money is so widely used. Take money away, however, and it is easy to see how the process of exchange and economic development could not take place. Because most of the money used today is taken from bank deposits, it is important to understand how banks accept, use and even create money.

THE DEVELOPMENT OF BANKS

Fig. 5.5 How bank notes first came into being – the introduction of 'paper money' was initially greeted with great suspicion as the cartoon shows

Banks originated as goldsmiths, keeping safe the amounts of gold deposited by their customers. Some of the early goldsmiths originated from Lombardy in Italy where they flourished as pawn-brokers and money lenders. In Lombardy they had always done business on simple wooden benches and that was why the Italian word for bench – *banco* – became 'bank'. The word 'bank-rupt' came from the old Italian *banca rotta* indicating 'the bench is broken'. Goldsmiths soon began to realise that because deposits of gold were not all withdrawn at once, some could be loaned out at interest. Also the receipt that the goldsmiths issued to depositors in return for their gold, was used as money to settle debts in the knowledge that the receipt could be exchanged for gold when required. This receipt provided the origins of the banknote which individual banks issued (Fig. 5.5)

until the Bank Charter Act of 1844 gave the Bank of England control over the issue of banknotes in England and Wales.

Banks also authorised orders written and signed by depositors asking for stated amounts of money to be paid to another named person. This represented the original version of the modern day cheque. Cheques soon became so widely used that during the 19th century printed cheques became commonplace.

Today there are four major banks in England – Barclays, Lloyds, National Westminster and the Midland – which together control over 90% of the total banking deposits. Increasingly, however, other institutions are offering banking services (particularly building societies) making the whole business of attracting deposits much more competitive.

THINGS TO DO

1 Explain what is meant by the **double coincidence of wants**. Why would it be difficult for economic development to take place under a system of barter?

2 What is **money**? Distinguish between **legal** and **non-legal tender** money.

3 Under what circumstances can money be a poor store of value?

4 Describe how far the following commodities would be satisfactory as forms of money using the terms described on p. 47:
   (a) pebbles on the beach;
   (b) cattle;
   (c) apples;
   (d) wine;
   (e) diamonds;
   (f) notes.

5 Legal tender limits for coins and notes are set as follows:
   – copper – 1p, 2p pieces up to 20p;
   – silver – 5p, 10p, 20p, 50p pieces up to £5;
   – bank notes and £1 and £2 coins – up to any amount.

Which of the following sums offered by a buyer are legal tender?
   (a) $5 \times £5$, $21 \times 50p$, $4 \times 10p$
   (b) $31 \times £10$, $15 \times 50p$, $30 \times 20p$, $10 \times 10p$
   (c) $2 \times £1$, $14 \times 20p$, $23 \times 10p$, $100 \times £2$

6 Explain the importance of money acting as a standard for deferred payments.

7 Martin just caught the last bus home from the disco. The fare was 40p, but he had no change and offered the bus conductor a £10 note. The bus conductor refused to accept it, and told him he would have to get off the bus. Martin refused and a row broke out.
   (a) Who was right under the law, the bus conductor or Martin, and why?
   (b) Can you suggest how the matter might have been resolved with less bad feeling?

(reprinted from the Banking Information Service leaflet *Money is our business*)

OPENING A BANK ACCOUNT

There are two principal types of bank account: current and deposit. A **current account** has three important features:

1 A chequebook is provided which can be used as a safe and convenient way of spending money compared to cash. Cheques are safe because if they are lost or mislaid they can be cancelled by notifying the bank. A stolen chequebook is also of limited use to a thief because cheques have to carry the signature of the account holder to be valid. They are convenient to use because they avoid the need to carry large amounts of cash about. Cheques can also be easily sent through the post to pay bills.

There are two types of cheque. The **open** cheque, which has no lines written across it, can be cashed at the payer's branch straightaway making it more acceptable to the payee but risky for the payer if the cheque is lost or stolen. Much more common is the **crossed** cheque which has to be paid into a bank account and cannot be exchanged for cash therefore making it much safer (Fig. 5.6a and b overleaf).

2 Money can be withdrawn from a current account straight away. If cash is required a cheque can be made payable to 'cash' and handed across the bank counter to receive money. A cashcard is also available to obtain money from a cash dispenser machine when the bank is closed.

3 Because a current account is used for spending rather than saving, banks do not normally pay interest on it. Indeed sometimes banks make charges for cheques written on a current account if the balance is below a specified amount.

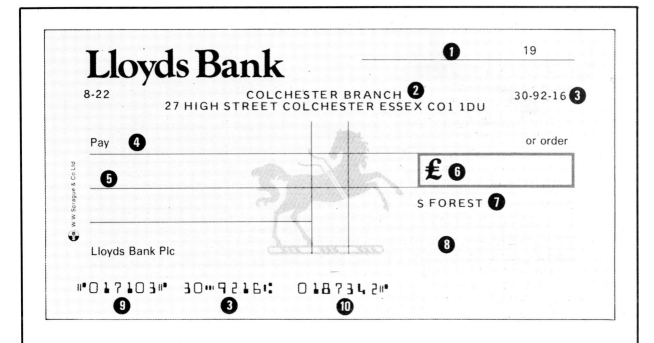

Lloyds Bank

8-22

COLCHESTER BRANCH ❷
27 HIGH STREET COLCHESTER ESSEX CO1 1DU

30-92-16 ❸

❶ 19

Pay ❹

or order

❺

£ ❻

S FOREST ❼

Lloyds Bank Plc

❽

⑈017103⑈ 30⑈9216⑈ 018734 2⑈

❾ ❸ ❿

(1)   Date.

(2)   Name of the account holding branch.

(3)   The sorting code number of Colchester Branch.

(4)   Payee's name — the person to whom you are paying the cheque.

(5)   The amount in words.

(6)   The amount in figures.

(7)   The name of the account.

(8)   Signature.

(9)   The cheque number.

(10)   The account number.

THE NUMBERS ALONG THE BOTTOM OF THE CHEQUE ARE WRITTEN WITH
SPECIAL MAGNETIC INK SO THAT THE COMPUTER CAN READ THESE FIGURES
WHEN IT IS SORTING CHEQUES.

Fig. 5.6a   A crossed cheque

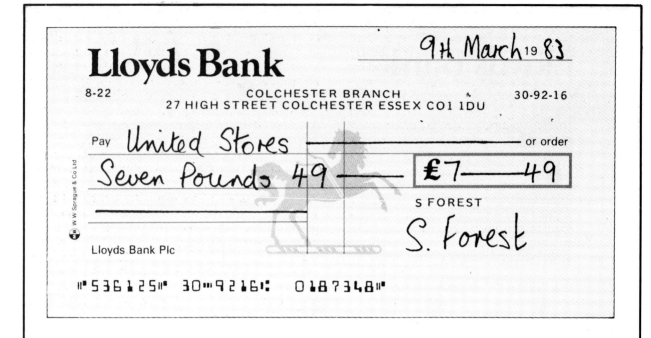

(1)   Always write in ink or ball-pen – NEVER pencil.

(2)   Write out the amount of the cheque in both words and figures – this gives us a double check on the amount you want to be paid, and prevents alteration of your cheques (particularly the figures).

(3)   Draw lines through any unused spaces (so that no-one can add anything to the amount you want to pay out).

(4)   Sign your cheque with your usual signature.

(5)   Don't forget to make a note of the cheque details on the special pages or stubs provided in the cheque book – this will be your record of what you've paid out, to whom and when.

(6)   **Crossings** – All cheque books we issue are "crossed" which gives extra protection. If an "open" cheque fell into the hands of a dishonest person, he might take it to your branch of Lloyds Bank and obtain cash for it. If your cheque is "crossed" then it has to be paid into a bank account.

Fig. 5.6b   How to fill in a cheque correctly

A **deposit account** is designed for saving money. Here the customer does not usually have a chequebook but interest is paid on the amount deposited. The rate of interest is determined by the bank's **base rate** which in turn is influenced by the total amount of saving and borrowing. If savings are greater than borrowings, the base rate may fall to attract more borrowers. If borrowing is excessive, the base rate will rise to attract more savers. The deposit rate is usually about 2% below base rate. Withdrawals from deposit accounts are often subject to seven days' notice, though small amounts can usually be withdrawn on demand. The Bank of England may wish to influence the level of bank base rates which it can do through its own **intervention rate** formerly known as the **minimum lending rate**. This is the rate of interest that the Bank charges for borrowers. For the High Street banks to stay competitive, they have to alter their base rates in line with the Bank of England's intervention rate.

Holders of bank accounts will receive a regular **statement** of their financial transactions sent out at monthly or quarterly intervals (Fig. 5.7). The statement details all withdrawals, deposits, standing orders, etc. which have taken place during the preceding period.

LOANS AND OVERDRAFTS

With the money banks receive from current and deposit accounts, income can be earned for the bank through loans and overdrafts. A **loan** can be either in the ordinary or personal category. **Ordinary loans** require some form of **security**. If a bank lends money, it has to have some assurance that it can get its money back and a security is some form of asset the borrower owns. It may be an insurance policy, the deeds to a house, share certificates, or valuable jewellery. The bank will keep the title to the security for the duration of the loan and if the borrower fails to repay, the bank will claim the security as settlement of the debt.

Ordinary loans can be negotiated for large sums, millions of pounds in some cases, but for smaller amounts a personal loan may be preferred because no security is required. A **personal loan** may pay for a foreign holiday or a new car, and usually involves a maximum of a few thousand pounds. Personal loans, however, carry higher interest rates than ordinary loans because of the absence of any security.

An **overdraft** arises when more money is taken out of a bank account than has been paid in. Overdrafts have to be arranged with a bank and are governed by agreed limits.

Overdrafts differ from loans in some important respects. Firstly a loan is *credited* to a current account whereas an overdraft represents a *debit* and is shown by symbols such as DR or OD on a bank statement (Fig. 5.7). Secondly, overdrafts tend to be periodic, especially for businesses, whereas a loan is repaid over a fixed time period. A business cannot always match together payments and receipts so that over certain periods an overdraft will arise as payments exceed receipts. At other times of the year the opposite situation will occur. A further difference between a loan and an overdraft comes in the interest calculation. Overdrafts are charged on a daily basis whereas a loan is estimated on an annual basis. It is much more expensive to have a £200 overdraft for a year than to take out a £200 loan for the same time period. This is because the daily interest on an overdraft may be as high as $\frac{1}{2}$% which over a year would amount to over 150% interest! However, overdraft facilities are essential for business customers: without them if on any single day money owed exceeded receipts, then the business could be forced to close down.

THE CHEQUE CLEARING SYSTEM

One of the complex operations banks perform is to transfer money throughout the country and indeed the world. The main ways in which cheques are credited to the payee and debited from the payer is through the **cheque clearing system**. It works as follows:

Adam Jones may write a cheque drawn on Lloyds Bank for a new car bought from High Street Motors Ltd. They pay the cheque into their Barclays Bank account which credits the company with the amount on the cheque. That cheque leaves the branch the next day for London where it arrives at Barclays Clearing House in the City. It is sorted and sent firstly to the Central Clearing House and then to Lloyds Clearing House where it is further sorted into a pile to be sent to the Lloyds branch where Adam Jones has his account. The next day it arrives at his branch to be debited from his account (Fig. 5.8 overleaf). Altogether an average of four million cheques a day are cleared in London. To put this into proportion, one million cheques piled on top of each other would reach the top of the Post Office Tower in London. The total value of each day's cheques averages over £10 000m which is almost as much as is spent on the whole of education by the government during a year!

Banks taking part in the clearing system are more correctly called **clearing** banks. They include the four major banks, Williams & Glyns, Coutts and the Cooperative Bank.

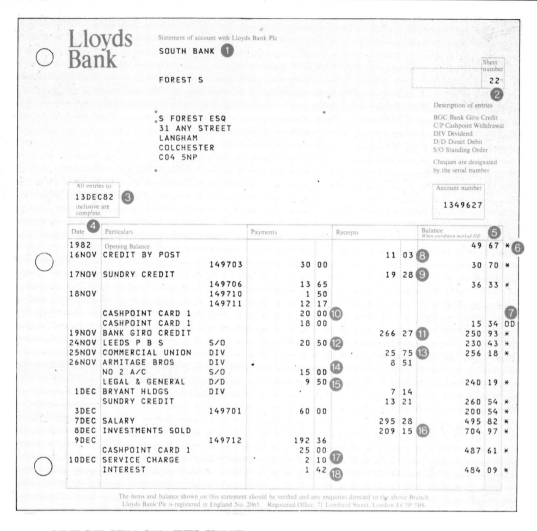

SPECIMEN STATEMENT

1 Name of the account-holding branch

2 Statement number

3 Date on which the statement is produced

4 Date on which account has been debited or credited for each transaction

5 Balance on the account after day's transactions have been completed

6 Symbol denoting credit balance

7 Symbol denoting overdrawn balance

8 Items received by post for the credit of customer's account

9 Credits paid in at customer's own bank branch

10 Entry denoting withdrawal, using the bank's Cashpoint machine (an automated cash dispenser)

11 Credits paid in at another bank or branch, either by the customer or by a third party (other than salary)

12 Standing order – regular payment made automatically by the bank in accordance with customer's instructions

13 Dividend – credit received from a company representing income earned from the customer's shares

14 Regular payment made by standing order to repay customer's loan from the bank

15 Direct debit – a regular payment like a standing order, but payment is originated by the named company. The bank holds the customer's instructions to debit the account

16 Entry denoting investments (e.g. shares) sold by the bank for the customer, under his instructions

17 Bank charge levied for operating the account during the quarterly period September 1982 to December 1982.

18 Interest charge levied on any overdrawn balance on the account during the quarterly period September 1982 to December 1982.

Fig. 5.7 A bank statement showing the usual transactions of a current account

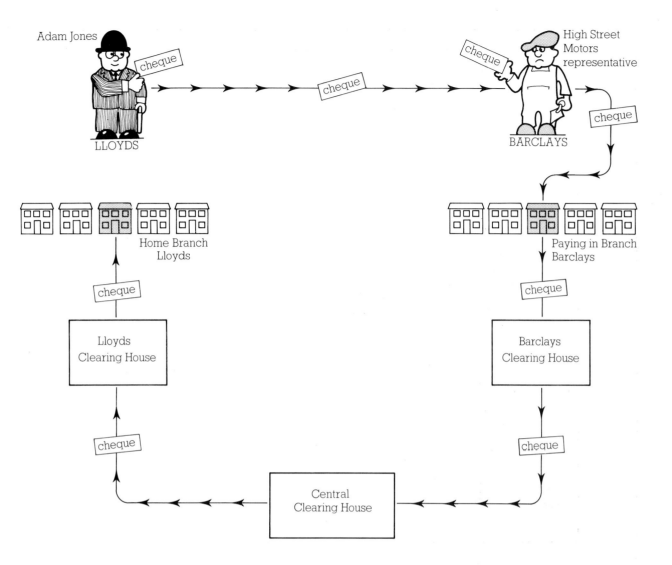

Fig. 5.8 The process of cheque clearing via the Central Clearing House

A SUMMARY OF THE MAIN FUNCTIONS OF BANKS

Banks have four principal economic functions.

1 They *distribute* all legal tender money on behalf of the Bank of England. It is important to understand that the Bank of England has the sole right to *issue* legal tender notes in England and Wales, but it relies on the clearing banks for distribution. Over the year each bank keeps a record of how much of each type of coin is needed at any time of the year. In December much more is requested than at other times, when people draw out money for Christmas shopping. In general the banks play an important role in making sure that cash is available where and when it is wanted, and that anyone can get change in a bank.

2 Banks accept *deposits* of money into current and deposit accounts. These deposits are known as **liabilities** since the banks are liable to pay this money back on demand to current account holders and after 7 days to deposit account holders.

3 Banks *lend* out money. Banks regard the money they lend out as part of their **assets** since it represents money owed back to them. By charging a higher rate of interest to borrowers than that given to savers banks make their profits.

4 Banks *collect* and *transfer* money via the cheque clearing system. The efficiency of this system means that generally cheques only take three days to clear. Thus the cheque system is the most widely used form of money in the UK and in most other industrialised nations.

THINGS TO DO

1 Identify the bank signs in Fig. 5.9.

 (a)

 (b)

 (c)

 (d)

 (e)

 (f)

Fig. 5.9

2 Identify the errors in the cheques in Fig. 5.10.

3 What are the main differences between a **current account** and a **deposit account**?

4 What is the origin of the term **bank**?

5 Distinguish between an **open** cheque and a **crossed** cheque.

6 'A loan and an overdraft are merely different words for the same type of borrowing.' What is wrong with this statement?

7 Why is **security** asked for when a loan is negotiated?

Fig. 5.10a

A

15 Feb 19   **20-87-29**

BARCLAYS

BARCLAYS BANK LIMITED
236 Tottenham Court Road W1A 2JF

Pay ~~Sports suppliers~~ _Sportsline Ltd_   or order

Two hundred and ten pounds   £ _210—00_

M. OWENS

M OWENS.

| Cheque No. | Branch No. | Account No. |

⑈488168⑈   30⑈1840:   29064010⑈

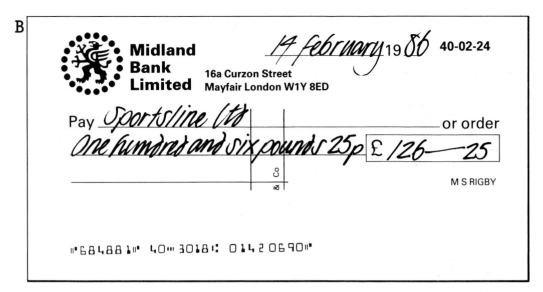

Fig. 5.10b

8 What are the main influences on the level of a bank's **base rate**?

9 Describe briefly the process of **cheque clearing**.

10 What other financial institutions perform similar functions to those of banks? Why are they growing in importance?

SOME IMPORTANT BANK SERVICES

A CHEQUE CARD

Fig. 5.11   A cheque card

A **cheque card** (Fig. 5.11) is used to guarantee that a cheque written up to £50 in value will be honoured by the payer's bank. Since cheques are not legal tender a shopkeeper may be uncertain about accepting a cheque in case there is not enough money in the holder's account to cover the transaction. If this is the case the cheque will 'bounce' and be returned to the shopkeeper with its value unpaid. The same problem does not arise when a cheque card is used since a guaranteed cheque up to £50 cannot be stopped. Cheque cards are normally only issued after the account holder has shown competence in managing money by not running up unnotified overdrafts.

A CREDIT CARD

A **credit card** (Fig. 5.12 overleaf) allows the holder to buy goods or obtain services at any shop, restaurant, garage, etc. which has joined the scheme, without paying cash or using a cheque at the time of purchase. Instead, a plastic card is used embossed with the customer's name and credit number, and carrying his specimen signature. The card is presented and a voucher signed by the cardholder. At the end of the month a statement is sent to the cardholder showing all transactions made during that month. These can then be paid in full with one cheque, or by instalments in which case interest will be charged.

Fig. 5.12 Examples of the most well-known credit cards. In the case of American Express, cardholders have to pay a yearly fee to use the card in addition to normal charges

The big two credit card companies in Britain are Barclaycard, which has over $3\frac{1}{2}$ million card holders, and Access, which has slightly more, drawn from the other three big clearing banks (Midland, Lloyds and National Westminster) which own it. More sophisticated cards include Diners Club and American Express which are directed more towards the needs of travelling business people because a large number of outlets worldwide accept them. Increasingly large stores are promoting their own credit cards and the Marks & Spencer chargecard is now beginning to rival Barclaycard and Access in terms of membership.

The advantages of credit cards are that they remove the need to carry around large amounts of cash; they are useful in emergencies; and they enable you to delay payment for a short period of time without paying interest. In all cases the interest rates are lower than on hire purchase schemes. The disadvantages are that the longer you delay payment, the higher the interest charges become; every cardholder has a credit limit (which can be as low as £100); and that if they are not used carefully the credit cardholder can get into debt.

A CASH DISPENSER CARD

Fig. 5.13 A cash card

A **cash dispenser** is a machine set in the wall of a bank branch, building society or retail store, which is stocked with banknotes. The customer is given a personal code number and a card which can be inserted into the machine to withdraw cash (Fig. 5.13), provided the customer types in the code correctly and the account balance is sufficient to meet the withdrawal. Some cash dispenser machines are more sophisticated, allowing details of the account to be given and, if required, a chequebook to be forwarded to the customer. Cash dispenser machines are very useful when the bank is closed as they may be open 24 hours a day, 7 days a week (Fig. 5.14).

STANDING ORDER

If amounts of money have to be paid out at regular intervals, for insurance premiums, subscriptions, etc. then the bank can take on this responsibility via a **standing order** payment. The account holder simply fills in a form with the details of the payee's bank, the amount and when it has to be paid and the bank will then transfer the stated amount on the due dates. Standing orders avoid the danger of forgetting to pay and are clearly itemised on a bank statement which the account holder receives periodically (Fig. 5.7).

BANK GIRO CREDIT

A **paying-in** or **credit slip** is used for cheques or cash that are deposited in the account holder's name. A **bank giro credit form** (Fig. 5.15 overleaf) is used when the account holder wishes to make a payment to an account held at another branch or even another bank. As Fig. 5.15 shows, space is allowed to write in the code number, branch and bank name of the payee, together with their account number and the amount to be paid. This system saves the trouble of posting cheques or sending cash in payment for bills. Companies can by a series of giro credits pay all their employees' salaries using just one cheque overall to cover the total of salary credits.

Fig. 5.14 A cash dispenser machine means money can be withdrawn 24 hours a day, 7 days a week

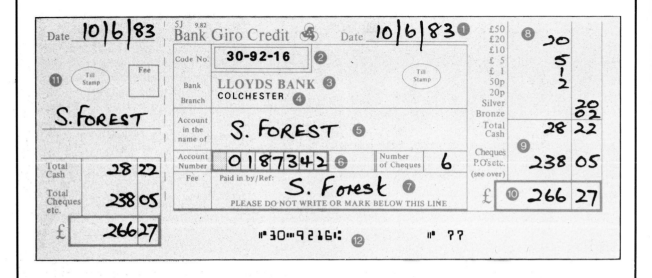

(1)   Date.

(2)   Sorting code number of the account holding branch (as at (3) on specimen cheque).

(3)   Name of account holding bank.

(4)   Name of account holding branch (as at (2) on specimen cheque).

(5)   Account holder's name (as at (7) on specimen cheque).

(6)   Account number (as at (10) on specimen cheque).

(7)   Signature of person paying the money in.

(8)   Breakdown of cash paid in.

(9)   Total of cheques paid in, details of which are listed on the back.

(10)   Total of the credit to the account (cash and cheques).

(11)   Counterfoil (your record of what you've paid in).

(12)   Magnetic ink symbols to enable automatic processing by the computer.

THIS BANK GIRO CREDIT SHOULD BE USED WHEN PAYING MONEY INTO YOUR ACCOUNT AT ANOTHER BANK OR AT ANOTHER BRANCH OF LLOYDS BANK.

Fig. 5.15   A giro credit slip

Fig. 5.16 Traveller's cheques are one of the safer forms of money with which to travel abroad since if they are stolen their value can be reclaimed

Traveller's cheques are a safe and convenient way of taking money abroad. Anyone can buy them at a bank (or travel agency) and they are available in various denominations (Fig. 5.16). Each cheque has to be signed when purchased and signed again when presented for payment abroad. Usually if traveller's cheques are lost or stolen, the issuing bank can cancel them and refund their value to the purchaser.

HOW BANKS CREATE CREDIT

Perhaps one of the most important points to understand about banks is that they can and do lend out more money than they have cash deposited at the bank. This happens because of the popularity of using cheques and credit cards as money. Banks have observed that if for example a Mr X has deposited £100 in cash in a current account, he is likely to spend £90 using his chequebook and will only require £10 in cash. Whilst this 10% **cash ratio** varies in different parts of the country, it is, if anything, becoming smaller as the popularity of using credit cards instead of cash grows. Logically a bank might then lend out the £90 not required but again if for example a Miss Y borrowed £90, on average 10% would be taken out in cash (£9) and the other £81 using cheques. Thus lending £90 leaves £81 cash still in the bank!

Some basic mental arithmetic can show that if banks really want to lend out all of the £90 cash, then they could in fact raise their limit for borrowing to £900 in total. If Miss Y borrowed £900 then on average £810 would be taken out using cheques and £90 in cash. Banks in this way can actually create credit to a much higher value than their cash base (Fig. 5.17).

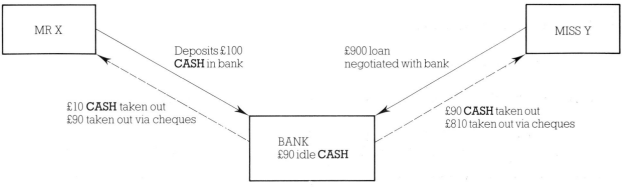

Fig. 5.17 The process of creating credit

LIABILITIES (Deposits)	£	ASSETS (Lending base)	£
Mr X deposits cash	100	Mr X's cash, available for withdrawals	100
Miss Y's loan creates a deposit	900	Loan or advance to Miss Y	900
TOTAL	1000	*TOTAL*	1000

How do banks balance their books if they are lending more than is being deposited? The answer lies in the fact that a loan is credited to an account where it actually counts as a deposit. The balance sheet for a bank which reflects the above transactions might look like the one above.

It is perhaps easier to understand now how banks contribute so much to the amount of money in an economy. They will want to create credit because they are in business to make a profit and additional lending earns additional interest. What is very important is that depositors trust banks with their money so that if they want to withdraw cash at anytime they are always able to. Clearly if people did not trust the bank and everyone tried to withdraw their deposits at once, the bank could only pay about 10% of customers.

The huge advantage of banks creating credit is that more money is available for business expansion and economic development without which new jobs could not be provided.

The Bank of England has to exercise some control over just how much credit banks create because too much money in relation to the goods produced can lead to inflation. This control is called **monetary policy** and is discussed in more detail in Chapters 14 and 16.

THE FUTURE OF BANKS

There are two major technical developments in banking. The first is the increasing automation in branch banking. In Sweden, for example, there are banks so highly automated that branch employees are only needed to give customers help in using the machines. Such banks can be opened with security cards for use outside normal hours.

The other major trend is towards 'home banking' which the Bank of Scotland has pioneered in the UK. Using a computer keyboard terminal linked to a phone line and television screen, bills can be paid, current account balance checked, standing order details given and interest moni-

tored as well as the ability to transfer money between current and deposit accounts. It is likely that other banks will develop similar facilities.

There have also been recent regulations introduced to encourage more competition between financial institutions which has led in particular to building societies introducing banking services such as chequebooks and cashcards. This wider competition may have some adverse effects on the growth of the clearing banks but it is good for the depositor who stands to gain a better service at a lower cost.

THINGS TO DO

1 What are the main differences between a **cheque card** and a **credit card**?

2 What is a **standing order**?

3 If Mr A deposits £250 cash in a bank and withdraws only 10% in the form of cash, how much can the bank make available for lending? If all the loan goes to Mr B show how the bank's balance sheet will look.

4 Why does the creation of **credit** depend on the trust of the depositor?

5 If a bank finds that only 8% of its cash deposits are withdrawn, how much credit can it create if total deposits are £300?

6 'The Bank of England controls the issue of notes in England and Wales, therefore it also controls the total supply of money.' Why is this statement inadequate?

6

DISTRIBUTING GOODS TO THE CONSUMER

INTRODUCTION

Having looked in some detail at how products are manufactured, it is important to look at the final stage in the production process: that of getting the product from the factory to the consumer. Traditionally there have been two stages in distribution, those of the **wholesaler** and **retailer**. The wholesaler is often called the 'middleman' in production, buying goods in bulk from the manufac-turer and selling in smaller quantities to the retailer. Today, however, the process of distribution is changing dramatically as large out-of-town 'superstores' combine the roles of warehousing and retailing to the public. The traditional 'High Street' shopping centre is now experiencing considerable competition from the out-of-town stores which are growing in popularity because of their low prices and easy parking (Fig. 6.1).

Fig. 6.1 A decaying high street – once a flourishing shopping centre

The face of retailing in the future will be an interesting battle between the centre and out-of-town units and already a number of traditional retailers have combined forces to set up out-of-town stores, seeing the potential growth that lies out of the High Street.

RETAILING – TYPES OF SHOPS

THE DEPARTMENT STORE

The **department store** has traditionally been the centre for buying 'everything under one roof'. The most famous and largest department store is Harrods in Knightsbridge, London. Other well known names include Selfridges, John Lewis and Fenwicks. Products are organised into departments with staff who provide expert advice and good service. A wide variety of goods will normally be sold, ranging from food and clothing to sports equipment and household goods. Department stores have the advantage of being convenient for the customer who can buy a wide range of goods from one shop with assistance from the sales staff. The disadvantages are the higher prices which result from a large number of personnel and a lower turnover on individual items which may not allow large bulk discounts from suppliers.

Department stores are less popular today than in the past because city centre parking is more difficult and, perhaps more important, out-of-town hypermarkets offer a wide range of low-priced goods with free and easy parking.

SUPERMARKETS

Twenty-five years ago supermarkets were still in their very early stages, mainly because before the Resale Price Maintenance Act in 1964, manufacturers could withhold supplies if retailers discounted on their directed selling price. The act abolished price maintenance, allowing retailers flexibility in their pricing and thus the idea of supermarkets grew rapidly as bulk buying and a high turnover allowed lower pricing. Statistics show that in 1957 there were only about 80 supermarkets but by 1978 this had grown to 6200. Supermarkets are characterised by self-service, attractive displays, a large number of checkouts and, above all, cheap prices. Stores are usually arranged so that the most commonly bought goods are at the back of the store thus attracting the customer well inside to buy other products.

Supermarkets are now much more than grocery shops diversifying into fresh foods, meats, wines and spirits, DIY goods, small electrical durables and clothing. In general groceries provide a low profit margin whereas non-foods give a much better return. For example, while profit margins on

Fig. 6.2b An Asda hypermarket – Asda has approximately 7% of the market share

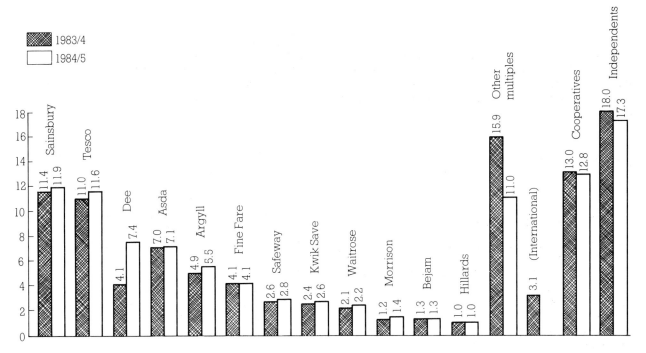

Fig. 6.2a Market shares in the grocery league 1983/4 and 1984/5 (% of total)

'dry groceries' (canned and packaged goods) average around 9%, with meat and vegetables around 13%, clothing, household textiles and electrical goods average around a 25% profit margin.

Supermarkets have the advantage of self-service and low prices for customers but where they are situated in town centres, they may be rather inconvenient for parking. Figure 6.2a shows the market share of the main grocery firms in the UK. It is likely that the newer firms with the large out-of-town stores (such as Asda – Fig. 6.2b) will increase their market share at the expense of the Co-op which has a legacy of small shops. Supermarkets in general are now making inroads into the independents' share of the UK grocery trade at around 3% a year.

HYPERMARKETS

The word hypermarket comes from the French *hypermarché* and the development of this type of store started much earlier on the continent than here in Britain. Hypermarkets, which are sometimes known as **superstores**, have a minimum size of around 3325 sq. m. (about the size of three football pitches) but some, such as the Tesco store at Irlam in Lancashire, are over 9300 sq. m. They are on the edge of town with free car parking and will sell, at a discount, a wide range of goods (Fig. 6.3 overleaf). Asda is one of the best known companies in the hypermarket growth league with around 85 stores, but other well-known names such as Fine Fare, Tesco, Sainsbury, BHS, Marks &

Spencer and Woolworths are all engaged in superstore development. Marks & Spencer, for example, have teamed up with Tesco to develop a number of sites including a large one at Cheshunt in Hertfordshire with almost 12 000 sq. m. of selling space and parking for at least 1000 cars, making it one of the biggest shopping complexes in the country. Most recently Asda have teamed up with MFI, the discount furniture retailers, and could overtake Marks & Spencer as Britain's biggest retailer. The merger firmly gets behind the idea that the future of retailing is out-of-town and the only limitation to hypermarket expansion comes in the scarcity of large out-of-town sites especially in the South-East of England. Local authorities in the South-East are worried about the impact of hypermarkets on local shops and have refused planning permission for several developments for this reason. Geographically in the North-East there is one hypermarket for every 110 000 people, but in the South-East there is only one store per 400 000 people.

Hypermarkets now cover a wide variety of retail areas besides groceries. DIY stores are fast growing (B & Q, Texas, Homebase, etc.) as well as carpets (Queensway, Allied Carpets, etc.) and electrical goods (Comet, Ultimate, etc.).

Hypermarkets have the advantages of cheap prices, everything being under one roof, easy parking and convenient locations, since driving is away from city centres. Their main disadvantage comes in the large amount of land they use up, and the problems they create for the High Street shops, but since many High Street retailers are now involved in hypermarket development this argument is less valid and it may be the smaller multiple that is worst hit.

Fig. 6.3 Easy parking in an edge of town hypermarket – Sainsbury's had the largest share of the grocery market in 1985

MULTIPLE CHAIN STORES

Multiple chain stores are those where one company owns a large number of branches throughout the country. In this sense some large supermarket chains are also multiples but in general a wide variety of products are marketed through multiples. Well-known names include Boots the chemists, W H Smith for books and stationery, and C & A for clothing. The multiple sector in the retail trade has been growing fast over the last decade (by over 200%) but sales of the ten largest firms grew by over 270% showing that this sector is becoming increasingly dominated by a few large firms. These firms have tended to diversify their range of products and W H Smith, Boots and Marks & Spencer in particular have moved well away from their original trading base. Multiples have the advantage of being able to buy standard lines in bulk and thus offer low prices. They can standardise shop operations, carefully monitor the performance of each retail unit and be systematic in the search for new retail techniques, stores and product lines. The main disadvantages are for the manufacturers supplying the multiples who can be put out of business by the withdrawal of an order. They are often dictated to and work with minimal profit margins.

INDEPENDENTS

Independent retailers are those who own just a few or perhaps one shop. Many are sole traders or partnerships and they cover the whole range of retailing from food to musical instruments.

Share of retail trade 1961–82

	1961	1966	1971	1978	1982
cooperatives	10.9	9.1	7.1	6.8	5.8
multiples	29.2	34.5	38.5	46.5	63.0
independents	59.9	56.4	54.4	46.7	31.2

Shop numbers 1971–82

	1971	1982	% change
cooperatives	16 480	8 556	− 48.1
multiples	71 162	66 013	− 7.2
large independents	83 996	80 141	− 4.6
one-shop independents	338 210	208 185	− 38.4

Source: *Annual Abstract of Statistics*

The tables above show that the *number* of independents has been declining rapidly and also (more slowly) their *share* of retail trade. Their decline has been particularly marked in the field of groceries. Labour costs as a percentage of sales tend to be higher in small shops which also do not have the advantage of being able to buy in bulk at a discount. There are some advantages for the owner – flexible opening hours, the personal retainment of profits, personal control over the organisation of the shop and the requirement of only a small amount of start-up capital. There are some disadvantages for the consumer principally in the form of the higher prices paid at the independents and the smaller variety of stock compared to a supermarket, although the personal service element and the possibility of credit may compensate for this.

MAIL ORDER

Mail order selling involves the customer ordering goods by post or over the telephone. It is a growth industry because sales over the last ten years have almost quadrupled from around £550m to over £2.5 billion. Much of the attraction has come from traditional catalogue retailers like Great Universal Stores (Janet Frazer, Marshall Ward, etc.) and Littlewoods, whose appeal to customers has been not so much cut prices as free credit together with the convenience of 'shopping' in their own homes.

More recently the fastest growing sector has been **direct response** mail order – special offers of individual products where buyers have to send cash with orders. Annual sales bring in about £300m in total. One of the most successful firms has been Scotcade, started in Shropshire in 1972. Turnover in 1983 was around £15m.

The main disadvantage of catalogue mail order buying comes in the higher prices generally charged for items and the problem of not being able to see the goods before buying them. For 'direct response' mail order, there is the possibility of the exploitation of customers where offers are not quite as genuine as they may seem!

COOPERATIVES

The **cooperative movement** dates back to 1844 when a group of men in Rochdale opened a shop in Toad Lane with an initial capital of £28. Cooperatives today are organised into regional groupings and are registered as friendly societies having different principles from most private enterprise companies. Those principles can be summarised as follows:

1 Membership of a cooperative society should be open to anyone without social, political or religious discrimination.

2 Cooperative societies are democratic organisations with the principle of one member, one vote.

3 Share capital should have a strictly limited rate of interest, if any.

4 Any surplus arising out of trading should be distributed back to cusomers via a **dividend**.

5 All cooperative societies should make provision for the education of their members.

6 There should be international cooperation between cooperative societies.

Perhaps because loyalty to the 'Co-op' rests with an older generation (who saw it as a movement representing the interests of working people) its customers tend to be rather elderly and it has suffered from the legacy of owning a lot of small uneconomic shops. The newer retailers such as Asda, with economies of scale and no outdated shops to close, have encroached on the Co-op's market severely reducing its share of the grocery trade. The Co-op has attempted to update its organisation by reducing the number of societies, closing small shops and opening 'superstores'. The Co-op is still the nation's largest milk retailer and farmer and operates around 8000 shops, still far and away the biggest retail chain. Whether it can survive the competition from the newer out-of-town hypermarket-orientated companies is rather doubtful.

THE MAIN FUNCTIONS OF THE RETAILER

Retailers are very diverse in size and in the type of good or service they offer. Increased car ownership and the widespread use of refrigerators and freezers has meant fewer shopping trips and a movement to out-of-town sites where parking is easy and prices are cheaper. In general, however, retailers perform a number of useful functions:

1 They are located in a convenient place for customers. The corner shop is close for small purchases, the out-of-town store for larger purchases and the High Street for a variety of shops and products.

2 They provide after-sales service. Consumer durables (long lasting goods) may require servicing or a repair under guarantee; the retailer will normally carry this task out.

3 They can provide advice to the manufacturer. Any shortcomings in a product can be relayed back to the firm making the product.

REGIONAL SHOPPING CENTRES

A growing trend, especially in large conurbations, has been to develop regional shopping centres away from city centres. The aim has been to reduce congestion and provide a wide variety of shops with easy parking. The concept is well established in London and Fig. 6.4a shows the main regional shopping centres which have developed around the capital.

Brent Cross opened in 1976 as a purpose-built shopping centre aiming to put the best of the West End in northwest London (Fig. 6.4b). There are around 90 shops in the centre with a total selling space equivalent to about seven football pitches and the added attraction of free parking for about 3500 cars. Prices, though, are not cheap and opponents of the centre believe it would have been better to encourage discount shopping in the form of hypermarkets.

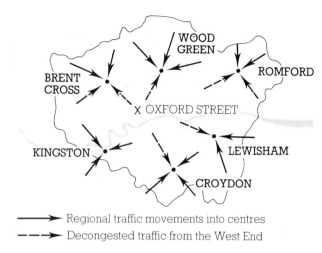

→ Regional traffic movements into centres
--→ Decongested traffic from the West End

Fig. 6.4a Regional shopping centres in London

Fig. 6.4b Brent Cross – modern, warm and dry, a purpose-built regional shopping centre

THINGS TO DO

1 Explain why 'out-of-town' shopping has become so popular in recent years.

2 'Since 1971 the number of retail outlets has fallen by almost 25%.' Why has this happened and in which retail sectors has it been most marked?

3 Why did the Resale Price Maintenance Act in 1964 affect the growth of supermarkets?

4 What factors explain the growth of mail order retailing over the last 10 years?

5 In what ways do Cooperative principles differ from those of limited companies? Why has the Co-op found it difficult to compete with hypermarket development?

6 Look at Fig. 6.5. Suggest how the supermarket's layout is designed to maximise consumer purchases.

7 Visit your local High Street shopping centre and make a chart comparing the good and bad features of different types of store such as Woolworths, Marks & Spencer, a boutique, a multiple shoe shop, etc.

Fig. 6.5 A possible layout of a supermarket

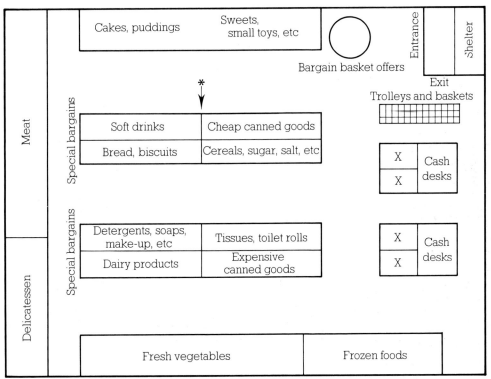

X sweets, tobacco, matches, etc. displayed near cash tills
*no space between sections means walking past other food areas to get to the other side

THE WHOLESALER

The **wholesaler** is the 'middleman' in distribution, buying in bulk from the manufacturer and selling in smaller quantities to the retailer. The more recent economies of scale in retailing have led to the decline in importance of the wholesaler who now serves mainly the small shop which cannot afford to buy in bulk direct from the manufacturer. The wholesaler also plays a very important role in the distribution of farm produce, particularly where processing or grading is required. The marketing boards set up by the government play a valuable role in this respect, for example the Milk Marketing Board is responsible for pasturising and the egg marketing board for grading. Wholesalers may also import goods from abroad which need grading and packing.

The main functions of the wholesaler are to provide warehousing facilities in order to hold the large stocks of products and, though less common today, to prepare some goods for sale by packaging them into smaller quantities. Wholesalers also make distribution easier for the manufacturer since a smaller number of journeys are required with full loads to wholesalers, than if every single retailer took delivery direct from the manufacturer.

Wholesalers are adapting to the challenge of hypermarket selling by setting up **'cash and carry' warehouses** open to the public and by organising voluntary chains of retailers, such as SPAR, who are served and controlled by them.

CONSUMER PROTECTION

Over the last 20 years the consumer has benefited from increased protection against unfair trading practices caused by retailers and manufacturers. A number of consumer laws have been introduced and a wide variety of consumer organisations are available to give help and advice. The most significant laws for the consumer have come in the form of the Trades Description Act 1968 and the Sale of Goods Act originating in 1893 but amended in 1973. The Trades Description Act makes it a criminal offence for traders to make false or misleading statements about goods or services, including their prices, whether by word of mouth, in writing or through illustrations. Fines and imprisonments can result from prosecutions. The Trading Standards Department of the local council will often prosecute on the consumer's behalf if they feel there is a valid case to answer. Figure 6.6 shows one example of how the law was broken.

The Sale of Goods Act states that goods must be: of 'merchantable quality' meaning they must not be broken or damaged; 'as described' meaning no false descriptions can be made about materials or colour for example; and 'fit for any particular purpose' meaning that they must do the job they

LAWRENCE SHEPHERD set off for his vacation by the seaside convinced that he had found his ideal holiday retreat. The brochure said that at the Courtlands Holiday Inn at Torquay, holiday-makers could expect a weekly cabaret, a new solarium, a putting green and nightly dancing to a resident band.

But when Mr. Shepherd and his wife, of Stockport, booked in, they found that the hotel was not all it was made out to be, Stockport magistrates were told today.

Bertram Hunt and his mother, Jeannie, of the Courtlands Holiday Inn, Rawlyn Road, Chelston, Torquay, admitted making false statements in their hotel brochure. They were each fined £40 and ordered to pay £7 compensation and £13 costs.

Holiday retreat was not ideal

Letter

The defendants did not appear, but in a letter to the court, they said that the brochure had been sent out by genuine mistake after the facilities had been withdrawn, and new brochures had been prepared.

Mr. Terence Price, for the Trading Standards Department of Greater Manchester Council, told the court that on the first night, Mr. Shepherd was told:

The solarium was being used as a drinks store; The nightly dancing had been abandoned for reasons of economy; The putting green had been vandalised by guests and their children.

Fig. 6.6 Some of the problems of buying by brochure

are supposed to do. If a good or service purchased does not conform to the above standards then the purchaser is entitled to claim his money back. If the purchaser is unsuccessful there are a number of organisations that may be able to help.

1 **Trading Standards or Consumer Protection Departments**
These are run by the local authority and make sure that traders work within the various laws made to protect shoppers. In addition checks are made on weights and measures and some aspects of the safety and price of goods.

2 **Consumer Advice Centres**
These are usually situated close to main shopping areas and trained staff can give both pre- and post-shopping advice. They are very useful when the purchase of an expensive consumer durable is being considered, providing help on safety, reliability, value for money, etc.

3 **Office of Fair Trading**
Set up under the 1973 Fair Trading Act to investigate aspects of unfair competition, this Office also works closely with local Trading Standards Departments to identify unscrupulous traders.

4 **Advertising Standards Authority**
This is an independent body but financed by the advertising industry to ensure that adverts con-

form to the standards of being 'legal, decent, honest and truthful'. The ASA monitors all newspaper, magazine and poster campaigns but not advertisements on radio and television which come under the control of the Independent Broadcasting Authority. The ASA publishes regular reports about the results of investigations into complaints about adverts from outside bodies, together with any appropriate action it proposes to take. The main criticism of the ASA comes from its claims to be 'independent' when only half of its members come from outside the industry. It also has no absolute powers over advertisers to make them comply with its recommendations.

5 The Consumers Association
This association is perhaps best known for its publication *Which?* with a subscription of over 600 000 people. The magazine evaluates different makes of a particular product to give a 'Which best buy'. Very often newspapers publish any particularly important findings.

6 Small Claims Court
In England and Wales claims against someone selling faulty goods or for faulty service provided by, for example, a builder or dry cleaner, can be made in the county court provided that the amount claimed is not more than £2000. This can be done without reference to a solicitor and legal knowledge is not necessary.

7 The media
One of the best examples in the past of the media giving publicity to consumer complaints was Radio 4's 'Checkpoint' programme. During the course of his investigations the programme's presenter often found himself in violent confrontations with unscrupulous businessmen!

8 British Standards Institute
The BSI sets certain specifications which products have to comply with to be labelled safe and reliable. Those which conform to the BSI standard are awarded the 'Kitemark' (Fig. 6.7). Samples are regularly tested in laboratories. Safety belts and electrical goods are just two examples of a range of products carrying the Kitemark.

Fig. 6.7
The BSI
Kitemark

ADVERTISING

Advertising is a method of creating **product differentiation**. This is a term which refers to the characteristics which distinguish one product from another. If a manufacturer, through advertising, can convince people that his soap powder washes whiter than any other and consumers believe him, then he has achieved product differentiation. The fact that the soap powder may not actually be any better than other brands is not so important in this context: product differentiation is achieved providing the consumer *believes* there is a difference.

There are two types of advertising: **informative** and **persuasive**. Informative adverts attempt to achieve product differentiation by giving specific information about the product which describe its important features. Persuasive adverts tend to glamourise or exaggerate a product's features to induce a purchase. Perfumes and aftershaves fall very much into this latter category where in any case simply describing the aroma for information would be difficult! Informative advertising is also typically done for public bodies such as the Health Education Council who may want to display factual information or warn the public, for example about the dangers of smoking. In this context informative advertising is very useful and valuable, allowing consumers to make a more considered judgement. Persuasive advertising is more typical for luxury goods or where in a highly competitive market, product differentiation is important to increase sales. Figure 6.8 (overleaf) shows the different types of advertising.

One major criticism of advertising is that it has to be paid for by the consumer in the form of higher prices and therefore it is wasteful. In the soap powder market the two major manufacturers, Lever Brothers and Proctor & Gamble, mark up prices by about 25% on average to cover advertising costs. It can be argued that the consumer should be able to make his or her mind up about a product without being influenced by advertising and that adverts simply erode this consumer 'sovereignty'. The case for advertising perhaps rests on the notion that adverts may increase overall sales and allow firms to gain greater economies of scale which may in turn lead to lower prices. The balance of the argument suggests that advertising may have some role to play in assisting consumer choice but that persuasive advertising needs to be monitored to ensure consumers are not misled into buying undesirable products. The ban on the television advertising of cigarettes is a good example of the government exercising influence on the suitability of this type of advertising.

Polo ~ Ralph Lauren   Eau de Toilette

Do you always tidy things away before your husband comes home?

It starts with a nip of something stronger than afternoon tea to help you through the housework.

Before you know where you are, your little nip turns into two or three or four. Or more.

And you feel so guilty, that you start to hide the evidence of your drinking from your husband.

Suddenly, you've got a big drink problem. Your health, your relationships, everything starts to suffer.

Of course, the best way to get out of this problem is not to get into it.

If you feel bored or lonely or depressed, don't expect drink to get you out of it. Whatever you may have heard, alcohol is actually a 'downer' so it won't help in the long run.

Instead, talk your problems over with your husband or a friend.

If you're already showing some of the signs outlined above, you almost certainly need outside help.

Pick up a telephone and ring Newcastle 20797. That's the number of the North East Council on Alcoholism.

They've got people who really understand your problem.

They won't criticise you.

They'll help you.

The same way they've done with hundreds of other women in your predicament.

And don't despair. Drinking problems can be cured.

🕪 The Health Education Council.

Fig. 6.8a (left) An example of persuasive advertising which is designed to make people want to buy something by associating it with exclusivity and wealth

Fig. 6.8b (above) An example of informative advertising which is designed to make people more aware of the dangers of various courses of action – in this case the problem of alcoholism in the home. Figures 7.1b and 7.3 are further examples of informative advertising

THINGS TO DO

1 'Economies of scale in retailing have meant the wholesaler is no longer necessary.' Comment on this statement.

2 The Trades Descriptions Act states it is an offence to make (*a*) false statements about goods; (*b*) false statements about prices; (*c*) false statements about services, accommodation or facilities. Look at Fig. 6.9 and decide which kind of offence, (*a*), (*b*) or (*c*), applies to each.

3 If you think a trader has made an untrue statement about something you have bought, would you:
   (*a*) go to the police;
   (*b*) ask the trader for your money back;
   (*c*) take the case to your local Trading Standards Department;
   (*d*) go to a Consumer Advice Centre?

4 What is happening in Fig. 6.10? Has the dealer committed an offence? If so, in which picture?

Fig. 6.9

Fig. 6.10

5 Explain the difference between **persuasive** and **informative** advertising. Give some examples of each type of advertising.

6 Outline the role of three organisations connected with consumer protection.

7 Look at Fig. 6.11. Could you answer the letters in a way which would be helpful to the writers?

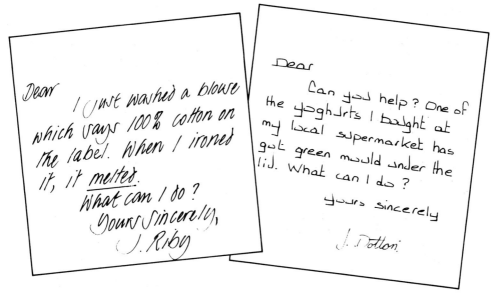

Dear

I just washed a blouse which says 100% cotton on the label. When I ironed it, it melted. What can I do?

Yours Sincerely,
J. Riby

Dear

Can you help? One of the yoghurts I bought at my local supermarket has got green mould under the lid. What can I do?

Yours sincerely
J. Dutton

Fig. 6.11a

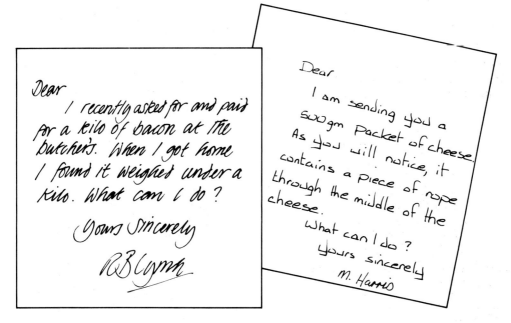

Dear

I recently asked for and paid for a kilo of bacon at the butcher's. When I got home I found it weighed under a kilo. What can I do?

Yours Sincerely
RB Lynch

Dear

I am sending you a 500gm packet of cheese. As you will notice, it contains a piece of rope through the middle of the cheese.

What can I do?
Yours sincerely
M. Harris

Fig. 6.11b

8 Study Fig. 6.12 (overleaf) then answer the following questions.
(a) In what ways are the nature of products being sold by Marks & Spencer changing?
(b) What social trends have emerged to influence the 'new look' Marks & Spencer?
(c) What ingredients does the article suggest have led to Marks & Spencer being Britain's most successful retailer?

Fig. 6.12

M & S: flattened – but fattened

by Ian Williams

MARKS & SPENCER has found a new way of squashing duvets flat. Which may sound a curious announcement in the week the High Street giant announced its best financial results ever. But it has every bearing on radical changes that could soon transform the face of retailing.

"I've seen a pillow as thin as this", says Brian Howard, the deputy chairman, as he lifts a copy of the end of year results from his desk. The pillow – or duvet – inflates as it comes out of its packet, and is one space-saving technique the store is pioneering as its sales move increasingly into bulky household goods and food.

M&S last week became the first British retail stores group to earn more than £300m in pre-tax profits. It remains firmly established as Britain's leading retailer: the profit total of £303.4m is £24.1m up on 1983/4 on a best-ever turnover of £3.21 billion. But behind the figures is the continued shift in the profile of goods sold, away from the traditional clothing. And an M&S face-lift will be central to a record £480m two-year investment plan outlined last week.

For the first time, clothing – although up in volume terms – accounts for less than half of sales, at 49.1%. Underwear sales were up – M&S has 34% of the total lingerie market, but as far as things to wear over the top are concerned, "we've had a disappointing outerwear year", says Howard. M&S still holds 15% of the total market, though.

Food and household goods are both up, now ac-counting for 40.4% and 10.5% of sales respectively. "Food has grown at a faster rate than the rest of the business for 20 years", says Howard, increasing by 75% in volume in the last five years.

But the challenge clearly lies in the future, and M&S has been undertaking a number of small pilot schemes that led to last week's investment an-nouncement. "It's the coming together of a number of experiments we have been discussing and effecting over the past two years", says Howard. At the heart of the new-look M&S will be:

● "Satellite" stores. Smaller, and "down-the-road" from the main store, these are likely to specialise in specific products. An experimental satellite was opened in York in March and is al-ready being hailed a success. They are seen as the answer to "land-locked" big stores which cannot be extended.

● Out-of-town stores, bigger and with more parking facilities and a wider range of goods. The first is to be opened in the Metro Shopping Centre – which will be the biggest out-of-town shopping centre in Britain – at Gateshead by the end of next year.

● Shops-within-shops. Small self-contained mini-stores – for household plants, for example, of which M&S is the UK's biggest supplier – within big stores.

● Financial services. Continued extension of the charge-card scheme, and wider use of the data-base on customers it provides for promotion activities.

● Mail order. An experiment in the West Country, whereby a mail order form was provided with a standard M&S household cata-logue, may be extended to other branches that do not carry the full product range.

● Refurbishment on a large scale to improve the decor of existing stores. The emphasis will be on main-taining a friendly at-mosphere. "It's very much our intention that we remain a personal business", says Howard.

● More export business and contained development in clothing lines (later this year M&S will begin to stock ski gear for the first time).

"You're going to see a wider range of goods other than food and textiles. They're going to be more to do with the home," says Howard. And what has been the biggest influence? "We're reacting to social trends … it's about atmosphere, it's about leisure," he adds. No longer is M&S catering sole-ly to a housewife; "More women work and younger married couples shop much more as a couple than did their parents".

The investment plan en-visages a 700,000 sq ft expansion of selling space – equivalent to an extra 30 stores on top of the existing 264. More specific details of M&S's property plans are to be revealed over the next year.

Clearly St Michael is changing his armour. And if the market leader becomes a trend setter, the High Street may never be the same again.

The Sunday Times 12.5.1985

9 Read the passage on 'Retail trade trends' carefully, then answer the following questions.

   (*a*) Explain what is meant by 'niche marketing'. How will it be reflected in shop design?

   (*b*) In new out-of-town shopping developments, such as the one in Gateshead Enterprise Zone, leisure amenities have been combined with shops. Why?

   (*c*) What is 'personnel' management? Why is it particularly important in the retail sector?

Fig. 6.13

Retail trade trends

David Sands **looks at the latest changes in the pattern of British shopping and the career opportunities they offer.**

A BETTER-educated, better informed and more discerning customer has stretched the retailer's imagination to provide better value and more attractive facilities. The retail sector today is vastly superior and more adaptable than it was even five years ago. A consumer-led retail revolution has taken place and the sector now provides challenging, rewarding and exciting careers for many people.

Design has played an important role in changing the face of many of our high streets and shopping centres. Initiatives first mooted by Fitch & Co, Europe's largest design house, and applied to the Burton Group, mean that few new ventures or shopping developments are now considered without close co-operation with a design team. This has ensured that such groups as Burton have remained in the forefront of the market place with a policy of constantly up-dating this image. In their bid to win and keep more market share, forward-thinking traders and retail developers have followed the design bandwagon to compete with names like Next, Next Interiors, Laura Ashley, Storehouse (Habitat, Mothercare, British Home Stores) and Benetton.

Another factor which all the above groups have in common is a commitment to effective and selective merchandising. An Americanism to embrace these terms is niche marketing. It means identifying a market and a lifestyle, assessing its needs, designing a range of merchandise for it and the type of outlet and image to sell it. For those who do this well the rewards are high.

Over the past twenty years consumer spending has risen steadily and is confidently expected to continue its increase. John Richards, senior retail analyst at Wood MacKenzie & Co says that this increased spending will be tapped most successfully by the retailers with multi-strategy or 'multi-niche' formulae. "The power base has shifted from buying to marketing requiring clarity of offer and identification of market gaps." It seems that the new breed of retailer is aware of the constant need to engineer their offer to move in line with retail trends. Everyone has to be different and an important key to this is product development, adding value and fashion, rather than just selling a commodity.

The last few years has seen an unprecedented rise in the amount of out of town shopping space in the UK. It is estimated that six per cent of retail sales takes place in superstores, hypermarkets, retail warehouses and shopping centres located outside or on the edge of town. That figure is expected to increase to 15 per cent within the next ten years. The number of superstores will rise from 1,460 to an estimated 3,100 in 1995. Retailing in the form of retail parks and out-of-town shopping centres has only just begun to make it in a big, and controversial, way.

Most of our big cities and towns currently have before the planners enormous competing schemes running into millions of square feet. One has already opened in an Enterprise Zone in Gateshead. Called the Metro-Centre, the first stage began trading earlier this year and it comprises a Carrefour superstore and six shops—a mere tenth the size of the proposed development due to be completed in October 1987.

In October the second stage of 210 shops will open whilst the third stage contains the leisure and lifestyle elements which will be so important to successful retailing in the very near future. It will be anchored by C&A, backed up by a 10 screen cinema complex, cafes, restaurants, food court and a 'leisure box' of 70,000 sq ft, centred on typical seaside fun rides. The scheme has attracted £100 million of private investment and the developer, John Hall of Cameron Hall Developments, hopes to increase the average shopping trip from 1–2 hours to 3–5 hours. This concept of

[continued over]

modern retailing harks back to the street scene, the bazaar and the square where trading also played a social role of an event and where more was acted out than a simple financial transaction. For those wishing a career in retail management John Hall has tough requirements: for his centre manager he needs an accountant, a personnel manager, a marketer and a prophet – all in one person.

Opportunities

Retailing is one of the largest employment sectors in the U.K. Government figures up to March 1985 give the total number employed in retail distribution at 2,129,000. This is 10.3 per cent of the total employed in industry and service sectors. There is an increasing amount of employment for high powered store management where a considerable amount of centralised buying takes place, although there is still a certain amount of scope at local level for management and merchandising tasks; management at local level is given stock and profit parameters within which to manage.

Large numbers of staff mean opportunities for those wishing to enter personnel management. With large scale hypermarkets and shopping centres management has a variety of functions, from stock and people movement to questions of hygiene. As many retail sector employees are part-timers, personnel management takes up a large proportion of resources. High staff turnover is still a problem for many retail companies.

Self employment in retailing is often the quickest way to part with your savings. In a small shop the hours are long and the rewards not particularly good. But traders with specialist product knowledge, such as hi fi, are always in demand. The number of small shops declined in 1980 to 1984 from 878,000 to 836,000 and the trend is still towards multiple groups. An entrant into the market needs a good new idea, money, sound business sense and a lot of luck. Franchising is often seen as an entry to retailing but again it is the larger groups like cosmetics and jewellery who dominate the market. Fast food franchising is the likeliest way in.

Executive Post

7

OUR CHANGING POPULATION

INTRODUCTION

Population is an important topic in Economics because it looks at the factor of production – labour – in more detail. If the economy is to be planned properly it is important for the government to know whether the number of schools needs to be increased, whether more pensions are going to be required in the future, etc. Businesses need to be able to estimate the future demand for their products and if, for example, fewer babies are being born a firm manufacturing prams will see its demand drop and it may need to diversify into other products.

On a world scale, the total population is about 4500 million which is an increase of nearly half since 1961 and one fifth since 1971. By the year 2000 the world population is estimated to exceed 6000 million, double the 1961 population. The consequences of this dramatic rise have to be considered, in particular, how the world is going to feed itself.

THE CENSUS

Every 10 years in the UK there is a national census to count the number of people. The first census was taken in 1801 although it could be argued that the Domesday Book completed in 1086 was the first official count of our population!

The census means more than just adding up the total population. It counts the numbers of men and women and whether they are single, married, widowed or divorced; how many children there are, how many teenagers, people in their twenties, thirties, forties, ... retired people and so on. The census counts people by the kind of housing they live in, the country in which they were born, the kind of job they do and how they travel to work.

The census is used to work out present and future housing needs, and to assess the size of the grants the government gives to the Health Service and local authorities. It is used to work out the amount needed for pensions and allowances, and for planning. The census shows how many people have moved from one area to another and how the local workforce is changing. This information is used when factories, offices, shops, public transport and places for leisure are being planned. Most UK population statistics are derived from census figures.

THE MAIN FACTORS AFFECTING THE SIZE OF A COUNTRY'S POPULATION

There are three main factors which affect the size of a country's population: the number of babies being born, the number of people dying, and the amount of immigration (people coming into the country) and emigration (people leaving the country).

1 BIRTHS

In the UK, births are measured by the **crude birth rate**. It is defined as:

$$\frac{\text{number of live births}}{\text{total population}} \times 1000.$$

If, for example, the total number of live births in a year is 1 million and the total population is 50 million, then the crude birth rate would be:

$$\frac{1 \text{ million}}{50 \text{ million}} \times 1000 \quad \text{or} \quad 20.$$

This is really saying that for every 1000 people in the country, an average of 20 babies are born during a year. In 1982 the birth rate for the UK was 12.6 and there were 692 000 live births. The term 'live' births is used because some babies are stillborn and therefore cannot be counted. The **infant mortality rate** measures the number of infants that die before the age of one year, per 1000 live births. It gives an indication of post natal (after birth) care facilities. Infant mortality rates tend to be high in LDCs although the UK has quite high figures compared to other European countries. The main changes in live births since 1950 are shown in Fig. 7.1a (overleaf).

The birth rate is affected both by the number of marriages and the size of families. Both were increasing after World War 2, a trend which continued up to 1964. Larger families probably arose because of increased government support for the family through the introduction of child allowances, a comprehensive National Health Service and free secondary education. These reforms were introduced by the Labour government during the period 1945–50. There was also increased prosperity after the War with virtually

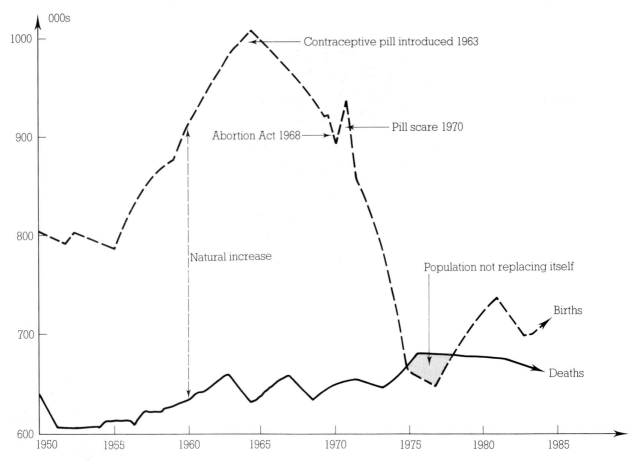

Fig. 7.1a Live births and deaths 1950–85

full employment, meaning couples could afford to have larger families.

As Fig. 7.1a shows, the picture changes dramatically after 1964 and the birth rate plunged to its lowest ever recorded level in 1977.

The reasons for the fall were probably due to a variety of factors. Certainly increased publicity about family planning (Fig. 7.1b), the introduction of the contraceptive pill in 1963 and the Abortion Act in 1968 all played a part (indeed a pill scare in 1970 connecting it with thrombosis (blood clotting leading to heart attacks), caused a temporary surge in the birth rate as women stopped taking it). The introduction of the pill and the Abortion Act do not by themselves, however, explain why women actually wanted fewer children. The pill provides the means but not the motive. The answer to this question has more to do with the increased employment opportunities for women which for many meant the postponement of a family until a later age. This postponement might explain the rise in births after 1977 as women entering their early thirties started families. Inevitably starting a family late in years has meant a reduction in family size which is perhaps why births only recovered slightly until 1980 after which they fell again until 1985. It is also possible that increased living standards and the vast range of consumer goods available has helped to compete against the costs of having a large family. Elec-

tronic goods in particular, such as colour televisions, stereo systems, video recorders and home computers, have all made an impact. In addition most families now expect to own their home, drive a car and afford a foreign holiday at least once a year. All this puts a constraint on having a large family.

The effects of the falling birth rate in the 1960s and 1970s have been highly significant. Businesses with a strong stake in the baby market have had to get used to a situation where the number of customers for their products has actually fallen. Companies like H J Heinz and Johnson & Johnson have been supporting sales by promoting their products to older age groups (e.g. 'Johnson's "Baby Powder" is for anyone who wants to keep their skin soft'), but the longterm scope for this kind of strategy is limited. Planning assumptions had to change quite dramatically once the downward trend in the birth rate became continuous. Projected new towns were scrapped (e.g. Maplin, a development to the north of Southend originally designed to coincide with the development of London's third airport), and in education the number of teacher training places were cut dramatically. In 1972 the government estimated a school population in 1986 of 9.7 million. Two years later the downward drop in the birth rate meant a revised estimate of 8 million pupils and 43 000 fewer teachers needed. Teacher training colleges

Fig. 7.1b   A campaign poster encouraging the use of contraception in the 1970s

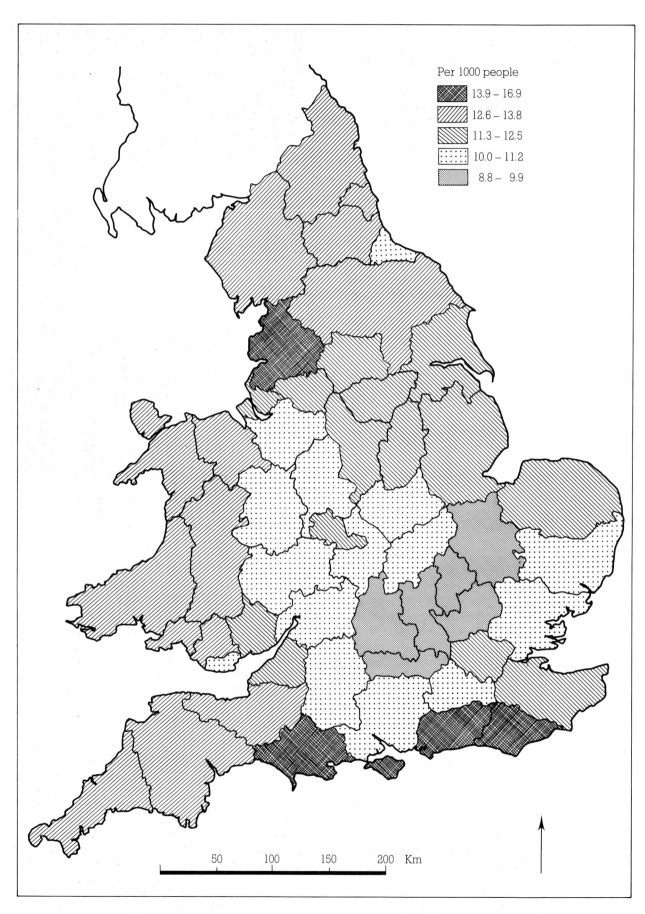

Fig. 7.2 Crude death rate, 1980

were closed and schools amalgamated to cope with the falling roles. Housing has also been affected: fewer family homes have been built. Hospitals have closed maternity wards and Youth and Community budgets have been cut back. It is interesting to consider the consequence of the present generation of young children reaching child bearing age and themselves having smaller families. The future population of the UK would then decline quite dramatically. This is already happening in West Germany where the present population of about 59 million is expected to contract to 39 million by the year 2000.

2 DEATHS

In the UK deaths are measured by the **crude death rate**. This is defined as:

$$\frac{\text{number of deaths}}{\text{total population}} \times 1000.$$

If, for example, 750 000 people die per annum in a country with a total population of 50 million, then the crude death rate will be:

$$\frac{750\,000}{50\,000\,000} \times 1000 \quad \text{or} \quad 15.$$

This means that for every 1000 people in the country an average of 15 people die every year. In 1982 the death rate was 11.7 with 663 000 actual deaths.

If the death rate is subtracted from the birth rate the **rate of natural increase** can be found. In the examples above, with a birth rate of 20 and a death rate of 15, the rate of natural increase would be 5 per 1000 population. Figure 7.1a shows deaths since 1950 combined with the number of births, the gap being the natural increase. It is interesting to note that the natural increase was negative from 1974 to 1978 showing the population was not replacing itself.

Regional variations in the death rate are shown in Fig. 7.2. The large number of retired people on the South coast explain the high figures for Sussex and Dorset. Over a long period the death rate has fallen consistently which is only to be expected with rising living standards, progress in medical knowledge and the expansion and improvement in health services. The most significant fall in the death rate has come in the area of infant mortality where from 1941 to 1979 the infant mortality rate dropped from 60 to 12.8. Attitudes towards preserving good health have become more positive, particularly in the form of anti-smoking campaigns (Fig. 7.3), and with greater medical improvements it is likely that a further gradual fall in the death rate will take place in the future. Some common causes of death in 1982 were heart disease (223 633), cancer (146 095), respiratory diseases (95 639) and road accidents (6050).

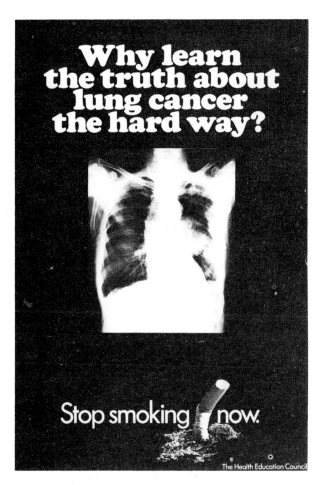

Fig. 7.3 An anti-smoking advertisement designed to promote a positive attitude to good health. (This and Fig. 7.1b are both further examples of informative advertising.)

3 MIGRATION

Migration is concerned with flows of people entering and leaving the country. **Immigration** is connected with people moving into Britain, **emigration** with British people moving abroad. **Net migration** is found by subtracting emigration from immigration. Figure 7.4 (overleaf) shows net migration trends since 1950. In the early part of this period there was a net outflow of Britons to Australia, New Zealand and Canada. This trend was reversed by mainly Commonwealth immigration in the next few years, but since 1961 net migration has been negative partly due to tighter immigration controls, especially the Commonwealth Immigrants Act 1962 which put a quota (fixed number) on people coming into the UK. Undoubtedly the more recent economic slump in Britain and high unemployment, has encouraged people to find work abroad. In the decade to 1982 an average 227 400 people have emigrated each year, offset by about 184 000 immigrants. In total during those ten years the population of the UK was reduced nearly 430 000 by net migration.

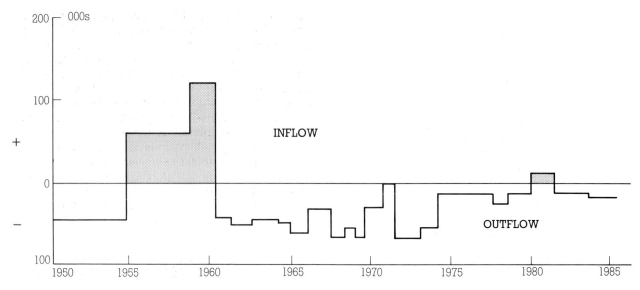

Fig. 7.4 Net migration since 1950. Note that in recent years emigration has generally exceeded immigration

Subtracting deaths from births, then adding net migration figures gives the overall growth of a country's population. Figure 7.5 shows changes in the size of population from 1971 to 1982. It is interesting because between 1974 and 1978 the size of the UK population actually fell, implying a negative growth rate between those years. This confirms the observations about deaths being higher than births during that period, with additional net outward migration to further emphasise the fall in population. Population also fell slightly between 1981 and 1982. Growth rates give a good indication of how fast the size of a country's population is changing; negative growth means overall size is declining. The population of the UK today is 56.3 million which is the world's 14th largest.

The rapid growth of the UK's population towards the end of the 18th century prompted a now

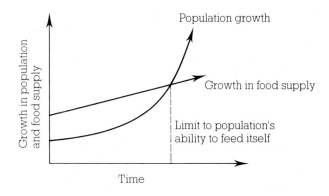

Fig. 7.6a (above)   The Malthusian view – population grows at an exponential (multiplying) rate but food supply at a constant rate. When the two converge mass starvation results

Fig. 7.5 (below)   UK population trends 1971–82

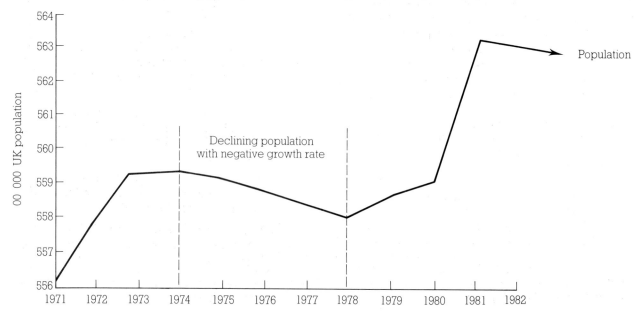

Fig. 7.6b Thomas Malthus

famous book *Essay on the Principle of Population* to be written by the Reverend Thomas Malthus in 1798. He believed the rate of growth of population would outstrip the growth of food production creating widespread starvation (Fig. 7.6). He thought that since land is a fixed factor, increasing the variable factor labour would lead to a lower output per head, the essence of an economic principle called the 'Law of Diminishing Returns'. The pessimism of Malthus proved unfounded in the 19th century mainly because many new lands were discovered such as the Canadian Prairies, and the technologically-based agricultural revolution dramatically improved crop yields. Nevertheless Malthusian ideas still have credibility today because in many parts of the world the limits to cultivation have now been reached.

OPTIMUM POPULATION

Optimum population as a term means 'best size' population. But what exactly counts as best size? Best size in this context means the size of popu-lation that produces the largest output per head. Figure 7.7 shows where optimum population lies and suggests that if the population is too small it may not be able to exploit fully the potential of the division of labour and economies of scale. Beyond the optimum, diseconomies of scale occur and since land is a fixed factor, natural resources may become very limited, congestion increases and output per head further declines.

Optimum population is easy to illustrate graphically, but not so easy to determine in practice. It is not a static concept because technology is always changing to increase output per head and experiments cannot be made with the size of population to see how output per head might vary.

THINGS TO DO

1 Explain why the census is more than just a count of the country's population.

2 Define the terms (*a*) **birth rate**; (*b*) **death rate**;(*c*) **infant mortality rate**.

3 What are the economic implications of a continued fall in the birth rate?

4 Why was the introduction of the contraceptive pill not by itself an adequate explanation of the declining birth rate after 1964?

5 Using Fig. 7.8 (overleaf):
   (*a*) describe the regional variations in the take up of the six durable goods between 1969 and 1980;
   (*b*) what do the graphs show about regional variations in the quality of life?

6 With reference to Fig. 7.9 (overleaf), explain why regional differences might occur, in particular contrasting urban and rural variations.

7 What is meant by the term **rate of natural increase**? When has it been negative for the UK population after 1950?

8 What major factor has played a major contribution to the fall in the death rate after World War 2?

9 What is **optimum population**? Why is it easier to define in theory than in practice?

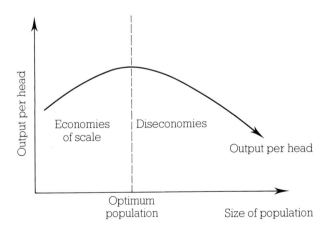

Fig. 7.7 Optimum population

85

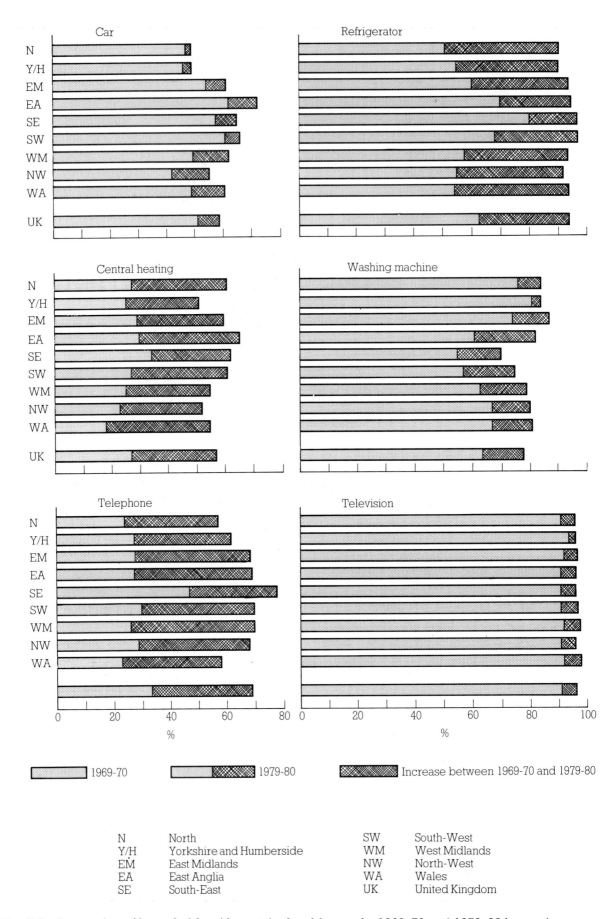

Fig. 7.8 Proportion of households with certain durable goods, 1969–70 and 1979–80 by region

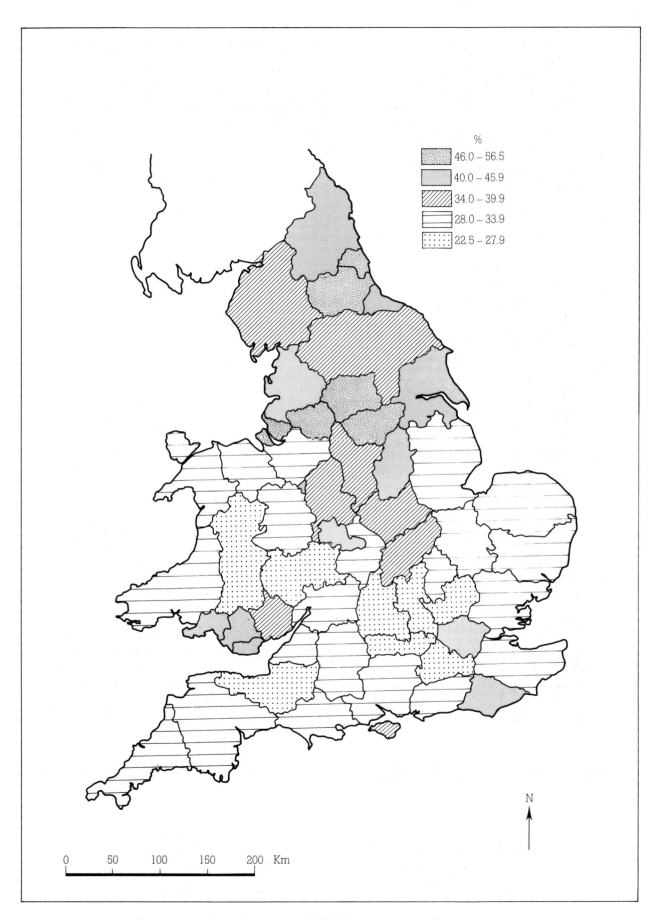

Fig. 7.9 Proportion of households with no car, 1981, by county

Legend:
%
46.0 – 56.5
40.0 – 45.9
34.0 – 39.9
28.0 – 33.9
22.5 – 27.9

N

0   50   100   150   200   Km

AGE DISTRIBUTION

Breaking down the population size into different age groups is very useful for planning purposes. The main groupings used are broadly the child population from 0–16 years, the working population aged 16–65 years, and the retired population aged 65 and over. The groupings give a general indication of trends and are not absolutely accurate. For example college students over 16 and the unemployed are not strictly 'working' and people over 65 may have full or part-time jobs so they are not strictly retired.

In the UK the broad groupings can be used to compare the age structure of the population over different time periods. This is particularly useful in terms of predicting the future working and retired population from present and past statistics. Look at Fig. 7.10. It shows clearly an 'ageing' population as the proportion of retired people increase and the child population falls. In fact life expectancy now averages 70 years for males and 76 years for females.

The working population has started to decline more rapidly, falling by nearly 400 000 between 1979 and 1981. In September 1981 the working population totalled about 26 million people of whom 23 million were in employment and 3 million were unemployed. The other interesting and marked change within the working population comes in the percentages of men and women actually employed. Such changes are measured by male and female **activity rates**. Whereas male activity rates have declined, female rates have increased very sharply. Females accounted for nearly 42% of the labour force in 1983 compared to 30% in 1950 and nearly all of this increase was accounted for by married women working, as the table below shows. Some of the reasons for increased female activity include the reduction of sex discrimination in the labour market, smaller family size and social attitudes changing to become increasingly tolerant of wives, and even mothers, working. It is also true that industrial expansion has been particularly marked in industries employing a high proportion of female to male workers.

Wives' activity rates (%) by age, Great Britain

Age group	1951	1976	1979	1981
16–19	38	52	41	49
20–24	37	55	58	57
25–44	25	56	58	59
45–69	22	61	61	67
60+	5	14	10	12
all ages	22	49	50	50

Source: *Social Trends* 1979 and 1984

THE CONSEQUENCES OF THE CHANGING AGE DISTRIBUTION

1 **The increased burden of pensions**
The baby boom of the 1950s and 1960s translates into the 'granny' boom of the 2010s and 2020s. Between now and 2005 the number of pensioners will rise only from 9.2 million to 9.5 million but by 2030 it will have reached 12 million. If the working population gradually declines as well, then the burden of paying the extra pensions will be considerable. The **dependency ratio** is the term used to describe the proportion of dependents in the population relative to the working population.

i.e.
$$\frac{\text{number of dependents}}{\text{number of workers}}$$

The increased number of pensioners will create a rise in the dependency ratio which will be moderated by any changes in births. Estimates have suggested a possible 9p in the £

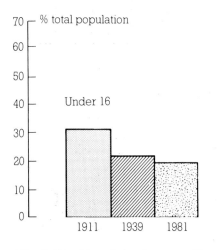
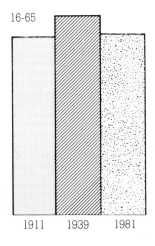
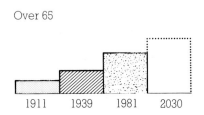

Fig. 7.10 The changing age distribution of population – 1911, 1939 and 1981

increase in income tax will be needed to pay the extra pensions and since in fact working people pay National Insurance contributions to fund their state retirement pension, it may mean these contributions sharply rising. Many working people also contribute to private pension schemes which invest these savings in stocks and shares. Because more people are living longer, the value of the shares will need to rise if pension funds are going to be able to pay out the required sums. This means industry making higher profits and consumers having to pay more for the goods they buy. Workers may have to take less of the fruits of their labour in wages. Thus the future consumer and worker could well end up financing a large part of the pensions after the year 2000.

2 A changing pattern of consumption

Just as the sharp decline in the birth rate after 1964 produced a drop in demand for baby products, so the increase in the retired population will produce an expansion in the demand for goods and services appropriate to this age group. Clothing manufacturers, for example, might benefit from shifting production of high fashion products aimed at teenagers to the more

conservative styles of an older generation. In addition a change in the pattern of housing will need to take place so that more appropriate accommodation is provided for old people such as supervised homes and sheltered housing.

3 Decreased mobility

As working people born during the baby boom period of 1951–64 get older, so their mobility in occupational and geographical terms will decline. Similarly the falling birth rate after 1964 has meant and will mean a smaller proportion of younger working people who tend to be more mobile. A less mobile workforce limits economic expansion because declining industries will create a surplus of labour which will not easily adapt to the demands of newer industries with labour shortages.

4 A less dynamic economy

A growing economy depends on new initiatives, improving technology and increased risk-taking. Much of this is pioneered by young people and an ageing population is likely to reduce the amount of economic change that otherwise would have taken place with a younger age profile.

CHANGES IN THE OCCUPATIONAL DISTRIBUTION

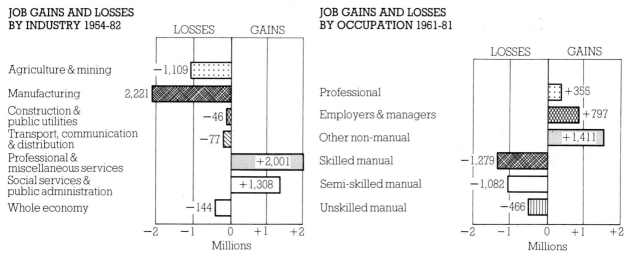

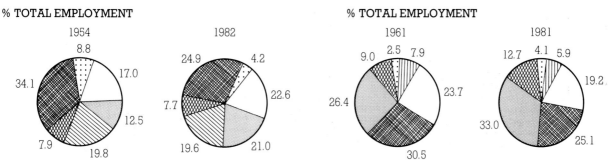

Fig. 7.11 Changes in the occupational distribution during the period 1954–82

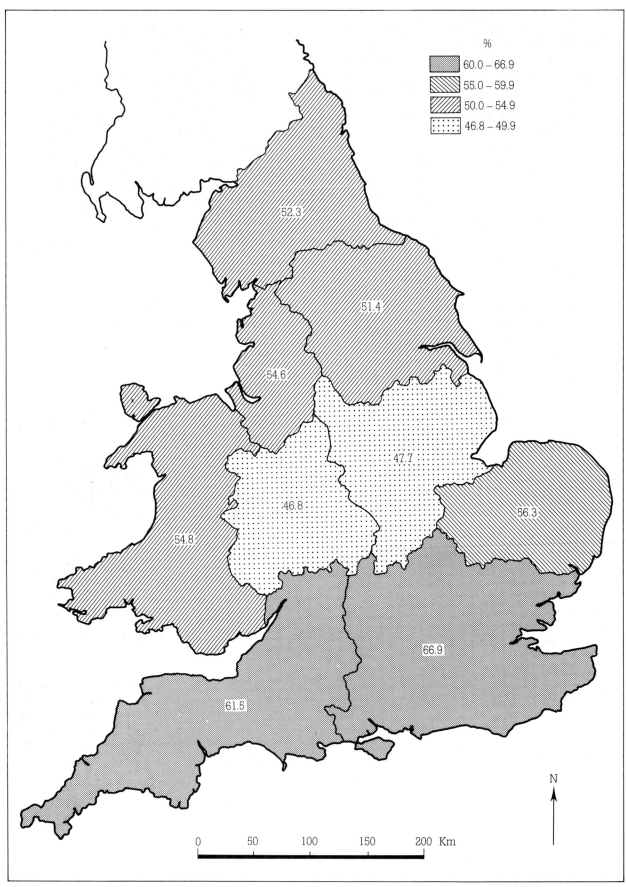

Fig. 7.12 Proportion of employees in services, by region. Can you account for the differences between the regions?

In September 1981 the manufacturing sector of the British economy employed less than 29% of all those at work. Adding the number of employees in agriculture, mining, construction and gas, electricity and water, the total still comes to less than 39%, implying that the service sector now accounts for well over half the employment in the country. Figure 7.11 shows where the main gains and losses have come from.

Within the service sector the main growth areas have been professional and scientific services particularly in the fields of education, medicine and dentistry. In the 12 years to June 1981, the numbers employed in professional and scientific services rose by nearly 750 000. Figure 7.12 shows the proportion of employees in services in various parts of the country. The higher incidence of manufacturing and unemployment in the Midlands and the North is reflected in the regional differences.

Manufacturing employment has declined principally because of a falling demand for products and improved labour productivity. The falling demand for products was probably affected by the high exchange rate in the early 1970s but since the UK is now almost self-sufficient in oil, there is less need for a large manufacturing base. This contrasts with the position prior to 1970 when manufacturing exports were vital to pay for the large quantity of imported oil. Labour productivity measures the output produced with a given amount of labour. In manufacturing, improved working practices and better use of machinery have helped to better productivity, but with vastly reduced labour requirements.

The expansion in the service sector has also brought with it the growth of female employment. Nearly 70% of employees in professional and scientific services are female, compared with 24% in agriculture and 4% in mining. In the public sector, local authority employment grew sharply by 61% between 1961 and 1980, mainly due to the expansion in education. This trend has now been reversed as the falling birth rate requires a smaller teaching force.

An interesting trend in the occupational distribution of 16–18 year olds is the declining number with full-time jobs. Only one in five 16 year olds had a full-time job in 1984, compared with more than three in five a decade earlier. The biggest drop in the number going into employment has occurred since 1979 and Fig. 7.13 compares activ-

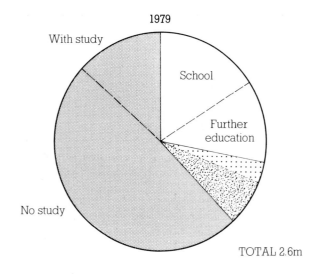

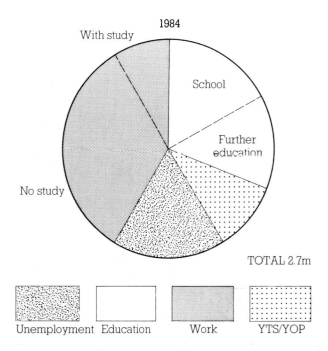

Fig. 7.13 16–18 year olds; occupational activities in 1979 and 1984

ities in that year with 1984. Overall in 1984, 76% of 16 year olds were taking part in some form of education or training and the extension of the Youth Training Scheme to two years from 1985 means that the effective working population starts at 18 and not 16 years.

THE GEOGRAPHICAL DISTRIBUTION OF POPULATION

The geographical distribution of population is measured by the density of people per square kilometre. Figure 7.14 shows that Britain's population is concentrated in a few main urban districts called conurbations. The main conurbations are those around London, the West Midlands (Birmingham and Coventry), South East Lanca-

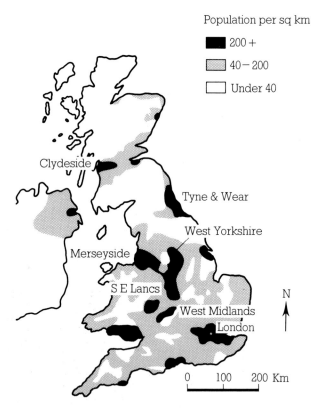

Population per sq km

■ 200 +

▨ 40 − 200

□ Under 40

Fig. 7.14 The geographical distribution of population in the UK, showing the major conurbations

shire (Manchester), West Yorkshire (Leeds and Bradford), Clydeside (Glasgow), Merseyside (Liverpool) and Tyne & Wear (Newcastle and Sunderland). Together these seven conurbations make up about a third of the UK's total population. This concentration of population is largely a result of the Industrial Revolution which brought factories to the coalfields. The exception was London which owes its importance to being the capital city and major port.

RECENT CHANGES IN THE GEOGRAPHICAL DISTRIBUTION OF POPULATION

Broadly the main changes in the geographical distribution of population since 1945 have been from the North of the country to the Midlands and South-East. Even at present, Scotland and the North are losing their male working population at the rate of 2% every five years.

The Midlands gained people because of the development of light engineering and in particular the motor industry centred around Birmingham, Coventry and Oxford. London and the South-East gained population with a diverse number of new industries ranging from the motor and electronics industries to aerospace, cosmetics and household goods. The South-East area as a whole has become attractive to industry because it is a wealthy consumption centre enjoying a high standard of living compared to the rest of the country and it is close to the EC where the majority of international trade takes place. The opening of the London orbital motorway has further improved communications in the area and is likely to provide a further attraction for new industry.

Looking more closely at population movements between 1971 and 1981 (Fig. 7.15), it is fairly clear that the large conurbations such as Greater London and the West Midlands lost people and that a number of rural areas became net gainers of population. Part of this rural gain can be explained by a movement from the inner city to the surrounding countryside where living conditions are generally better and housing costs usually lower. This movement has also been possible because of the increase in car ownership and better road communications. The 'urban rural fringe' as it is sometimes called, gained 30% more people between 1961 and 1981. The other explanation for the rural gain in population comes in the movement of the retired population to coastal areas, particularly West Sussex, Cornwall and East Anglia.

Government attempts to influence the geographical distribution of population have largely come in the form of **new town development, location of industry policy** (see Chapter 10), and the establishment of **green belts** around major urban areas, particularly London. New town development came as a move to relieve congested inner city areas and to establish new regional growth points. Many of the new towns in the South-East (e.g. Harlow, Basildon and Stevenage) were designed for the London overspill whereas Milton Keynes, Telford and Peterborough were designed to create new areas of growth with low cost housing.

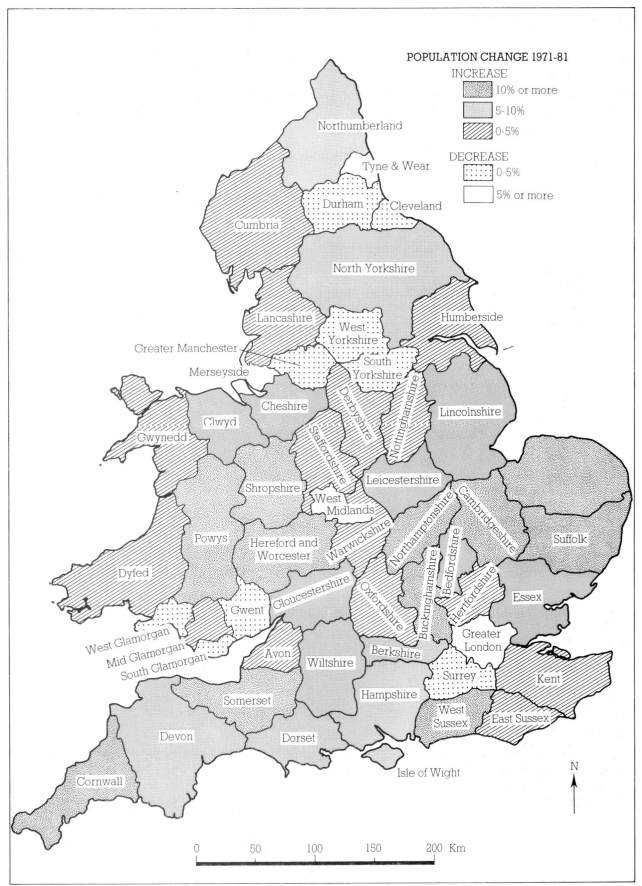

Fig. 7.15 The percentage population change during the period 1971–81; counties of England and Wales

WORLD POPULATION PROBLEMS

The world's population at current growth rates is doubling every 35 years. Every year the equivalent population to a country larger than the size of the UK comes into being, and a child born today could see the population of the world quadruple in his lifetime. Thus the concerns of Malthus about how a growing number of people would be fed and supported, present a real challenge today. The implication is that unless world food supply increases at the same rate as population growth, there will be famine on a large scale. Furthermore since at present a large percentage of the world's population is suffering from malnutrition, food supply needs to increase *faster* than population.

In total on a world scale food production is keeping pace with population growth but not necessarily in individual areas where dramatic improvements in yields are required to solve the problem of malnutrition: the EC continually produces large surpluses of grain and dairy products whereas African countries at the southern fringe of the Sahara desert have experienced ever frequent crop failures. Opinions are divided as to what the future holds. Some researchers demonstrate that Africa has only 30% of its land under cultivation, China 29% and Latin America 25%. Dramatic innovations in fertilisers, food strains and synthetic foods could increase food supply substantially in a short period of time.

The global problems are more intense in certain regions and even if there is more capacity to produce food, undoubtedly there will be famines in some areas with a possible massive loss of life. The main reason for the surge in world population growth has been the steady decline in the death rate which has been due to increased medical knowledge. The likelihood that this knowledge will go on expanding means that the future problem of feeding the world will be a real one and put much pressure on LDCs to reduce their birth rates (Fig. 7.16).

Fig. 7.16a Children scavenging in rubbish dumps in Calcutta. Children in LDCs are still seen as important sources of family income, and as a form of security in old age. They have to earn money however they can

Fig. 7.16b (top right) Instruction in family planning, Calcutta
Fig. 7.16c (bottom right) A family planning clinic in Katmandu

THINGS TO DO

1 Study the following figures which relate to a country's changing age distribution over time.

Age group	Population	
	Year 1	Year 31
0–16	8	11
16–65	25	24
65+	9	9

   (a) Does the country have an ageing population?

   (b) What are the economic implications of the changing age distribution?

   (c) Is the above country likely to be developed or less developed? Give reasons for your answer.

2 What is an **activity rate**? What has been happening to female activity rates over the last 30 years and why?

3 Why is the burden of paying pensions after the year 2000 likely to be very heavy for the working population?

4 Why are the economic consequences of an ageing population important to consider? What is the optimum age distribution in economic terms?

5 Using Fig. 7.11 explain some of the reasons for changes in the occupational distribution between 1954 and 1982.

6 Using Fig. 7.12, suggest reasons for the regional variations in those employed in the service sector.

7 Describe the urban nature of Britain's population. What problems might arise from the concentration of population in urban areas?

8 What economic effects might result from a large number of retired people moving to Eastbourne on the Sussex coast?

9 'World food supply can keep pace with population growth.' Does this mean malnutrition is not really a serious problem?

10 Using Fig. 7.17 describe the main changes in the educational and economic activity of 16 year olds in Great Britain from 1974 to 1984.

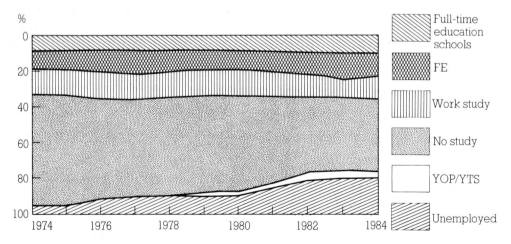

Fig. 7.17 Educational and economic activity of 16 year olds in Great Britain during the period 1974–84

8
ORGANISING PRODUCTION

INTRODUCTION

Figure 8.1 shows the main types of business enterprise which exist in Britain today. There are two broad categories, **private** and **public enterprise**, the former owned by private individuals, the latter being controlled by the government.

Private enterprise takes a number of different forms, usually related to the size of the business, ranging from the sole trader or proprietor (owned by one person) to the public company which can have an unlimited number of owners called shareholders. Private enterprise is characterised by the 'profit motive' which means that the principal aim of business is to maximise the reward earned from trading. This suggests that the firm will try to charge the highest price possible in order to achieve this objective. In fact it normally has to compete with other firms to stay in business and this limits its ability to exploit the consumer. This is the system of automatic balances and checks which the market economy relies on. The profit motive which threatens to lead to consumer exploitation is balanced by competition which forces firms to limit the prices they charge. The danger in private enterprise comes when competition disappears and a single producer controls the market. Such a single producer is known as a **monopoly** and in this case the desire to maximise profits can lead to higher prices. In the USA, where competition is seen as being vital to the public interest, monopolies are banned. In Britain a Monopolies Commission exists which investigates potentially harmful monopolies and action can be taken to limit their power, though they are not by themselves illegal.

Public enterprise can take a variety of different forms. The large nationalised industries may be financed through taxation and government borrowing or in some cases the government may be the majority shareholder. Some public services, such as the National Health Service, are run in the form of a government department. Other public undertakings, such as transport and cleaning, may be run by local authorities. The aim with much of public enterprise is not to maximise profits, but to provide goods and services at cost price. Since a number of nationalised industries are themselves monopolies they are subject to investigations by the Monopolies Commission if there is a suspicion of poor value for money being offered to the consumer.

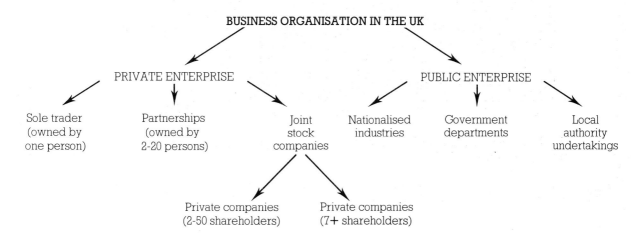

Fig. 8.1   Business organisation in the UK – private and public enterprise

PRIVATE ENTERPRISE

THE SOLE TRADER

Figure 8.2b shows just how much small firms dominate in terms of numbers compared to larger sized enterprise. The **sole trader** or proprietor is probably the oldest form of business and the easiest to start up. There are few legal formalities, often little capital is required and there are quite a large number of incentives from the government to start up, notably in the area of tax relief.

A sole proprietor business may have a large number of employees; the important characteristic is that the firm is owned by just one person. That person is responsible for the fortunes of the business and incurs what is known in economic terms as **unlimited liability**. This means that all the debts of the enterprise have to be met by the proprietor which, in the case of serious loss, may mean selling personal possessions such as their car or even their house. Thus the larger the business, the bigger the risks in terms of unlimited liability. The relatively high risk attached to this type of business means that finding sources of capital can be difficult. Much of the money will come from personal savings; banks may be prepared to help, but since the loan may be unsecured, a high rate of interest will be charged.

Sole proprietorships are commonly found in re-

Fig. 8.2a   Small shops such as these are typical examples of sole traders' businesses

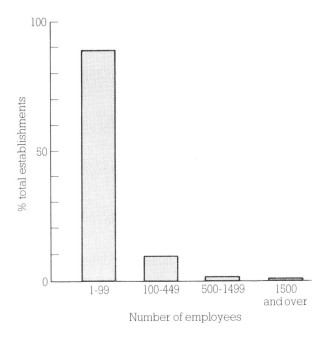

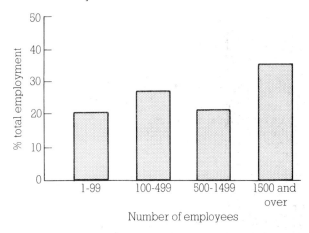

Fig. 8.2b How small firms dominate in terms of numbers compared to larger ones

tailing (corner shops), personal services (hairdressing), restaurants and home maintenance such as building and plumbing (Fig. 8.2a). They have a high mortality rate because often inexperienced people set such businesses up without adequate resources. They do offer certain advantages such as independence for the owner, a close relationship between effort and reward (if the business is successful) and some flexibility in working hours. The disadvantages stem from unlimited liability and the difficulty of obtaining large amounts of capital to expand, insecurity and potentially long working hours.

PARTNERSHIPS

Sharing the risks of business with other people is also a means of obtaining more capital and expertise which may give rise to a **partnership** being formed. Legally a partnership can consist of between 2 and 20 people, each liable for the activities of the other partners. Unlimited liability also applies to partnerships meaning all partners are liable for the debts of the company. It is possible to become a 'limited' or 'sleeping' partner where financial liability is restricted to the amount of capital invested but limited partners have no say in the management of the business. Partnerships, like sole proprietorships, are easy to set up and also easy to dissolve. By giving notice to the others a partner can dissolve the business; also the death of one of the partners creates automatic dissolution.

Partnerships are common where joint expertise

is useful, such as in accountancy, law and stock-broking. They still have the disadvantage of a limited capital base and rely largely on trading profits being **ploughed back**, for expansion. One special type of partnership comes in the John Lewis and Waitrose Partnership where every employee is a partner with profit sharing rights and a strong stake in the running of the company.

JOINT STOCK COMPANIES

Joint stock companies are characterised by the key features of stock or share issue and limited liability; they usually employ large numbers of people (Fig. 8.3). In order to raise the larger sums of money required to expand a business, individuals can be asked to subscribe to the capital of the company. The purchase of **stocks** represent a loan to the company, whilst **shares** give an entitlement to ownership. Share purchase represents a gift of money to a company, the return being a share in the profits of the company. The concept of **limited liability** goes back to 1855 when a parliamentary statute limited the financial liability of stock or shareholders to the capital they had subscribed. Prior to this **unlimited liability** meant it was virtually impossible to invest in a number of companies in case one went bankrupt with the resulting personal liability for the stockholder.

Fig. 8.3 How large firms dominate in terms of their contribution to total employment

Companies are regarded as 'legal persons' and can own land and property, employ people, sue and be sued in courts. When they are formed, a **Memorandum of Association** setting out the aims of the company and the **Articles of Association** setting out the rules and regulations under which it will run, have to be submitted to the Registrar of Companies for approval. Because stocks and shares can be transferred from one person to another, joint stock companies are assured of continuity in business, unlike sole traders and partnerships where a death means the business winding up.

RAISING THE CAPITAL

Companies can raise capital in the form of borrowing and share issue. A loan to a company is often referred to as a **debenture** (or stock), whilst shares can be of two types: **ordinary** and **preference**.

1 Debentures

Anyone making a loan to a company has the right to expect the loan to be paid back in full with interest. Debenture holders for that reason are 'creditors' of the company and their interest is paid first out of company profits. If this interest is not paid debenture holders can 'liquidate' the company forcing it out of business when they have first rights on the company's assets (stock, buildings, plant, machinery, etc.) as a means of recovering their money. The interest paid on debentures is fixed throughout the period of the loan.

2 Shares

There are two types of share: preference and ordinary. **Preference shares** are less popular but offer a balance between risk and security for the lender by offering a fixed **dividend** which is paid out of profits after debenture holders have received their interest. Because preference shareholders are part owners of the company, the dividend represents their share of profits and is a fixed percentage, usually just above that of the debenture holders. Voting rights in the company for preference shareholders are limited and the dividend is not guaranteed; it is related to the fortunes of the company. Preference shareholders are therefore not creditors like the debenture holders. Cumulative preference shareholders, however, do have their dividend made up in high profit years from any shortfall in low profit years and therefore give more security for the holder compared to standard preference shares.

Ordinary shares are the most popular medium for providing company capital. They carry the greatest risk but offer potentially the highest rewards. Ordinary shareholders are entitled to full voting rights in a company but are last in the queue for their share of profits. The dividend they receive is not 'fixed' but varies with the size of distributed profits. Thus some years they may receive only a small dividend or perhaps none at all. If the company is highly successful they may receive a very high dividend, far better than the amounts received by the preference share or debenture holders. Buying ordinary shares entails having some confidence about the company's future success and initially, in the case of a new company, may mean sacrificing an early return for more substantial rewards in the long run.

An illustration of the returns from company investment can be seen in the following example:

The 'Oasis' Mineral Water Company raises its capital as follows:

£2m	6% debentures
£2m	7% cumulative preference shares
£2m	ordinary shares

Distributed profits were announced as follows:

	Year 1	Year 2	Year 3
distributed profits (£)	200 000	350 000	800 000
6% debenture holders(£)	120 000	120 000	120 000
7% cum. pref. shares(£)	80 000	200 000	140 000
ordinary shares(£)	—	30 000	540 000

The debenture holders receive payment first from profits: 6% of £2m requiring a total payment of £120 000 each year. The cumulative preference shareholders are next to receive payment, 7% of £2m amounting to £140 000. In year 1 however, only £80 000 is available for payment which the preference shareholders receive, leaving no dividend for the ordinary shareholders. In year 2, the higher profit figures allow the preference shareholders to have the year 1 dividend made up to £140 000 by adding £60 000 to their year 2 amount. This only leaves £30 000 for the ordinary shareholders. In year 3, however, the company is beginning to establish itself and after the debenture and preference shareholders have been paid £540 000 remains for distribution to the ordinary shareholders. This amount is greater than the whole of the income received by debenture holders and preference shareholders up to the end of year 3 and is equivalent to a 27p in the £ return. The example illustrates the risk versus profitability element in ordinary shares and how debentures are a relatively safe investment, though less remunerative when a company does well.

PRIVATE AND PUBLIC COMPANIES

Joint stock companies can be of two types: private and public. **Private companies** tend to be smaller than public companies. They must have at least two shareholders but no more than 50. **Public companies**, on the other hand, must have at least 7 members but there is no maximum. Private companies are often family businesses and the amount of capital employed is often not very large. Public companies can raise capital directly from the public in large amounts. This is often done through a 'public issue by prospectus'. An advertisement is placed in two major newspapers setting out the details of the company's trading activities and accounts. The public is then invited to subscribe to the share issue and millions of pounds can be raised from just this one advertisement. Private companies cannot offer their shares to the public. Public companies also have their shares traded on the Stock Exchange so that existing shareholders can easily exchange their shares for cash. Equally members of the public can buy shares at the current market price in any quoted company. Transferability of shares is not achieved quite so easily in a private company where prior approval of other members is necessary before the transfer can take place. All companies have to draw up an annual report which is presented to shareholders at the Annual General Meeting, but public companies have to publish a summary of their report in a national newspaper.

THINGS TO DO

1 Explain the meaning of the term **unlimited liability**. To what extent are shareholders liable for the debts of a company?

2 From Fig. 8.2 suggest reasons why small businesses proliferate in the UK.

3 The following information relates to ICI:

Size of holding £	Number of stockholders' accounts	Amount £m
1–250	151 826	18
251–500	88 564	33
501–1 000	69 104	49
1 001–5 000	37 362	64
5 001–10 000	1 088	8
10 001–50 000	840	20
50 001–1 000 000	607	136
over 1 000 000	67	291
all holdings	349 458	619

At the end of 1984 the register of stockholders consisted of 349 458 Ordinary Stock accounts, 660 Preference Stock accounts and 163 598 accounts in respect of all classes of Loan Stock. The table analyses the holdings of Ordinary Stock.

(a) Which is the most widely-held form of investment in ICI?
(b) What is **loan stock** more popularly called?
(c) From the table of stockholders, to what extent is ICI owned and controlled by the numerical majority of shareholders with holdings of up to £500?

4 List the main differences between public and private companies under the headings of (a) size; (b) transferability of shares; and (c) methods of raising capital.

5 If a company raises capital in the following way and earns distributed profits as shown, calculate the returns for each group of investors. What assumptions might need to be made before purchasing ordinary shares?

Capital: £1m 8% debentures
£500 000 9% cumulative preference shares
£1m ordinary shares

Distributed profits:
Year 1 – £100 000
Year 2 – £120 000
Year 3 – £140 000
Year 4 – £160 000

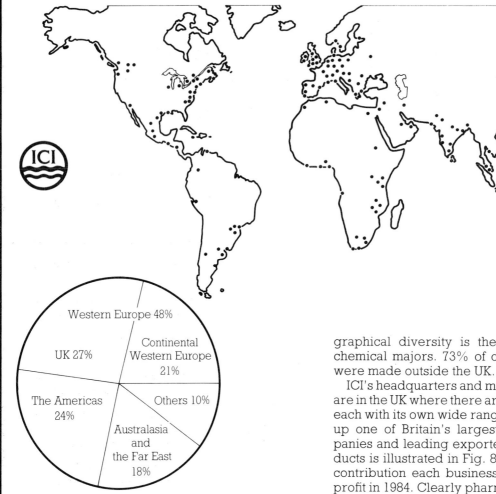

Fig. 8.4 ICI's 1984 chemicals' turnover worldwide showing % share of various territories – total value £8820m

A CASE STUDY OF A LARGE PUBLIC COMPANY – IMPERIAL CHEMICAL INDUSTRIES PLC

ICI is amongst the world's largest chemical companies and has one of the broadest and most varied product ranges in the industry. The parent company is British and the Group has manufacturing subsidiaries, sales organisations and related organisations throughout the world (Fig. 8.4). With manufacturing in over 40 countries and substantial sales organisations in more than 60, ICI's geographical diversity is the widest amongst the chemical majors. 73% of chemical sales in 1984 were made outside the UK.

ICI's headquarters and main technological base are in the UK where there are nine operating units, each with its own wide range of products, making up one of Britain's largest manufacturing companies and leading exporters. The range of products is illustrated in Fig. 8.5 which shows the % contribution each business sector made to total profit in 1984. Clearly pharmaceuticals and agricultural products (principally fertilisers and agrochemicals) were major contributors to ICI's 1984 performance.

ICI's turnover in 1984 was £9909m from which profits before interest and taxation amounted to £1134m. Figure 8.6 shows how these profits were divided up, taxation taking away a significant slice. Retained profits are reinvested in the business as a means of modernisation; dividends represent the profit distributed to shareholders. In 1984 the dividend paid to ordinary shareholders amounted to 30p in the £ or a 4.7% return on the stock market price of 636p at the beginning of the year.

The success of the company over time is shown by the graphs in Fig. 8.7. From a profit trough in 1982 the company has moved to record figures for both turnover and profit.

ICI's main objectives in business are outlined in Fig. 8.8 and are taken from the company's 1984 Annual Report.

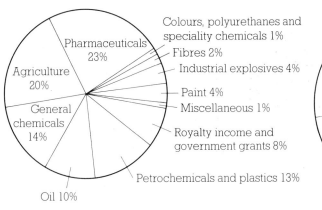

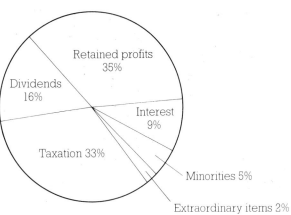

Fig. 8.5 (above) ICI's 1984 trading profit by business sectors – £1063m

Fig. 8.6 (right) Distribution of 1984 profits £1134m (from trading operations and related companies)

Fig. 8.7 ICI's turnover, dividend and profits – trends

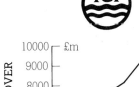

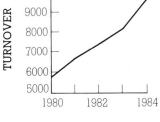

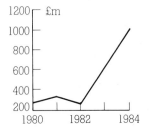

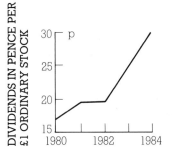

Objectives   Fig. 8.8

The diversity of ICI's products, its international spread and the breadth of its technological and commercial skills provide the Group with ample opportunities for profitable growth within its existing broad areas of activity. The Group's field of business will therefore continue to be the efficient manufacture and sale of chemical-based products, combined with other operations supported by its science base. Diversification into areas unrelated to ICI's strengths will not be sought.

ICI's principal objective is to improve the effectiveness of wealth creation within the Group and hence its financial performance, to the benefit of shareholders, employees, customers and the communities in which it operates.

In pursuing that objective the Group's main strategies are

– to maintain or increase ICI's position in its strong businesses throughout the world and to identify and develop profitable opportunities to increase the proportion of the Group's business in products with high added value

– to increase the Group's share of growth markets and to use its international marketing strength to create profitable business opportunities throughout the world. This includes:

continuing to develop participation in the overall West European market for chemicals;

increasing ICI's presence in its selected fields in the USA;

participating in the high growth areas of South East Asia; and

taking up opportunities to benefit from Japanese expansion and technological innovation

– to sustain the strength of the Group's technological base and earning ability within the UK while continuing to increase technological strength and earnings worldwide

– to make further advances in productivity, efficiency and cost effectiveness

– to continue to pursue appropriate opportunities for growth by acquisition and to make divestments where appropriate

– to maintain with vigour the Group's tradition of regeneration of its business portfolio through research, including specifically as current targets the establishment of growth businesses in advanced materials, products for the electronics industry, medical diagnostics, fermentation products and technology, and the application of bioscience to the development of crops.

PUBLIC ENTERPRISE

The market economy tends to suggest a *laissez-faire* (leave alone) approach to industry where firms respond to consumer preferences and competition between firms keeps prices down. There are, though, some forms of business organisation that justify state intervention. Take the case of electricity. If competition through private enterprise prevailed, there could be a lot of duplication of electricity cables with unprofitable rural areas being excluded from supply. If any supply company went bankrupt, it is possible that large numbers of people could be cut off for prolonged periods. It makes more sense to coordinate supply through one body regulated by the government to ensure a fair pricing policy. Nationalisation, however, is not universally accepted as the most appropriate method for organising major industries. Political parties have sharply differing attitudes about the issue and this has given rise to **privatisation** where nationalised industries have been returned to the private sector in terms of ownership and control. Sometimes a compromise is adopted, where state and privately owned bodies compete side by side. In broadcasting, for example, the BBC, set up as a public body in 1927, competes with the independent stations which earn all their income through advertising.

Nationalised industries are the principal form of public enterprise and the main period of nationalisation came with the 1945–51 post-war Labour government. The main industries taken into public ownership included coal, gas, electricity, steel and the railways.

Nationalised industries or public corporations differ in some important respects from private enterprise companies:

1 Aims

The principal aim of private enterprise is to maximise profits and usually the success of a business is judged on its profit performance. A nationalised industry has to operate much more in the public interest and should broadly aim to break even.

A summary of the main arguments for and against nationalised industries

Arguments *FOR*:

1 Losses do not lead to bankruptcy, so that essential services are continually provided.

2 A break-even pricing policy means consumers get a fair deal.

3 Economies of scale mean lower unit costs of production.

4 A state-run monopoly avoids duplicating resources, a possibility under private enterprise with competition between firms.

5 Nationalised industries can be used as instruments of economic policy by the government; expanding them in a recession, for example, will increase output and employment.

6 Nationalised industries all have consumer councils attached to them which provide a channel of communication between the industry and its users.

Arguments *AGAINST*:

1 Politicians do not always make good businessmen; misguided decisions may be made regarding nationalised industries.

2 Since nationalised industries have little or no competition they may become inefficient and provide a poor service to the consumer.

3 Longterm planning may be difficult as governments are subject to a general election at least every 5 years.

4 Decision-making is bureaucratic in nationalised industries and it is not always clear who runs the organisation. The chairman? The minister? Parliament?

5 Accountability is less easy to achieve in nationalised industries than in private enterprise companies where shareholders seek to ensure high profits for high dividends. The taxpayer who ultimately finances nationalised industries has little chance to directly monitor their performance.

6 Although nationalised industries run consumer councils, they have no say in policy decisions and are staffed mainly by part-timers.

2 Continuity

Since nationalised industries are responsible to the appropriate minister in government and governments are subject to re-election at least every 5 years, longterm planning may be difficult. An expansionary policy by one government could easily be reversed by another. Continuity is easier to achieve in private enterprise since ownership is unlikely to change hands as frequently as general elections!

3 Organisation

Nationalised industries have a board and a chairman similar to joint stock companies but the chairman of a nationalised industry is appointed by the government rather than the shareholders. In addition the chairman of a nationalised industry is responsible to an appropriate minister for policy whereas in private enterprise the chairman is responsible to the shareholders. There is another link in the chain of control of a nationalised industry involving parliament and, in particular, the appropriate select committee for the industry concerned. Thus the chairman is responsible to the minister who is in turn responsible to parliament. This bureaucratic organisation means decisions do take some time to effect and the divisions of responsibility in the chain are not always clear. The chairman is nominally responsible for the day-to-day running of the industry and the minister for policy, but in practice the two overlap. In the past there have been serious differences of opinion between chairmen and ministers over issues such as employment: a labour government may pursue a 'social employment policy' preserving jobs in nationalised industries to cushion a recession whereas a chairman may want manpower reductions to increase efficiency.

4 Capital

Whereas in joint stock companies new capital is raised largely from the issue of shares, nationalised industries rely on taxation for the bulk of their income. Some government borrowing is also diverted to investment for nationalised industries. It should also be noted that ploughed-back profits form a large source of investment in the private sector. This is also the case in nationalised industries where significant annual surpluses are made.

PRIVATISATION

The 1980s have seen a fairly radical change in government thinking away from nationalisation towards **privatisation** – the return of publicly owned industries to the private sector.

The arguments for privatisation partly stem from the disadvantages associated with nationalisation and more positively to encourage competition to break inefficient monopolies. What is not always clear is whether competition and privatisation always go hand in hand. The selling of government-owned shares in British Petroleum in November 1979 reduced its overall stake in the company from 51% to 31% and raised £817m but did little to promote competition. The British Telecom sale in 1984, where the state holding was reduced from 100% to 49%, raised about £4000m but simply transferred a public monopoly into a private one.

Privatisation does have the advantage of raising large sums of money for the government and where competition is promoted, it should increase industrial efficiency and increase consumer choice. It reduces the bureaucracy in decision-making and should allow new firms to enter markets previously made exclusive to state-owned monopolies. The improvements in efficiency though are likely to create some unemployment which has certainly made privatisation unpopular with Trade Unions.

MONOPOLY AND COMPETITION

If the best interests of the consumer are to be served, it is important that competition exists between producers to ensure fair pricing in the market. Pure **monopoly** is the clearest case of market power, where one firm is the sole supplier in a market. Where the monopoly exists in the private sector and the pursuit of maximum profits is the principal aim, the government needs to take action to prevent abuse of this form of market power. A monopolist in particular may try to keep prices as high as possible by restricting output to maximise total income. Barriers to entry for new firms may be put up where a monopolist discounts prices only to eliminate competition. A monopolist may also engage in **product differentiation** (the use of 'brand names') to try and disguise market power. Where there are no close substitutes for monopoly products, the monopolist may well be inefficient having little incentive to introduce new techniques compared to a highly competitive market. It has to be remembered that many nationalised industries are also monopolies and whilst they are not in pursuit of maximum profits, their market power can lead to inefficiencies in

A CASE STUDY OF NATIONALISED INDUSTRY ACCOUNTING: BRITISH RAIL

British Rail receives a considerable subsidy from the government each year which allows its accounts to break even. This subsidy averages around £300m a year. It could be argued that British Rail should become more efficient and close any loss-making lines to avoid the necessity of government financial help. However, what has to be taken into account is the fact that there are 'social costs', i.e. costs to the community, of closing unprofitable lines. Examples of such costs are the longer time incurred if travelling by road, the extra road accidents, and perhaps in a wider context, the additional unemployment created when people with no alternative means of transport have to forfeit their jobs. If all these social costs are given a monetary value then it could be the case that the social costs of closing a line are greater than the operating losses. If this is so then a subsidy may well be justified. Not all loss-making lines are in a position where the social costs of closing the line outweigh the operating deficits and here the problem regarding closure is more difficult. Such an example is shown in Fig. 8.9: the Cambrian Coast Line.

The operating losses amount to − £1 507 000 and the social costs of closure to only £752 000. Therefore retaining the line would give a negative benefit of − £755 000. It could be argued in this case that the social cost items are too narrowly defined. Certainly the more difficult and time consuming road journey resulting from the closure of the line could mean people giving up jobs and no allowance is made for the unemployment costs of all the railway staff made redundant. However, the cost-benefit study does show clearly that accounting losses on their own give a misleading indication of whether or not a railway line should close.

One other consideration regarding railways is that they are energy-saving compared to cars and in a national transport plan it may be worth considering taxing cars more heavily and increasing the subsidy on railways because there would be overall energy savings for the nation. Thus again operating losses may be justified if the nation as a whole makes substantial energy savings from the decreased use of the energy-wasteful car.

The idea of a national transport plan justifying greater subsidies for railways, could also be applied in a parallel way to the fuel and power industries. For example, since UK coal reserves are likely to last for at least another 200 years, but natural gas for only another 30 years, it would make sense to provide a subsidy to coal production to ensure its continued longterm future. Higher prices would be charged for gas to conserve supply. Thus again it is too simplistic to conclude that all nationalised industries should aim to break even with no government subsidy.

Fig. 8.10

A CASE STUDY OF PRIVATISATION: BRITISH TELECOM

British Telecom caters for 18 million customers and links 28 million phones. Its sale to the public in October 1984 raised about £4000m for the government (Fig. 8.10). The aim was to create a more efficient telephone service which under nationalisation had a legacy of outdated equipment. In 1983 for example 60% of the main telephone exchanges were based on the mechanical Strowger system, invented in the 1890s! Since BT, now in the private enterprise sector, still has a virtual monopoly position, the government set up OFTEL (the Office of Telecommunication) to regulate its activities. However OFTEL with a staff of only 30 may find it difficult to exert real influence over the

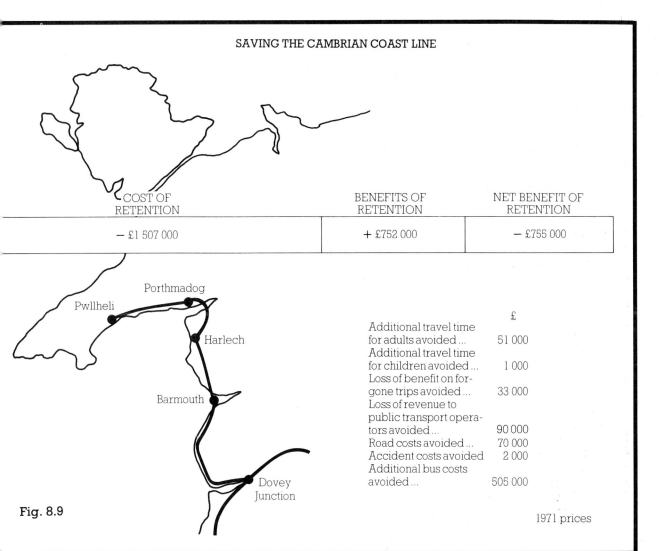

SAVING THE CAMBRIAN COAST LINE

COST OF RETENTION	BENEFITS OF RETENTION	NET BENEFIT OF RETENTION
− £1 507 000	+ £752 000	− £755 000

	£
Additional travel time for adults avoided ...	51 000
Additional travel time for children avoided ...	1 000
Loss of benefit on forgone trips avoided ...	33 000
Loss of revenue to public transport operators avoided ...	90 000
Road costs avoided ...	70 000
Accident costs avoided	2 000
Additional bus costs avoided ...	505 000

Fig. 8.9

1971 prices

whole range of BT's activities. The privatisation of BT has led to more competition between its major suppliers GEC, Plessey and STC. Foreign companies can now tender for contracts and some American firms have shown a keen interest to take advantage of this deregulation.

The main criticism of the BT privatisation comes in what is seen as the lost opportunity to create more competition in the telecommunications market. The announcement of record profits amounting to £1480m in 1984/5, the first year of privatisation, gives an indication of the market strength of BT and serves to confirm the suspicion that the government has converted a public monopoly into a private one simply to dial money.

The degree to which future competition is allowed to develop may well be the key to limiting the market power BT now has and reducing the excess profits which a private monopoly can all too easily make.

production and service which may require some form of monitoring by the government.

In the UK, monopolies are not banned in law (unlike in the USA), but are examined on their merits before any action is taken. There are, for example, a number of benefits which can be derived from monopolies such as economies of scale (monopolies tend to be large undertakings), the saving of wasteful advertising costs, and the security to spend money innovating new products.

The legal machinery for investigating monopolies was consolidated under the 1973 Fair Trading Act. This defined a monopoly in legal terms as a firm with more than 25% of the market share of a product or service. Any such firm can be investigated by the Monopolies Commission which reports its findings to the Director General of Fair Trading, set up under the Act to coordinate the application of competition and consumer law.

Action can be taken to remedy any trading policies which are found to be against the public interest. Mergers that create a 'legal' monopoly can also be investigated under the terms of the Act.

A further piece of legislation which is important comes in the form of the Restrictive Practices Act 1976. This Act made it illegal for companies to make restrictions on retailers relating to price, conditions of supply, quantity and persons supplied unless they could prove it would be in the 'public interest' to make such restrictions. The Competition Act of 1980 extended monopoly control to certain public bodies, in particular nationalised industries.

The evidence shows that the trend in UK industry is firmly towards concentrating production into larger units. A **concentration ratio** measures what share large firms have of the total market, a common ratio being the five firm sales concentration ratio. This shows for various markets what % of total market sales the five largest firms enjoy. Examples of heavily concentrated markets with high ratios are cigarettes and tobacco (99%), petroleum (93%) and vehicles (90%). Figure 8.11 shows how concentration in general in the UK is increasing, both in terms of production and employment.

Increased concentration may not necessarily be a bad thing – greater economies of scale can result. However, it is important to ensure that any resulting monopolies are carefully regulated and the evidence for this happening is not very convincing. From 1965 to 1975 for example only 3% of mergers which were eligible for investigation by the Monopolies Commission were actually taken up (see *A Review of Monopolies and Mergers Policy* Cmd 7198, 1978). There is thus the suspicion that mergers may well be taking place which act against the public interest. One problem with the existing legislation may be that companies are 'innocent until proved guilty' whereas if a merger or monopoly was assumed to be against the public interest unless firms proved otherwise, perhaps fewer unwanted mergers would actually take place.

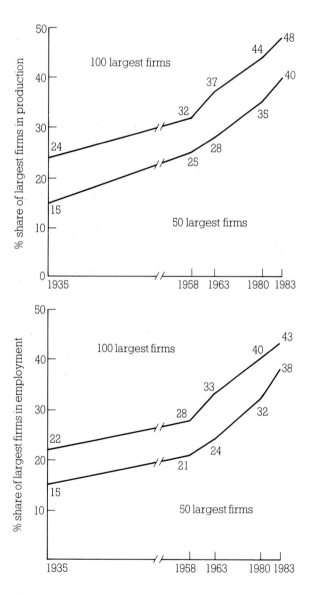

Fig. 8.11 Trends in concentration by employment and output

THE SPECTRUM OF COMPETITION

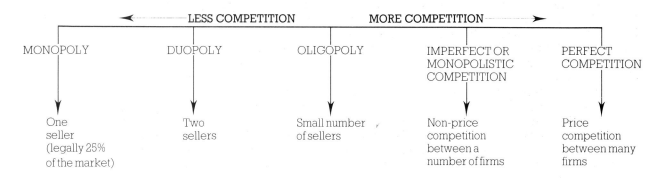

Fig. 8.12 The spectrum of competition

In Economics there are specialist terms which are used to describe the various forms of competition that can exist in a market (Fig. 8.12). **Perfect competition** assumes a large number of firms competing on the basis of price with a common product and that consumers have perfect knowledge in terms of producers' prices. This is the classic competition model which allows consumers sovereignty over producers. Where producers manage to differentiate their product by giving it special attributes such as 'extra strength' lager or 'fresh breath' toothpaste, competition may not be so much on the basis of price as the virtues of the products' characteristics. Competition becomes **imperfect** and is sometimes referred to as **monopolistic competition**. When only a few firms are in the same market together an **oligopoly** is said to exist. In the UK, car manufacturers, banks and breweries are examples of oligopolistic markets and the danger is that with only a few dominant firms, some collusion may take place over pricing or restricting output. Thus 'cartels' are started which are almost informal monopolies and need to be carefully monitored. A market with only two major firms is known as a **duopoly**. The UK soap market is a good example with just Proctor & Gamble and Lever Brothers supplying over 90% of the market. Pure **monopolies** with only one seller are difficult to find in the private sector though British Telecom is a good example. Firms that come near to the legal definition of a monopoly include the British Shoe Corporation which owns most of the High Street shops such as Dolcis, Saxone, Lilley & Skinner, Freeman Hardy & Willis, Truform and Manfield. Equally, examples of pure perfect competition are difficult to cite although the Stock Exchange used to boast near perfect competition between jobbers in the market for securities. Today mergers between traders have made competition very imperfect.

There needs to be some qualification to the conclusion that more competition is always better than less. The increased economies of scale that are achieved have to be balanced against the decreased efficiency that often comes with less competition. What evidence there is suggests that the improvement in scale economies from mergers is often small and that some diseconomies of coordination may result from a larger size. It does seem therefore that a more careful monitoring of the increase in concentration is called for, and that in general more competition is the best safeguard for the consumer against higher prices and restricted output.

THINGS TO DO

1 Give *two* examples in each case of a public sector body which is (*a*) organised through a government department; (*b*) run by a local authority; (*c*) organised as a nationalised industry.

2 Outline the main characteristics which distinguish **private** from **public** enterprise.

3 Under what circumstances might it be appropriate for a nationalised industry to receive a permanent subsidy?

4 Outline the principal advantages and disadvantages to the consumer of a **monopoly** market.

5 Read Fig. 8.13 relating to the Monopolies Commission Report on British Rail's London and South East Commuter Services. It was investigated as a result of the Competition Act 1980.

(*a*) Describe the main criticisms of the Monopolies Commission under the headings of efficiency; manpower; excess capacity; sex composition of workforce; and punctuality.

(*b*) What steps could British Rail take to improve conditions?

Fig. 8.13

British Rail is criticised for a list of failings. These include:

● Quality of commuter services – in terms of punctuality and level of cancellation this is now below the quality offered in 1974. Staff shortages, absenteeism and "a degree of deterioration of the asset base" are contributory factors.

The commission sees little scope for improvement without timetable changes, more success in recruiting and more efficient use of manpower.

Performance fell "well short" of the standards set out in BR's "Towards a commuters charter" issued last year.

BR had no targets aimed at reducing train cancellations.

Standards for carriage cleaning laid down by the British Railways Board are "not at present feasible."

● The efficiency with which BR uses its physical resources. BR did not analyse maintenance costs for vehicles in sufficient detail. Maintenance cost controls were based on control of labour costs "with no direct control of material costs." These "major weaknesses" have to be remedied.

● Poor cleaning of the insides of carriages – a result, in part, of "poor management monitoring procedures."

● Few women were employed on the railway. "The Board should re-examine the potential for meeting its labour needs by increasing the use of females in the workforce. This should include the employment of women on a part-time basis to help meet demand at commuter peak periods."

● Efficiency in the use of manpower must be increased in ways leading to cash savings. These savings must in some measure be used to increase pay levels and working conditions. But they must in part be available for the reduction, or holding, of costs.

● BR should consider increasing the use of contract labour for weekend working.

● BR should urgently consider cutting down the number of carriages operated. BR operated excess capacity on some peak hour inner rail services in 1979.

● Manpower problems. Labour turnover and absenteeism were not out of line with other industries. But they created special problems for the railways. Absenteeism among train crew led to train cancellations. Low basic wages, long, irregular and unsocial hours led to labour difficulties.

● BR is also criticised for not matching the recent decline in traffic with corresponding reductions in resources.

The Monopolies and Mergers Commission, "British Railways Board: London and South East Commuter Services," Cmnd. 8046, HMSO, £8.60, October 1980.

The Financial Times 3.10.1980

6 Read carefully the article on 'Rush-hour war as buses queue for passengers'.

List the advantages and disadvantages of privatising the Glasgow bus service (as stated by the article) in two columns as shown below.

Advantages of privatisation (deregulation)	Disadvantages of privatisation (deregulation)

Fig. 8.14

Rush-hour war as buses queue for passengers

A BUS war has broken out in Glasgow, striking fear and confusion into innocent bystanders and making Keystone Kops farce of the traffic flow in the city centre.

During rush hours last week, solid phalanxes of up to 30 buses, sporting the colours of five opposing companies, advanced on the bus stops, each jostling for pole position whenever a potential passenger hove into view. They have all joined in a rush for business.

The Glasgow chaos has been caused by the five firms jumping the gun on deregulation D-day October 26. On that day anyone in Britain can start a bus service going anywhere as long as it meets the safety standards of local traffic commissioners. None of the operators wanted to be left standing on the day.

The battle for new routes means that you can now go from a Glasgow housing estate direct to Loch Lomond. But instead of heading directly on the routes, most buses make a point of traversing the city centre, scouring the bus stops for fares.

Inevitably the chaos is already passing into folklore with tales of drivers who have to ask their way back to base, who make up their own routes as they go along, or who drive with maps spread out on their laps.

Four of the companies are bidding to compete with Strathclyde Buses, formerly the Strathclyde Passenger Transport Executive, which at present runs Glasgow's more regular services.

But as a prelude to the competition to come, pedestrians have found that the simple task of crossing the street is now an obstacle course around the buses.

Tony Conway, head of traffic and environment for the Automobile Association in Scotland, has been monitoring services in the centre and says: "I am concerned from the road safety aspect. Some buses are racing for stops to be first to pick up passengers. It's an unhappy situation, but it's early days yet, and I will be looking at it later in the month before making representations to the appropriate authorities."

The bus war may be bad news for pedestrians and city-centre car drivers, but not everyone is complaining. For deregulation has provided several hundred jobs, especially with the reintroduction of clippies. Conductors had been consigned to the story books by cost-cutting campaigns, leaving the city with only pay-as you enter vehicles. But bus companies believe the public prefers to avoid the kind of queues that can build up waiting to board that kind of vehicle.

Along with the clippies, the bus war has also brought back the trusty double-deckers. About 120 of the legendary London Route-masters, built around 1960, have had their liveries repainted in blues, reds and yellows and refurbished.

George Watson, Clydeside Scottish general manager, said: "People have welcomed the return of the double-decker and the conductor. London Transport looked after the buses really well. They are in great condition. The crew operations means that our buses can gulp up passengers and leave the stop without delay."

Mark McSherry

The Sunday Times
5.10.1986

ORGANISING LABOUR – TRADE UNIONS AND WAGES

INTRODUCTION

In Chapter 8 it was clear that much of British industry is run on private enterprise principles, with the aim of making a profit. In order to maximise profits, the costs of production need to be kept to a minimum. Since for many firms wages represent the largest single item of costs, it follows that firms will try to minimise their wages bill as far as possible.

Working people have the opposite interest. Since wages represent the means of supporting a family, paying a mortgage, etc., people will want to ensure they achieve the highest possible living standards consistent with what the firm can afford to pay. **Trade unions** are simply groups of working people who have joined together to defend their common interests. They try to ensure that working people are protected against any exploitation by employers who may not always have their employees' best interests at heart.

THE HISTORY OF TRADE UNIONS

The origins of modern trade unions in England go back to the 18th century as a response to the exploitation of working people, particularly women and children, during the Industrial Revolution. Figure 9.1 shows some of the working conditions which existed at the time though it was not until 1871 that trade unions were made legal. Some of the worst working conditions occurred in the mining industry where very young children were sent to work. 'We find that instances occur in which children are taken into these mines to work as early as four years of age, sometimes at five, and between five and six, not infrequently between six and seven, and often from seven to eight, while from eight to nine is the ordinary age at which employment in these mines commences' (From the 1843 report of the Children's Employment Commission).

In 1906 the Parliamentary Labour Party was born with strong support from the Trades Union Congress which itself had been formed in 1868.

The TUC had not made much progress in gaining reforms to help working people during its early years but with 54 Labour MPs in the 1906 election, it began to have an increasing influence on government policies. In 1926, however, the TUC called a general strike of its members in response to the then Conservative government's attempt to cut wages of workers as a means of boosting Britain's trade. The strike failed and the government then passed a law forbidding general strikes. In addition a part of union member subscriptions had automatically gone towards Labour Party funds; in the 1927 Trade Unions Act union members had to give permission (contract-in) for their money to be used to support the Party. After World War 2 the TUC worked closely with the Labour government, helping to set up the Welfare State with a National Health Service and a National Insurance scheme for sickness and unemployment. More recently the influence of trade unions on government policy has diminished. The 1980 Employment Act passed by a Conservative government, made picketing more difficult, encouraged secret ballots to be held before strikes were called and made closed shops (where union membership is a condition of employment) more difficult to introduce. Today trade unions can also be required to pay compensation to an employer for lost earnings during the period of a strike.

TYPES OF TRADE UNIONS

Trade unions consist of many groups from dockers to doctors, from school caretakers to school teachers and from lorry drivers to senior civil servants. There are about 10 million trade union members in Britain out of a total workforce of about 27 million. Unions can be divided into four main types.

1 **Craft unions**
   Craft unions join together workers who have a particular skill or craft. Normally an apprenticeship has to be served before membership can be obtained. Craft unions formed the foundation of modern unionism in the 1850s. Few wholly craft unions exist today but examples include

Fig. 9.1 These illustrations show examples of the exploitation of workers during the Industrial Revolution. Child labour, horrific working conditions in the coalmines and the factories, long hours and very little pay were all injustices that trade unions set out to fight against

Fig. 9.2 A rail crash in 1874 – crashes such as these led to the setting up of ASLEF

the Associated Society of Locomotive Engineers and Firemen (ASLEF) and the Society of Graphical and Allied Trades (SOGAT). Figure 9.2 shows one of the important reasons for the setting up of ASLEF: throughout most of the late 19th century no regulations existed governing the working hours of train drivers and firemen and consequently there were many tragic accidents. The Union has long campaigned for shorter working hours and safer conditions in the railway industry.

2 Industrial unions

Industrial unions were formed in the early part of this century with the aim of representing all the workers in a single industry. Industrial unionism grew out of the desire to achieve greater workers' control of a particular industry. There are several large industrial unions in Britain; most have the prefix 'National Union of'. Examples are the National Union of Mine-

workers (NUM), the National Union of Railway-men (NUR), and the National Union of Seamen (NUS).

3 General unions

After World War 1 (1914–18), many unions amalgamated and the large **general unions** were formed. Nowadays British trade unionism is dominated by these large general unions. The largest, the Transport & General Workers' Union (TGWU) has 1 547 443 members and represents workers in all industries. The second largest union, the Amalgamated Union of Engineering Workers (AUEW) represents 943 538 workers and has become a general engineering union. The third largest union, the General, Municipal, Boilermarkers & Allied Trades Union (GMBATU) represents 875 187 members mainly in gas, local government, engineering and boilermaking.

4 'White collar' or non-manual unions

This is the most rapidly expanding sector of the trade union movement, a trend which reflects the growth in white collar occupations since the war. As Fig. 9.3 shows, over a third of all unionists are now in this category. Important white collar unions include the National Association of Local Government Officers (NALGO) with 780 000 members and the Association of Scientific, Technical and Managerial Staffs (ASTMS) with 390 000 members.

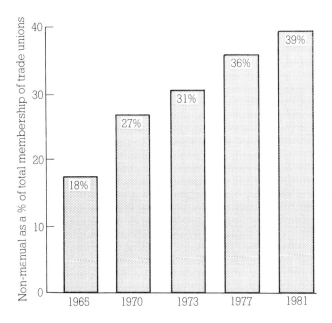

Fig. 9.3   The growth of white collar unions

THE CONFEDERATION OF BRITISH INDUSTRY

The **Confederation of British Industry** (CBI) is the opposite number to the TUC. It represents the employers and has a membership of 11 900 companies. It has a permanent staff headed by the Director General and again advises the government on a wide range of issues. Its views tend to find more favour with a Conservative government.

THE TRADES UNION CONGRESS

The **Trades Union Congress** (TUC) is a permanent organisation based at Congress House in London. All the major unions are affiliated to the TUC which puts forward the collective view of the movement. The TUC tends to work more closely with a Labour government on a wide variety of interests ranging from economic policy to health, education and international affairs. Even with a Conservative government, it acts as a very important pressure group representing the views of working people.

An annual congress, attended by over 1000 delegates representing the affiliated unions, decides TUC policy. The General Council with 51 members is elected to carry out conference policies and the TUC General Secretary is the public spokesperson for the Council.

IMPORTANT UNION TERMS

There are a number of important terms used in connection with trade union activity. The general name given to union activity in a dispute is **industrial action** (Fig. 9.5 overleaf). This can cover anything from a strike with picketing to a work to rule. Some important terms are described below.

UNOFFICIAL STRIKE

A **strike** that has not gained the approval of the union is called **unofficial**. Unofficial strikes often occur when members in a particular plant or factory feel strongly about an issue (e.g. future redundancies) and come out on strike before the union has decided its official policy. Unofficial strikes may be made official if the union, having assessed the situation, feels the workers have a good case. Unofficial strikes have been common in the car industry in the past where local grievances have caused friction between management and unions.

WORK TO RULE OR 'GO SLOW'

If a union does engage in a dispute with the management, strike action may be a rather drastic step to take, causing a total disruption of business as well as a loss of earnings for union members. A halfway step may be to stop any overtime being worked (an **overtime ban**) or work strictly to any rules laid down as part of working practice (**work to rule**). In the railways, for instance, train drivers could keep train speeds down and rigidly adhere to safety procedures; this is sometimes called a **go slow**. Teachers have in the past worked to rule by undertaking not to supervise out-of-school activities when involved in a pay dispute.

PICKETING

When a strike takes place, to make it more effective, union members may stand outside the place of work persuading other workers to join them (Fig. 9.4). Such a group is known as a **picket** and picketing is a legal right of trade unions. In the past unions not directly involved in a dispute have sometimes engaged in **secondary picketing**, giving added support to a cause they believed to be just. In 1979, when a large number of steel workers

THINGS TO DO

1 From the pictures of children working during the Industrial Revolution, describe their working conditions. Suggest how trade unions could improve such conditions.

2 Look at the following trade union names then classify them into craft, industrial, general or white collar.
   Amalgamated Society of Woodworkers
   National Union of Agricultural Workers
   Union of Post Office Workers
   Iron & Steel Trades Confederation
   Bakers' Union
   Inland Revenue Staff Federation

3 What is the main role of the TUC? How are TUC policies determined?

4 Look at the following table showing membership of the largest trade unions in 1982. Represent their relative importance graphically.

Transport & General Workers Unions	1 547 443
Amalgamated Union of Engineering Workers	943 538
General, Municipal, Boilermakers & Allied Trades Union	875 187
National & Local Government Officers Association	780 000
National Union of Public Employees	703 998
Union of Shop Distributive & Allied Workers	437 854
Electrical Electronic Telecommunications & Plumbing Union	428 595
Association of Scientific Technical & Managerial Staffs	390 000

were on strike, threatened with redundancy from plant closures, miners engaged in supportive picketing. Such secondary picketing is now illegal and unions can incur heavy fines if this law is broken.

CLOSED SHOP

A **closed shop** arises when union membership is a condition of employment. Examples of unions with closed shop agreements are the National Union of Mineworkers and the National Union of Firemen. Closed shops can give rise to divided emotions. On the one hand objections are that people should have the freedom to decide whether or not they wish to belong to a union. On the other hand, a number of employers have expressed a favourable attitude towards closed shops on the grounds that all negotiations about pay and conditions of work can be channelled through one set of union officials, simplifying the consultation procedure. From the unions' point of view a closed shop is desirable because all workers in the industry or occupation can be called upon for support in the event of a dispute. In teaching there is no closed shop so union membership is voluntary. However any pay rise awarded as a result of union pressure is paid to all teachers regardless of whether they are in a union or not. The 1980 Employment Act made closed shop agreements more difficult to enter into and gave individuals who may have suffered from such agreements the right to take legal action against the trade union.

"Hello – our work can't be too shoddy after all."

Fig. 9.4

Fig. 9.5 The ETA/ABS secretarial and clerical staff national rally in London for better pay and fairer conditions

COLLECTIVE BARGAINING

Collective bargaining takes place when management and unions sit around a table to negotiate the settlement of a disagreement. Such bargaining is usually related to pay and conditions of work with the union submitting an initial claim and the management making a counter offer. The process of collective bargaining can be looked at graphically by means of a **union resistance curve** and **employer's concession curve** (Fig. 9.6).

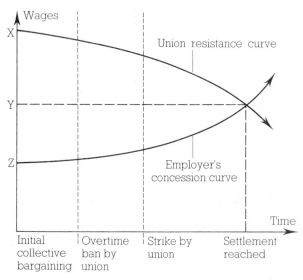

X – initial union wage claim
Z – initial employer's offer
Y – final agreed compromise wage after
    a negotiated settlement

Fig. 9.6   The process of collective bargaining

The union may put forward an initial wages claim of £X per week with the employer responding by offering £Z per week. Negotiations then take place to resolve the difference, the union 're-sisting' as far as possible a downward settlement, the employer 'conceding' as little as possible in an upwards direction. If no immediate agreement is reached the union may start an overtime ban followed later by a strike. Finally a compromise is reached and through the process of collective bargaining an agreed increase of £Y per week is paid to employees. In the majority of cases collective bargaining enables wage settlements to be reached without the need for industrial action, in which case the 'resistance' and 'concession' curves merge fairly quickly.

Collective bargaining takes place in nearly all industries though in the past some governments have suspended it in favour of wage restraint via an **incomes policy**. This may be introduced in times when pay rises are very high leading to the price of goods rising fast, the feature of inflation. The government may insist that wage rises cannot

go up beyond a laid down % in order to reduce inflation. Such policies have not been wholly successful in the past because unions much prefer the process of collective bargaining and are not prepared to accept wage restraint for too long.

CONCILIATION AND ARBITRATION

Sometimes the two sides engaged in collective bargaining cannot agree a compromise and a third party has to be brought in to resolve the dispute. **Conciliation** arises when the third party tries to bring the other two together by looking for the common ground between them. If the two sides are not too far apart, the conciliator will often persuade them to make further concessions to close the gap. If this does not work the third party may have to make a decision on what is the fairest solution. This is known as **arbitration** and it can be made more effective if both sides agree to be bound by the decision of the arbitrator (Fig. 9.7).

The **Advisory, Conciliation and Arbitration Service** (ACAS) was formally set up by the government in 1974 to provide a channel for mediation in disputes. Although it is paid for by the government, it is completely independent so that employers and workers see it as being impartial. ACAS is managed by a nine member council, three from the TUC, three from the employers' federation (the CBI) and three independent industrial relations experts. ACAS provides arbitration facilities and employs officers to act as conciliators who can take an outside view of the dispute.

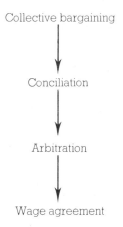

Fig. 9.7   Stages involved in settling a dispute

DEMARCATION DISPUTES

Demarcation disputes are about which job is appropriate for certain categories of skilled and unskilled workers. An electrician in a car assembly plant will not be prepared to cover for an absent worker in the body pressing plant who is unskilled. Disputes arise when unskilled workers are asked to undertake jobs normally reserved for skilled people, but at a lower rate of pay.

WAGE DIFFERENTIALS

Each year, normally starting around October, a new round of collective bargaining takes place in industry. Traditionally the first major group of workers to negotiate a pay claim are those at the Ford Motor Company and their pay award sets the pattern for other groups of workers. Skilled workers try to preserve a difference in their settlements from those negotiated by unskilled workers. Such differences are called **wage differentials**. The differential between a doctor and a bus conductor will be quite high and any narrowing of the differential is bound to be resisted by the higher paid group. In the annual wage round, therefore, workers in related occupations try to negotiate similar settlements to maintain differentials.

BLACKLEG

Workers who act against union policy (particularly in relation to strike action by going to work) are sometimes called **blacklegs**. They may in extreme cases be expelled from the union or sent to Coventry – when other union members will not speak to them. Generally trade unions expect solidarity when decisions are made and this may mean that a minority accept decisions made by the majority.

THE ORGANISATION OF TRADE UNIONS

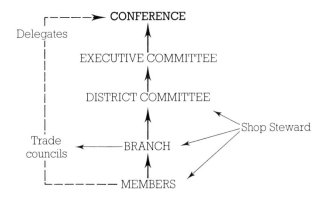

Fig. 9.8 How a union is structured

Although each trade union has its own pattern of organisation, Fig. 9.8 shows a typical structure. At its basic level there are the members who meet at branch level. In some occupations where factory work is common a shop steward is elected by his or her fellow union members to present their interests to the management. They are not paid by the union and they work at their own job when not on union business. They are trained by the union to carry out their union duties. The shop steward addresses union meetings and takes part in wage negotiations and other deals; he or she also finds new members, helps settle disputes with the foreman (the management supervisor) and keeps everyone in the factory informed (Fig. 9.9 overleaf).

The district committee will usually be regionally based, covering a large number of branches. Nationally the executive committee will carry out policies approved at the union conference. Conference policy is decided by delegates nominated by the branches or districts. They are not strictly representatives since they take motions approved by local areas to the conference which they must support regardless of their personal viewpoint. In this way democracy is achieved in the union by ordinary branch members deciding union policy. (By contrast, Members of Parliament are representatives of their constituencies. They do not have to agree with their constituents on all issues and can speak more freely in Parliament.)

THE MAIN FUNCTIONS OF TRADE UNIONS

It sometimes appears that trade unions have only one main function which is to negotiate higher wages for their members. Whilst this is an important objective and a well publicised one, they do perform a wide variety of other functions as Fig. 9.10 (overleaf) shows.

Trade unions run training courses for members to educate them in the organisation of union work. They provide strike pay for members where it can be afforded. Larger unions make contact with similar unions abroad to compare wages and working conditions. It is perhaps not always understood that unions may sponsor MPs where the union has a large membership in a particular region. The National Union of Mineworkers has several sponsored MPs representing localities where mining is the dominant occupation. More centrally, a union may carry out research on wages and prices and perhaps the profitability of an employer. Legal departments of unions will support industrial cases in court. Large unions can also afford to finance convalescent homes for members recovering from occupational accidents. All unions are keen to improve working conditions which apply to heating, lighting, ventilation, health and safety. In their organisation, unions also hold regular branch meetings and send representatives to sit on TUC committees.

In a wider sense trade unions try to ensure that the income earned by the nation as a whole is shared more equally amongst the community and that they share in the planning and control of industry. This is tied to their desire to achieve full employment. They also aim to eliminate boring

Greenwich Means Recruiting Time

GREENWICH local authority branch is distinguished by two achievements. Firstly it has grown in six years from a minority union position with 400 members to a majority union with over 1000 members. Secondly, it claims the biggest group of home-help staff in the country, with 400 members and 25 to 30 regularly at branch meetings.

Part of the secret of this success is a novel bonus scheme run by the branch, only this time the bonus is for shop stewards who recruit members.

District secretary Ted Sheehan explained how several years ago the branch decided to give a 25p bonus to shop stewards for every member they got onto payroll deductions.

The money came from the branch fund, and now the scheme is even self-financing.

Full-time convenor and branch secretary Bill Corbett, and branch chairman Will Fancy are rightly pleased at their scheme. "You can never hold a good branch back," commented Ted Sheehan.

FINDS NEW MEMBERS............

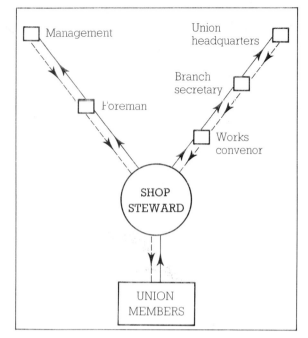

KEEPS EVERYONE INFORMED.....

'Just because I stopped for a few beers when I slipped out to the bet-shop he says me income's outstripping me production.'

Giles

"You're not happy here, are you, Parkinson?"

HELPS SETTLE DISPUTES WITH THE FOREMAN...   Birkett

Fig. 9.9 The functions of a shop steward

WHAT YOUR UNION DOES....

1 Runs training courses
2 Provides strike pay
3 Makes contact with unions abroad
4 Sponsors Members of Parliament
5 Carries out research on prices and wages
6 Supports industrial cases in court
7 Sets up convalescent homes
8 Presses for safer workshops
9 Sits on TUC Committees
10 Holds regular branch meetings

Fig. 9.10 The functions of a trade union are far more wide-ranging than the traditional media image of strikes and violent picketing

repetitive work so that jobs can be created which provide satisfaction, prospects and personal fulfilment. Trade unions aim to achieve income security for employees when work is interrupted by illness, accident, old age, redundancy or unemployment. Finally they promote equal opportunities for women and racial equality.

Clearly the role of trade unions is very broad and these functions represent the main advantages to members. Are there any disadvantages in joining a union? Perhaps for the individual the fact that the decisions of the executive may have to be accepted even though a ballot of members may not have been taken, may cause resentment. The cost of union membership may also be high in some cases and may seem less than worthwhile if strike pay is not provided. On a general level unions can be accused of dragging their feet over new technology and working practices leaving Britain behind our international competitors (though unions would claim such developments can contribute to increased unemployment). Finally at present most unions devote part of their funds to providing finance for the Labour Party and members have to 'contract out' i.e. state in writing if they do not wish this to happen. In practice few people do contract out but not all union members would wish to support the Labour Party: a sizeable minority vote for the Conservative Party (Fig. 9.11).

THE STEREOTYPE IS ...	THE REALITY IS ...
A left wing ...	Only 51% of union members support Labour ...
unskilled manual worker ...	72% are white-collar or skilled manual ...
who lives in a council house ...	56% are owner-occupiers ...
blindly follows his union leadership ...	31% are dissatisfied with their union's national leadership ...
is wedded to the closed shop ...	59% oppose the closed shop ...
and prone to strike at the drop of a hat.	84% think strikes should be called only after a postal ballot.

Fig. 9.11 Some – perhaps surprising – results from an opinion poll which challenge the traditional sterotype of a trade unionist. What is your image of a trade unionist?

THINGS TO DO

1 Study the following table comparing days lost through illness and industrial disputes 1975–8:

	Days lost through illness (millions)	Days lost through disputes (millions)
1975	340	6
1976	362	3
1977	385	10
1978	420	9

For every one day lost through industrial action, how many are lost through illness each year (approximately)?

2 Study the following figures which show days lost through industrial action and unemployment 1978–83.

Year	People involved	Industrial action	Unemploy- ment
1978	1 001 000	9 405 000	1 382 000
1979*	4 583 000	29 474 000	1 295 000
1980	830 000	11 964 000	1 664 000
1981	1 499 000	4 266 000	2 615 000
1982	2 101 000	5 313 000	2 862 000
1983	538 000	3 593 000	3 100 000

(*17 863 000 days are accounted for by the 1979 action of the engineering unions)

(a) For each year, calculate the number of days lost per person (approximately).
(b) Represent these figures graphically.
(c) Discuss the relationship between unemployment and the days lost per person. If a government wishes to minimise industrial action, what might it be tempted to do in relation to unemployment?

3 Bill Clarke is a printer on an evening paper. Last week his machine broke down and he lost one edition's printing while it was being repaired. At the end of the week the money for the lost time was stopped out of his pay packet. He complained to the shop steward, Eddie Brown. Imagine you were the shop steward. Take the story of the dispute on from there and fill in the results on a form similar to the one shown in Fig. 9.12.

EXAMPLE OF A RECORD OF A GRIEVANCE CASE

(a) Name of Member(s) Involved

(b) Card and Branch Number

(c) Nature of Grievance
    Time, Place and Date Occurred

(d) Settlement Required

(e) Action Taken

(f) Decision Arrived at

(g) Any Further Action Necessary

Signed   Date

Fig. 9.12

4 With reference to a recent dispute, show the stages involved and how the process of collective bargaining eventually produced a settlement.

5 Distinguish between **conciliation** and **arbitration**. What is the main function of the **Advisory, Conciliation and Arbitration Service**?

6 What is the difference between a **delegate** and a **representative** of an organisation?

7 Read the article from the *Times Educational Supplement* which relates to industrial action by teachers (Fig. 9.13).

(a) What is 'no cover' action by teachers?
(b) Why is this form of industrial action more common than a strike?
(c) What are local authorities trying to do to discourage 'no cover' action? How might this affect relations between heads and teachers?

Fig. 9.13

Stop pay for no cover action – l.e.a.s advised

by David Lister

Teachers who refuse to cover for absent colleagues or attend staff meetings are likely to have pay deducted from now on.

A tough strategy to combat industrial action in schools has been set out in a confidential document by employers' leaders on the Council of Local Education Authorities.

The advice, being sent to every l.e.a. in the country, brings to a head the continuing controversy over which teacher activities are contractual and which are not.

It defines as a contractual duty any activity which the authority is satisfied is normally carried out by teachers. It says that in future if teachers refuse to carry out these activities they will be in breach of contract and pay can be deducted.

The new advice is highly significant as industrial action over pay is a distinct likelihood this year and there is a constant stream of local disputes which result in no

cover action and a ban on activities that are believed to be voluntary.

No cover is the most common form of industrial action in schools. It was widely used in last year's pay dispute by the National Union of Teachers, but few NUT members lost pay because of it.

It was during that dispute that several authorities asked for advice on how to combat industrial action.

The new advice makes clear that it will be up to individual l.e.a.s to decide what are breaches of contract. But it does point to no cover, refusal to attend staff meetings or stay at staff meetings which stretch past the end of school; refusal to invigilate exams which stretch out of school hours, and refusal to attend parents' evenings. Refusal to undertake midday supervision is unlikely to be seen as a breach of contract.

Authorities are being advised to

apply the sanctions "reasonably". And l.e.a.s will be expected to write to all teachers first, explaining what will be considered breaches of contract.

The NUT remains convinced that no cover action, and indeed all the other examples mentioned, are not breaches of contract.

Headteachers are likely to welcome much of the new CLEA strategy as they have long wanted clarification of their responsibilities in industrial disputes. However, some heads are bound to fear that their relationships with their staffs will be affected if, as seems likely, they have to give their l.e.a.s the names of teachers refusing to cover for absent colleagues.

The CLEA document makes clear, for the first time, that deputies standing in for heads in disputes take on the duties of the head.

Times Educational Supplement 25.1.1985

WHY DO SOME PEOPLE EARN MORE THAN OTHERS?

There are wide differences in the income people earn in this country and it is important to understand why this occurs. The **professions** (e.g. doctors, solicitors and accountants) are in general well paid whilst at the other end of the scale people such as nurses, school cleaners and railway porters are generally low paid.

The conditions that give rise to wage differentials can be explained by concepts already discussed, namely those of demand and supply. So far these concepts have been used in relation to the **product market** but they can equally be applied to the **factor market**, in this case labour. Generally the demand for labour is *derived* from the demand for the product that the labour produces. If the demand for cars is similar to that shown, then the demand for car workers will also be downward sloping (Fig. 9.14). Note that in the case of car workers the *price* of labour is the *wage* they receive: this explains the difference in the labelling of the vertical axes on the graphs. Demand curves for particular occupations are bound to vary greatly according to the differing needs of industry and the community in general. For example the demand for electrical engineers is very high because the demand for the products they help to create is continually increasing (e.g. computers, word processers, video recorders). Unfortunately the opposite is true for steel workers. As UK demand for steel has fallen so too has the demand for steel workers. The two demands can be represented together on a diagram to illustrate differences in the conditions of demand for each type of workers (Fig. 9.15).

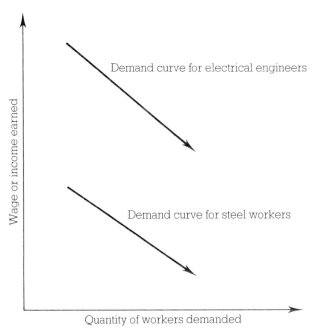

Fig. 9.15

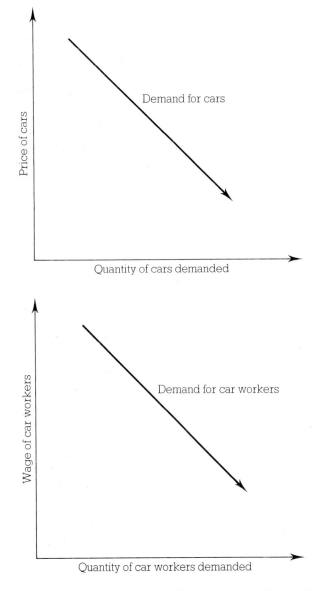

Fig. 9.14 How the demand for labour is derived from the demand for the final product

As far as the supply of labour is concerned, it depends to a large extent on the qualifications and training required to undertake a particular job. The higher the qualifications required the more difficult it will be for people to achieve them which explains why the supply of doctors is small relative to school cleaners. To become a doctor three good 'A' levels are required followed by five years training at university and a further year in a hospital. There are no formal qualifications needed to become a school cleaner. Similarly most electrical engineers will have good 'A' levels and a degree whereas steel workers may simply require physical strength and fitness. For these reasons the supply curves will show small or large quantities of workers, depending on quali-

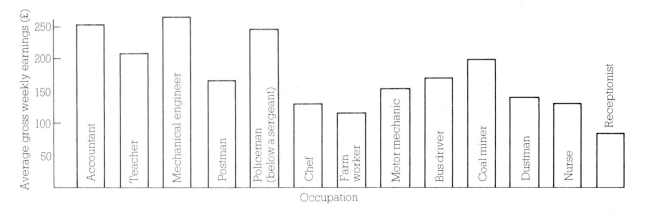

Fig. 9.17 Actual differentials in pay between groups of workers in 1985

fications. Likewise where a large amount of training has been undertaken, the supply price (wage) of labour is going to be generally higher than where no training or skill is required. To attract more workers into an industry or profession a higher wage will have to be offered so that the supply curve will slope upwards to the right in a similar way to the product supply curve. Figure 9.16 shows the reason for the large differential between electrical engineers and steel workers.

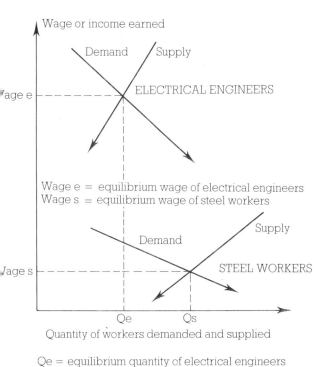

Wage e = equilibrium wage of electrical engineers
Wage s = equilibrium wage of steel workers

Qe = equilibrium quantity of electrical engineers
Qs = equilibrium quantity of steel workers

Fig. 9.16 Why electrical engineers earn more than steelworkers

Not all wages are determined entirely by market forces. Many public sector employees such as teachers have their wages determined by the government although demand and supply conditions still have some influence. For example the large fall in the birth rate from 1964 through the 1970s produced a large drop in the demand for teachers resulting in a sizeable number being encouraged to take early retirement to reduce the surplus supply.

Figure 9.17 shows some of the actual differentials in pay between groups of workers in 1985. Clearly the more highly skilled occupations receive higher rates of pay than unskilled areas such as farmworkers.

MINIMUM WAGE LEGISLATION

Sometimes a government may feel that where the market conditions of demand and supply produce a very low wage, legislation should be brought in to ensure that wages do not fall below a certain agreed level. This **minimum wage** should ensure that an acceptable standard of living is achieved in a low paid industry. However, demand and supply analysis can show why such legislation can create problems as well as solving some!

In Fig. 9.18 (overleaf) the original equilibrium wage is W_1 with Q_e workers being employed. If the government introduces a minimum wage of W_2 then at W_2 demand for workers contracts from Z to Y but at the higher wage more people are willing to work and supply extends from Z to X. Unfortunately the supply of workers is now greater than the demand for them resulting in un-

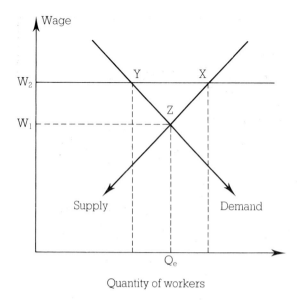

Fig. 9.18 Possible results of minimum wage legislation

employment of YX. Thus although the minimum wage legislation improves the wages earned by some workers, others may lose their jobs as employers find they cannot afford to keep on all workers at the higher wage.

1 Why is it that a solicitor earns much more than a hotel waiter? (Use a diagram to illustrate your answer.)

2 Plot a graph with a demand and supply curve for textile workers from the following tables. Show the equilibrium wage.

Demand for textile workers	Supply of textile workers	Wage(£)
4 000	7 000	80
6 000	6 000	70
8 000	5 000	60
10 000	4 000	50
12 000	3 000	40

What according to the graph would happen if the workers negotiated a wage increase taking them to £75 per week?

3 How much should people be paid? In each of the following jobs the person doing it is aged 40 years. Bearing in mind such factors as the amount of education and training necessary, the value of the work to the community and country, the danger involved in the work, the working hours, and the responsibility involved, decide how much each should earn. The minimum is £50 per week. The maximum is £500 per week. Be prepared to defend your decision! solicitor   miner   MP   social worker   secretary   doctor factory manager   teacher air hostess   factory worker

4 Study the job advertisements (Fig. 9.19). Work out (where necessary) the weekly wage in each occupation and suggest reasons for the differentials in terms of the conditions of demand and supply.

PRINT ROOM OPPORTUNITIES
PRINTING TECHNICIAN
Salary £5,400 – £6,175

We require an operator with experience at operating offset print machines. The successful applicant will also operate other printing and copying machines together with a range of finishing equipment. There is regular overtime during peak production periods.

FINISHING ROOM ASSISTANT
Salary £5,007 – £5,751

A vacancy exists to provide a service in the finishing section. There is a variety of equipment for stitching, binding, collating etc. Previous experience in a print-room environment preferred. Regular overtime is available during peak production periods.

Both jobs offer a five-day week, 33 days annual paid holiday, an attractive pension scheme, generous sick pay provisions, a canteen and various welfare and sports provisions. We enjoy good conditions of work in modern, centrally situated office.

Full-time
BOX OFFICE ASSISTANT

required at the Arts Theatre, 38 hours per week, Monday to Saturday, on rota basis, £2.30 per hour.

BREAKFAST CHEF

required for 100-150 Catering breakfasts daily, and then assisting in general duties as directed. 6.30 am-3 pm. 5 day week. Previous catering experience essential.

INSTRUMENT REPRESENTATIVE
£9,000 + 1.6 Cavalier

Extensive advertising of these quality products means you role is one of PR rather than sales.

MULTI PURPOSE CENTRE
DRIVER

required 39 hours per week (split duty). Wages £2.2179 per hour plus split duty allowance of 5p per hour if full-time (would consider 2 part-time applicants).
Duties involve transporting clients to and from the Centre, using the Centre's mini-bus. Some driving duties for the area will be included. You must be reliable, over 21 years of age and have a clean driving licence.

CARE ASSISTANT

required 20 hours per week. Wages £2.3269 per hour.
This temporary post is to be reviewed after six months. The duties involve helping physically handicapped people and assisting with their personal needs. A caring attitude is essential.

SALES MANAGER
(Director Designate)
£20,000 + car.

Motivating a team to sell non-technical planning systems means your own organisational skills are paramount

PRODUCTION MANAGER
£17,000 plus

This top level position in one of Cambridge's most successful firms requires full background knowledge and experience in all aspects of print for publishing. The manager is responsible for overall co-ordination of all print buying and progress control of books, directories and magazines into production.

A trained and experienced production staff of eight report to the manager; the manager reports to the board.

Good conditions and benefits include company car, pension scheme, BUPA and share option scheme.

GATE PORTER

required, aged 30-50. 40 hour week with shift work, meals on duty, 5 weeks holiday per annum, £96 per week, plus unsocial hours payment.

School of Clinical Medicine
ACCOUNTS CLERK

required to assist senior over the whole range of Clinical School accounts but with certain special responsibilities.
Interesting and varied duties involving contacts with university and hospital personnel. Previous experience essential. Social and many other facilities on site.
Salary: £5,779-£6,740.

RECEPTIONIST/TELEPHONIST/TYPIST
£5,000-£5,500

Suit applicant 18-25 years, smartly presented. Lots of contact with clients in professional company in city centre.

South Shields

PROJECT CO-ORDINATOR
£129.56 per week

South Tyne CP Agency require a Project Co-ordinator for their 'Warm-up' project which gives information on home insulation, heating problems and provides a low cost heating service to the disabled, elderly and low income families.
You will be responsible for the day to day management of the project and its staff — comprising of 24 workers.
Duties will include the promotion and co-ordination of the project, supervision of ordering and pricing, organisation of finance, liaison with the Management Committee, attendance at training courses and other duties as required.
You should have supervisory experience together with a knowledge of financial matters. An interest in the provision of insulation and heating would be useful.

Fig. 9.19

10
DECIDING WHERE TO PUT THE FACTORY

INTRODUCTION

The decision about where a firm should locate its factory is influenced by many considerations. Historically, during the Industrial Revolution several factors were important in determining **location**, namely nearness to raw materials, power, labour, markets and good communications. Thus the woollen industry in Yorkshire was initially sited in upland areas of the Pennines where fast flowing streams were important for water power, later moving downstream to the coalfields when steam power developed. The steel industry was located close to local supplies of iron ore, coal and limestone – the key raw materials in production. In some industries climate played an important role in location: the cotton industry in Lancashire required a humid climate for spinning and so went to the wetter west coast. Today, however, some of these 'traditional' influences are no longer important. Power is available anywhere in the country in the form of electricity and a comprehensive nationwide motorway network has meant that good communications are available over wide areas. Whilst some traditional factors remain significant – for example, the pull of the market – a large number of more recent influences will be considered before a company makes a final decision about where to put its factory.

IMPORTANT LOCATION INFLUENCES

Nowadays the large number of people unemployed in particular parts of the country has led to the government influencing where industrial expansion takes place to a considerable extent, but there are still some important 'natural' factors affecting location.

1 NEARNESS TO MARKETS

In some industries during the manufacturing process the product being made gains weight or bulk. Good examples of this come in the brewing industry where the raw materials mainly comprise hops, yeast, sugar and barley. These are fairly light in relation to the finished beer because nearly 90% of the product comprises water, which is added during production (Fig. 10.1). In the bakery industry the finished product, bread, is much more bulky than its main ingredient, flour. Clearly it is expensive to transport such items to their main consumer markets so these 'weight gaining' industries are normally located near to or within large population centres. They are known as **dispersed** industries because firms are scattered widely over the country wherever large towns occur.

Today, since nearly half of Britain's overseas trade is with the EC, the market 'pull' tends to attract firms to the South-East of the country for easier access to the continent. In addition, this part of Britain has one of the largest regional populations and also enjoys the highest living standards in the country, both factors reinforcing the market pull. In the EC as a whole, the market pull has tended to attract industry into what is known as the 'golden triangle' of major population centres. This is bounded by Birmingham, Dusseldorf and Milan, leaving regions at the extreme edge of the EC unattractive to industry (Fig. 10.2).

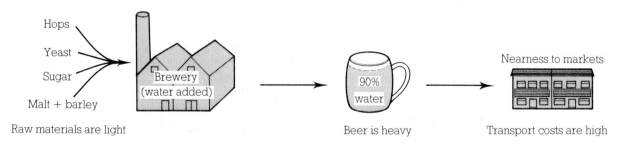

Hops
Yeast
Sugar
Malt + barley

Brewery (water added)

90% water

Nearness to markets

Raw materials are light　　　　Beer is heavy　　　Transport costs are high

Fig. 10.1 A weight-gaining industry – light raw materials and a heavy finished product means a location near to the point of sale

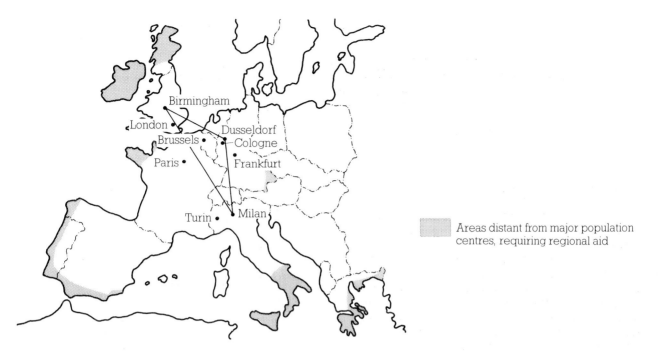

Fig. 10.2 (above)   The 'golden triangle' of the European Community – what measures could be taken to develop the poorer regions?

Fig. 10.3a (below)   The changing location and increased concentration of the steel industry – what factors have contributed to the changing face of Britain's steel industry? What problems did the towns where the steelworks closed down have to face?

2   NEARNESS TO RAW MATERIALS

Where raw materials are very bulky in relation to the final product a firm is likely to locate near to the source of the materials. Such industries are known as 'weight losing', and are **concentrated** near to raw materials. Perhaps the best example of such an industry is British Steel which is now concentrated in just a few centres in Britain (Fig. 10.3).

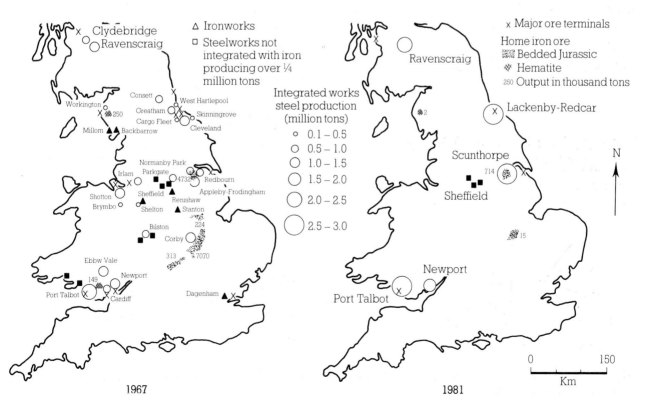

The main raw materials required to produce steel are iron ore, coal and limestone, and traditionally the steel industry was located where all three were locally found. Thus Corby in Northamptonshire used iron ore and limestone from the local Jurassic beds with coal coming from the East Midlands. Today, however, most of the iron ore comes from abroad since it is of much higher quality and so coastal sites have become more important, for example, Redcar. To make steel profitable large-scale economies are required so that as Fig. 10.3a shows, many of the smaller plants have been closed down leaving serious unemployment problems in some towns. The large-scale economies that exist in the plants that remain are well illustrated at Redcar where the blast furnace is larger than St Paul's Cathedral (Fig. 10.4)!

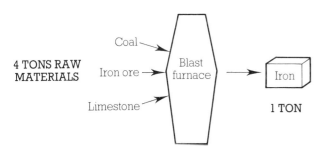

Fig. 10.3b Steel as a weight-losing industry – heavy raw materials and a lighter finished product

3 EXTERNAL ECONOMIES

Often a firm may wish to locate near to firms making the same or a similar product. It may need specialist labour which the area possesses, the machinery it uses may be manufactured or serviced locally, and the financial help it may require from the bank (e.g. export credit) may have already been given to other firms. External economies of concentration apply to the electronics industry at Cambridge and the computer software industry centered around Reading. They also apply to traditional industries like wool and woollen products in West Yorkshire where Leeds University has one of the largest textile departments in the world (Fig. 3.7).

Fig. 10.4a (top left) The coastal site of Redcar steelworks at the mouth of the River Tees. The blast furnace is show on the left
Fig. 10.4b (bottom left) The blast furnace at Redcar steelworks, which is larger than St Paul's Cathedral. The vehicles in the foreground give some idea of scale

4 INDUSTRIAL INERTIA

Sometimes a firm may remain in an area after the best location has moved elsewhere. This may be due to the personal ties of the entrepreneur or because the firm has built up a reputation for its product and does not wish to disrupt the labour force that has brought this about. The best example of such industrial inertia comes in the location of Stoke-on-Trent which is famous for its pottery, particularly that bearing the Wedgwood name. The local supplies of clay on which the original industry was founded have long since been exhausted and much of the raw material now comes from near St Austell in Cornwall, but the reputation of the product and the local skills of the labour force have kept the industry at Stoke.

5 RURAL AREAS

A more recent and important change in the location of manufacturing industry comes in the massive shift from large conurbations (population centres) to small towns and rural areas. The reasons for this are not clear but perhaps the lower land costs, lower rates and lower wage costs all help to attract industry away from the cities, as well as the difficulties of expanding city sites compared to rural ones. The table below shows how dramatic this movement has been.

% change in manufacturing employment 1968–78

Area	% change
London	− 42.5
conurbations	− 26.5
free standing cities	− 13.5
large towns	− 2.2
small towns	+ 15.7
rural areas	+ 38.0
Great Britain	− 11.5

Source: S Fothergill, Department of Land Economy, Cambridge

6 DIVISION OF LABOUR

Many firms now are separating their production plants from administrative offices so that London and the South-East has a concentration of financial and business services whilst northern regions tend to specialise in more routine branch plant activities. This also has the effect in a recession of producing higher unemployment in the northern regions than in the South-East.

7 SCIENCE PARKS

Another more recent development in location influences has been the setting up of science parks sponsored in part by the major British universities. The most successful is at Cambridge with about 30 companies operating (Fig. 10.5a), but such parks also exist at Herriot-Watt in Edinburgh, Aston in Birmingham, Surrey, Swansea, Keele, Warwick, Newcastle, Leeds, Bradford, Salford and Southampton. The big drive towards expanding science parks means they should make a significant contribution towards regional economic growth (Fig. 10.5b).

Fig. 10.5a Cambridge Science Park and the sci-fi architecture of Napp Laboratories

Science in the Park

Mike Lewis looks at a
modern expression of
industrial and academic
co-operation

UNIVERSITIES eager to develop their technology transfer activities have developed organisations to act as a shop window for outsiders of what the academic institution has on offer. In some cases the shop window organisation has evolved into a fully fledged trading company selling products to the outside world. The reverse side of the coin is an increased interest in tapping university work by established companies. For example, London University researchers working at Middlesex Hospital have developed a technique to detect the presence of Aids in blood supplies for Wellcome, the UK drug company.

Increasingly the most efficient method of helping the transfer of information is seen as the science park—an industrial estate built near the university or polytechnic campuses to house commercial organisations. The aim of a science park is that ideas and people from the technology and science departments of the academic institution should spill over to the companies on the estate, aiding later development. Science parks are diverse, having different structures and backing depending on where they are located.

Currently 21 parks are completed with six more to be opened this year. Over 300 firms, of which a third are actually new companies setting up, are located on these sites. Six of the parks are in partnership with a university alone, ten have involved a government department or agency, six a local authority, four private and public sector institutions and one solely a private sector institution.

Total employment on science parks now stands at around 4,000. The biggest park, and the first to be established, is Cambridge, going back to 1972. It covers no less than 130 acres, with 450,000 sq ft of property already completed and 90,000 more under construction. It has 56 companies and is in partnership with Trinity College.

Heriot-Watt is the only other science park established in the early 1970s. It has a good track record as well, but is smaller: 56 acres, 240,000 sq ft of buildings and 18 companies. In terms of number of companies Aston is the second biggest with 26. The park is in partnership with Aston University and the City of Birmingham. By contrast the smallest science park is the St Andrews Centre which occupies less than an acre. Most of the 'parks' which have less than five acres tend to be in a new sub-class, sometimes described as 'innovation centres'.

Wavertree Technology Park in Liverpool has unique characteristics. First, it combines a mixture of property designed and built to user requirements and 'spec' units to be let on easy terms to innovators starting up. Second, although it does have links with the university, the technology transfer opportunities are provided by a private company—Plessey.

Because each park touches on so many activities, research commercialisation, innovation, small firms, regional development, etc there are no simple criteria for success. Particularly as so many firms are less than a year old it is difficult to judge how well a park is doing. However, of 300 firms in the university/polytechnic linked parks only eight have failed.

Executive Post
1986

Fig. 10.5b   The development of science parks

8 COMMUNICATIONS

Good communications are obviously essential for a firm both to receive raw materials and send out the finished product. Today rail transport is fairly insignificant compared to road transport as Fig. 10.6 shows, perhaps because of the obvious difficulty of the railways in providing a door-to-door service. Figure 10.7, a map of Britain's motorways, shows quite a comprehensive communications system so that locating near to a motorway is not a difficult task. The completed M25 around London may be a further incentive for firms to locate in the South-East.

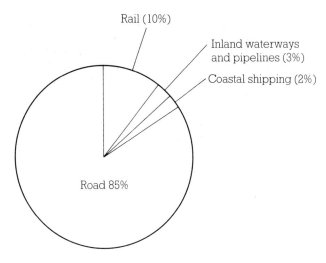

TOTAL: 1800m tonnes

Fig. 10.6 The freight market 1982 – the door-to-door services of road transport easily dominate the transport system, but what effect does this have on Britain's roads?

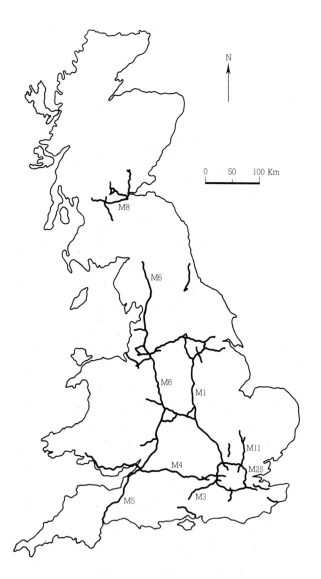

Fig. 10.7 Motorways in England, Scotland and Wales

LOCATION AND LOCALISATION

At this point it is important to distinguish between two terms often confused – location and localisation. It is also important to distinguish between the individual firm and the whole industry of which it is part. The location decisions of a firm may be influenced by any of the factors mentioned earlier and later on in this chapter. The location of the *whole* industry may be concentrated or dispersed throughout the country. If an industry is concentrated in just one area it is said to be **localised**. The cotton industry is localised in Lancashire, the woollen industry in West Yorkshire and to a considerable extent the motor industry is localised in the West Midlands. Today the localisation of an industry would not be encouraged because if demand for the industry's product falls, then a whole region is likely to suffer widespread unemployment. In all of the previous examples product demand has fallen, most recently for the West Midlands, a once highly prosperous region which now has an unemployment rate higher than Scotland's.

REGIONAL UNEMPLOYMENT

All of the above influences on location decisions tend to produce an uneven pattern of industry and employment throughout the country. Older industries are now in decline and the newer ones are increasingly gravitating towards the South. The table shows regional unemployment rates in 1977 and 1983 and it is clear that although all regions have experienced a large increase in the percentage unemployed, some have had dramatic rises. The West Midlands illustrates the point well with the unemployment percentage rising nearly to three times as much in this period. It is also clear that the South-East has been cushioned from the worst effects of rising unemployment compared to the North of England. Northern Ireland is a special case, the political problems of the region making it a high risk area for businessmen.

Clearly the government needs to step in to try and reduce the regional imbalance in unemployment.

Region	Unemployment %	
	1977	1983
North	7.9	16.3
Yorks & Humberside	5.4	13.1
East Midlands	4.7	11.1
East Anglia	5.0	10.0
South-East	4.2	9.1
South-West	6.5	10.8
West Midlands	5.2	14.5
North-West	6.8	15.0
Wales	7.5	14.0
Scotland	7.5	14.0
Northern Ireland	9.9	20.7
UK	5.7	12.3

THINGS TO DO

1 Why are some of the 'traditional' location influences not very important today?

2 Give two examples of (a) **weight gaining** industries; (b) **weight losing** industries.

3 Explain the meaning of **dispersed** and **concentrated** industries.

4 What is the 'golden triangle' of the EC? Why might firms be reluctant to put their factories in southern Italy?

5 Why is the steel industry much more concentrated today than in 1967?

6 Using the table on p. 131, draw a bar graph to show how rural areas have become an important location for industry.

7 What is meant by the term **industrial inertia**?

8 Explain why access to rail links is not an important locational influence today.

9 Study Fig. 10.8 (overleaf) and explain how it shows a regional occupational division of labour, particularly contrasting the South-East with the North-West of England.

10 Read the following extract carefully.
Explain the locational attractions of Cambridge for Napp Laboratories (Fig. 10.5).

Paul Manners can see the spires and towers of the colleges of Cambridge from the window of his office. He can also see the more modern buildings of his neighbours on the Cambridge Science Park.

Both university and science park are reasons why Mr Manners, who is managing director of Napp Laboratories, is where he is. 'We came here,' he says, 'because we wanted to be close to an academic centre of world renown. The company was spread among several locations in the UK and we wanted to put them all together on one site.

'There were other attractions. Cambridge offered us a large greenfield site. We occupy 20 acres now. We could get a long lease and the Science Park is well situated in terms of the motorway and the main roads around the city.

'Essentially we came because of the resources Cambridge offers. We have already established a lot of contact with people in the university and not only are some of them working in conjunction with us but the whole university has a marvellous attitude towards business. This is most encouraging. The university is very commercially orientated.'

Napp Laboratories are involved in the research, development, manufacturing and marketing of ethical pharmaceuticals. It already employs 250 on the Science Park, housed in a startling modern building, and is the biggest employer there.

Financial Times
11.1.1984

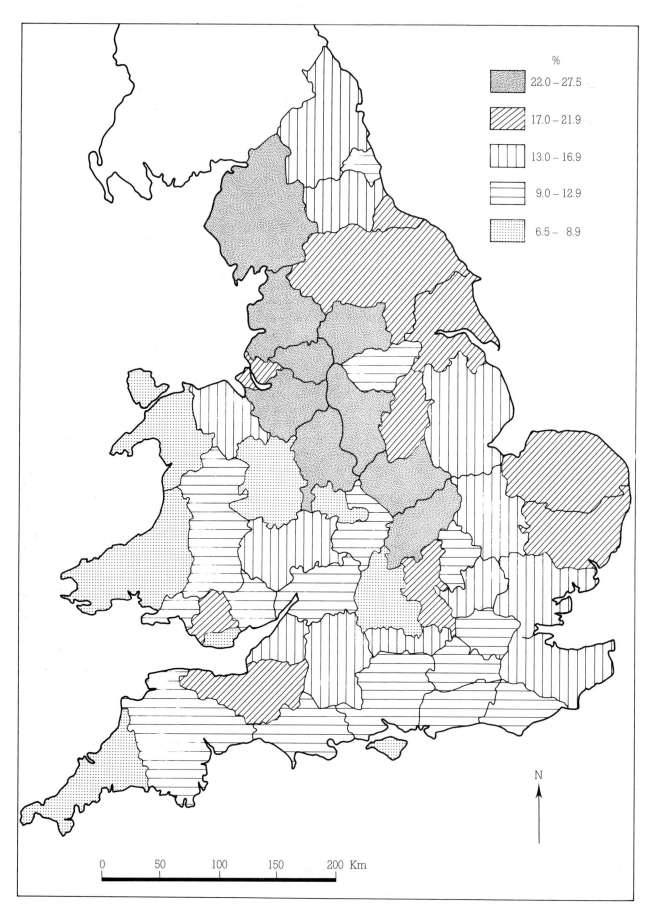

Fig. 10.8a Proportion of employees in services, by county

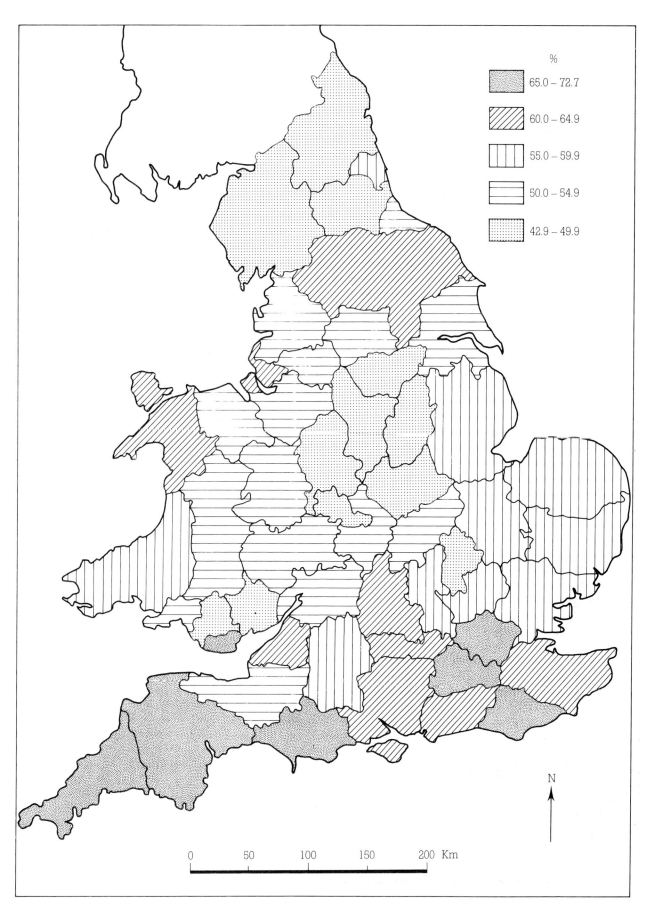

Fig. 10.8b Proportion of employees in other manufacturing, by county

THE INFLUENCE OF THE GOVERNMENT ON LOCATION DECISIONS

For the past 50 years the government has played a part in influencing industrial location because the regional development of industry has been uneven, creating large pockets of unemployment in certain parts of the country. The government has to decide whether to try and take 'work to the workers', that is encouraging firms to set up factories in areas of high unemployment, or take 'workers to the work', encouraging unemployed people to move to more prosperous regions.

The government has not adopted a 'workers to work' policy because congestion would only worsen in some areas. This would put pressure on housing (forcing up prices) as well as roads, schools and other parts of the infrastructure. (**Infrastructure** is a general term covering the main capital goods of a community, particularly transport and public services.) Another problem that would be difficult to solve relates to the geographical immobility of labour. This was discussed in some detail in Chapter 3. People generally are reluctant to move from areas they know well and may rather be unemployed in an area where they feel secure rather than risk going to a new area where they may be working amongst strangers. Furthermore most jobs are advertised locally and not nationally which means that mobility will be further hindered by lack of information. Finally the 'on your bike' approach is difficult because unemployment nationally may be high, leading to a scarcity of jobs in all areas. The government has therefore pursued a 'work to the workers' policy.

At first sight it might seem that high unemployment areas could be attractive to industry; there are reserves of cheap labour, low-priced housing, under utilised social amenities and a lack of congestion. However, in the real world labour in an area of declining industries will have the wrong skills and sometimes a history of divisive industrial relations. The social capital – housing, schools, hospitals – is likely to be of poor quality; the transport and communications system may be outdated; and if wages are negotiated on a national basis, they may turn out to be no lower than in any other region.

The government therefore needs to *persuade* industry to locate in areas of high unemployment which it does in a number of ways.

1 REGIONAL DEVELOPMENT POLICY

The government operates what is sometimes called a **carrot and stick** policy in regional development. The 'carrot' is connected with persuading industry to locate in certain **Assisted Areas** which receive financial aid; the 'stick' is related to what are known as **Industrial Development Certificates** (IDCs). These are required when any new

projects over a certain size take place in non-assisted areas. Through IDCs the government can carefully control industrial and commercial expansion in London and the South-East.

Figure 10.9 shows which parts of the country qualify for Assisted Area status and summarises the main UK investment incentives. Assisted Areas are divided into Development and Intermediate Areas. **Development Areas** qualify for 15% development grants and selective assistance; **Intermediate Areas** for selective assistance only. Development grants are given on capital (plant, buildings and machinery) but subject to a cost per job limit of £10 000. Alternatively there is a job grant of £3000 for each new job created in labour intensive projects. In the past, only manufacturing industry has qualified for assistance but since 1985 a number of service sectors have become eligible for regional development grants. In the past grants were heavily biased towards capital, often proving attractive to firms using a lot of plant and machinery but creating few new jobs. Cleveland,

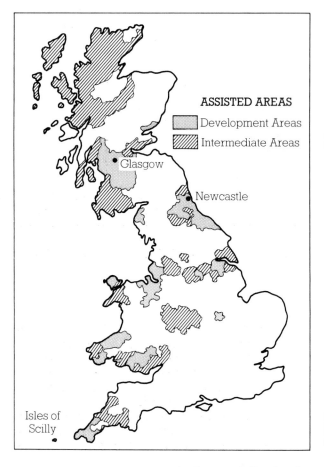

Fig. 10.9a Assisted Areas in England, Scotland and Wales

Type	Development Areas	Intermediate Areas	Northern Ireland
building grants	15%	nil	up to 50%
machinery and equipment grants	15%	nil	up to 50%
grants towards starting-up costs	Additional assistance on a discretionary basis. The level is related to the employment, location and capital requirements of the project.		Additional grants designed to provide new projects with an inflow of revenue during the build-up period are possible.
factory rents (per sq metre per annum)	£10.80 to £26.90 New projects may qualify for an initial rent-free period.		£8.30 to £18.80 related to size and location of factory.
venture capital	Various forms can be made available.		
interest relief grants	nil		Available to reduce the commercial costs of borrowing for up to 7 years – 3 years at a broadly commercial rate followed by 4 years at 3% per year.
help for transferred workers	grants, free fares and lodging allowances and help with finding houses		Fares, household removal costs or lodging allowance plus substantial settling-in grants for key-workers from outside Northern Ireland.
training grants	40% of basic wages and training costs		Employees per week aged under 18 £20 aged 18 to 49 £30 aged 50 and over £40 (previously unemployed)
industrial derating (remission of taxation imposed by local authorities)	England and Wales: nil Scotland: 50%		75% (100% in all Enterprise Zones)
research and development grants	up to $33\frac{1}{3}$%. The total cost of eligible projects will normally be not less than £25 000 or more than £5m.		40% to 50% – assistance limited to £250 000 per project.

Fig. 10.9b   The main UK investment incentives

Source: *Department of Trade and Industry*

for example, has been an Assisted Area for more than 20 years attracting industrial giants like ICI and British Steel, but now having the highest unemployment rate of any county in Britain. The job grant of £3000 should help to attract more labour intensive firms to Assisted Areas.

Regional development policy over the years has not been wholly successful. There is still a widening gap in living standards between the North and the South. This may be due to too little emphasis being put on the retraining of workers in the Assisted Areas and the lack of encouragement given to service industries in the past, which tend to be more labour intensive. It has already been mentioned that the emphasis on capital grants tends to encourage firms using a lot of machinery to go to Assisted Areas, often at the expense of the labour market. It is also often the case that the machines are purchased abroad thus promoting industrial development in another country at the expense of the British taxpayer!

2   ENTERPRISE ZONES

Whilst regional development policy is administered by the Department of Trade and Industry, **Enterprise Zones** are sponsored by the Department of the Environment which is much more concerned about inner city development. They are really a collection of plots of land which enjoy certain benefits such as no rates charged for 10 years; tax allowances for capital expenditure on buildings; simplified planning procedures for new buildings; and exemption from industrial training levies and from the requirement to supply information to industrial training boards. In 1985 there were 25 zones, many in steel closure areas (Hartlepool, Corby, Scunthorpe, Workington) and most in places suffering from industrial decline such as Dudley, Rotherham, Speke, Middlesbrough, Clydebank and the London Docklands (Fig. 10.10).

Enterprise Zones were started in 1980 as a 10 year experiment and in the first three years about 18 000 new jobs were created. However, the cost to the government was £133m in lost rates revenue and there is evidence that many firms moving into the zones are local, meaning jobs are simply being shifted from one part of town to another.

3   NEW TOWNS

Between 1946 and mid-1974, 32 UK **new towns** were designated, 11 of them within an 80-mile radius of London, whose housing problems they were intended to solve (Fig. 10.11). Their main attraction for industrialists is not financial; it is the availability of purpose-built factories and offices, on estates accessible to modern road systems, and often set in green fields with room for expansion. Another feature of the new towns attractive to many industrialists is their housing for key workers. However, the new town development corporations set up to attract industry to the areas, have in many cases now been wound up in favour of putting money into reviving the inner city areas of towns such as London and Liverpool. New towns are therefore beginning to make their own way in the world with reduced government assistance.

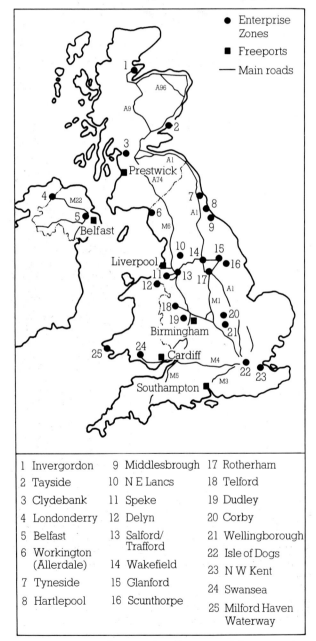

1 Invergordon	9 Middlesbrough	17 Rotherham
2 Tayside	10 N E Lancs	18 Telford
3 Clydebank	11 Speke	19 Dudley
4 Londonderry	12 Delyn	20 Corby
5 Belfast	13 Salford/ Trafford	21 Wellingborough
6 Workington (Allerdale)	14 Wakefield	22 Isle of Dogs
7 Tyneside	15 Glanford	23 N W Kent
8 Hartlepool	16 Scunthorpe	24 Swansea
		25 Milford Haven Waterway

Fig. 10.10   UK Enterprise Zones and freeports

4   FREEPORTS

Freeports are areas created by the government which are treated as being outside the customs frontiers of their host country. There are six in the UK: Birmingham, Belfast and Prestwick (all attached to airports), Southampton, Liverpool and Cardiff (all beside docks) (Fig. 10.10). They will attract firms connected with international trade because they allow tax payments on imports to be postponed with no duty at all being charged on goods which come in and later leave the country. Thus a foreign company wishing to organise European distribution from a freeport could do so without any tax penalties.

5   TRADING ESTATES

Finally, many local authorities construct **trading estates** with purpose-built roads, street lighting and warehouses to attract industry into an area.

Fig. 10.11 Milton Keynes new town. New towns are obviously 'planned' and do not evolve haphazardly like most urban and rural settlements. The needs and functions of the town are taken into account and allowed for from the earliest stages. Using Fig. 10.11, can you identify the areas set aside for housing, industry, recreation and part of the large, modern shopping centre? Has anything been forgotten? What might a new town lack?

THINGS TO DO

1 Study the table below which shows the number of workers being made redundant per 1000 employees between 1980 and 1982, with figures for 1977–9 in brackets:

Region	Average 1980–82	(1977–9)
South-East	34.2	(9.0)
East Anglia	37.6	(12.9)
South-West	51.3	(12.8)
West Midlands	57.2	(10.6)
East Midlands	53.4	(8.6)
Yorkshire & Humberside	74.9	(17.5)
North-West	77.1	(25.5)
North	76.4	(28.6)
Wales	104.2	(19.8)
Scotland	77.5	(33.8)
Great Britain	58.8	(16.9)

Source: *Employment Gazette* June 1983

(a) Which region experienced the greatest increase in redundancies between 1977–9 and 1980–82?

(b) Which of the above regions are *not* Assisted Areas?

(c) Which two regions showed the smallest increase in redundancies between 1977–9 and 1980–82?

(d) How far do the figures for 1980–82 confirm the areas that the government recognises as needing assistance, as shown in Fig. 10.9a?

2 Study the three advertisements (Fig. 10.12) which follow. They refer to three areas where the government gives financial incentives for industrial development. For each (Cumbria, Cwmbran and Merseyside), list the main advantages of locating there and decide from the information given which of the three you would choose if you were starting up a new factory. Give your reasons.

Fig. 10.12a

Cumbria ...home of an enlightened workforce.

Grasmere

Why not enjoy the good life – live and work in Cumbria. Life is good – exceptional even.

And there's never been a better opportunity for business, with a development area and enterprise zone set against the background of the Lake District National Park and the Solway Firth.

Rate free opportunities. Large capital allowances. Useful setting up and training grants. Attractive loans. Rents at almost peppercorn levels from £1/£1.50 sq. ft. Cumbria offers them all.

Long the home of an enlightened work force, absenteeism is half the UK average and there is an exceptionally low level of industrial stoppages.

Cumbria has extensive resources for underwater technology and offshore related activities, plus considerable modern dock and Ro Ro facilities at the Port of Workington.

Living in Cumbria provides a wealth of sporting activities – sailing, canoeing, skiing, climbing, fishing and all the more conventional sports. Something for everyone!

Cumbria really does provide a choice and has so much to offer industry, people and families.

So stop enjoying Cumbria from a distance. Start making it a way of life!

For full details of the business development opportunities in Cumbria contact the Industrial Development Officer at
Cumbria County Council, The Courts, Carlisle, Cumbria CA3 8NA. Tel: Carlisle (0228) 23456.

Cumbria, the natural choice.

142

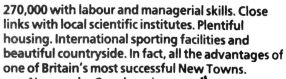
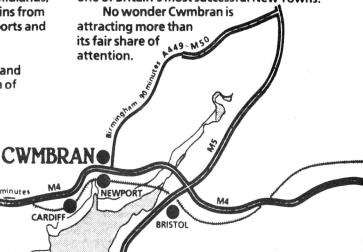

Fig. 10.12b

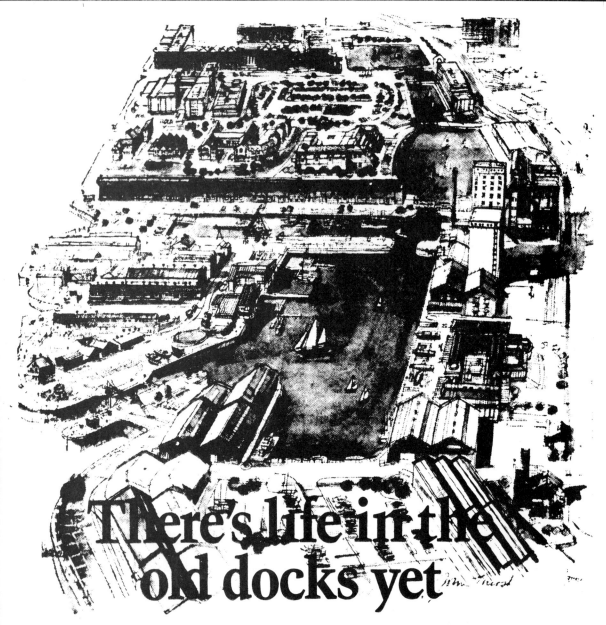

There's life in the old docks yet

Merseyside's docklands were once the heart of a thriving community.

The centre of its activities.

The source of its prosperity.

Today life is returning.

In a massive wave of activity we are clearing the docks of silt, creating almost 70 acres of superb enclosed waterspace.

On 125 acres of dereliction we've planted the world's premier Garden Festival of 1984.

We've moved mountains of rubbish and rubble and formed a bright new landscape on the once barren waterfront.

Derelict buildings have been demolished. Historic ones restored. Albert Dock, Britain's largest grade 1 listed building, is being transformed into a first class environment for commerce, housing and leisure.

Opportunities are here to be taken – the potential too great to be ignored.

Prime development land is now available – uniquely situated on the Mersey waterfront close to Liverpool city centre. Sites for industry, housing, commerce and leisure.

And with the new developments will come people. To work To live. To relax.

Every dock has its day. Our day is dawning.

Merseyside Development Corporation

TURNING THE TIDE ON MERSEYSIDE

Contact: Alex Anderson at
Merseyside Development Corporation Tel: 051-236 6090.

Fig. 10.12c

Fig. 10.13

3 Figure 10.13 shows ICI's Billingham works and an electricity generating station in the background near the mouth of the River Tees in Cleveland. Look carefully at the whole photograph and decide which features might be described as 'infrastructure'.

4 How does the government make it difficult for firms to set up new works which are *not* in Development Areas?

5 The government gives financial help to attract businessmen to set up factories in Development Areas. Describe *two* ways in which the government does this.

6 What are the main advantages of a company locating in an Enterprise Zone? In what way might such zones merely provide employment in one part of a town at the expense of another?

A CASE STUDY OF A MULTI-NATIONAL COMPANY:
THE FORD MOTOR COMPANY

Increasingly, large companies no longer make location decisions within only one country. **Multi-national companies** are those with sites in a number of different countries, sometimes throughout the world.

The Ford Motor Company is a good example of a multi-national with the parent company located in Detroit, but with a large number of plants located throughout Europe (Fig. 10.14). Altogether in Europe, Ford employs 140 000 people in 15 separate national companies.

Locating worldwide gives a company like Ford certain advantages. It can specialise internationally, for example at Bridgend all Escort engines for Europe are produced. Such economies of scale lower unit production costs. It can also expand where production costs are lowest. The Fiesta plant at Valencia was built partly as a result of lower Spanish labour costs. Multi-nationals can switch production from one plant to another, which may create some unemployment. Therefore governments need to monitor the locational activities of such companies carefully.

Worldwide Ford employs 494 000 people in more than 100 countries. It has manufacturing operations in North America, Europe, Asia, Latin America, the Middle East and Africa. Today, in addition to producing cars, tracks, tractors, engines, steel, glass and plastics, Ford companies are established in financing, insurance, vehicle replacement parts, electronics, communications and space technology.

In Britain Ford's major plant is at Dagenham (Fig. 10.14), chosen in 1925 because it gave a quick and easy outlet to European ports (it was originally conceived as a great exporting centre). It had deep water facilities and a ready-made pool of labour since the then London County Council was carrying out a great rehousing scheme centred on Dagenham. In Britain, Ford still has the largest enterprise outside that in the USA.

Fig. 10.14a (below) The Ford Motor Company works at Dagenham
Fig. 10.14b (right) Ford's European plants

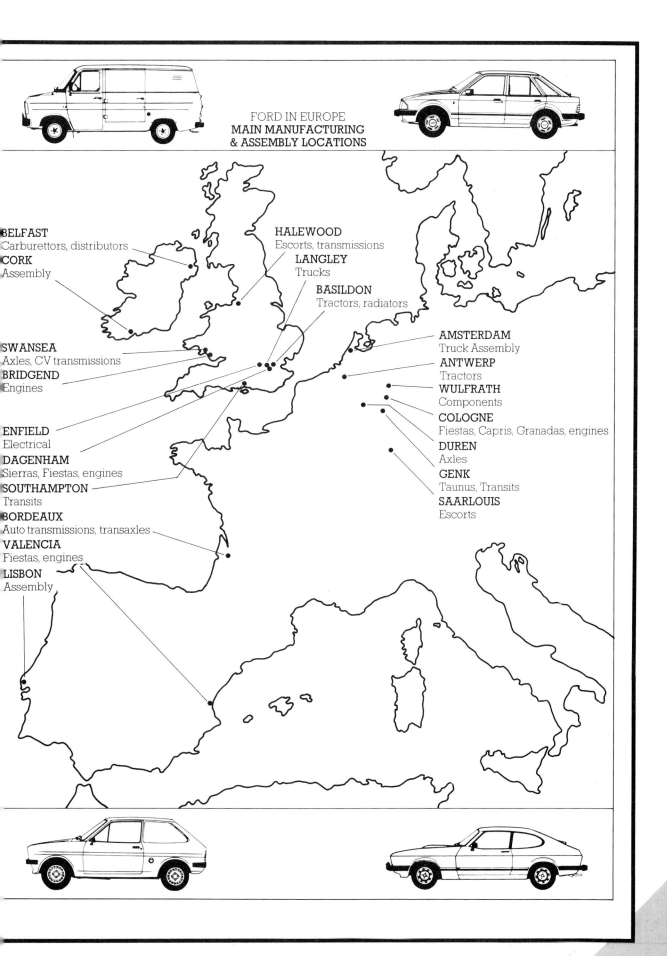

FORD IN EUROPE
**MAIN MANUFACTURING
& ASSEMBLY LOCATIONS**

BELFAST
Carburettors, distributors
CORK
Assembly

HALEWOOD
Escorts, transmissions
LANGLEY
Trucks
BASILDON
Tractors, radiators

SWANSEA
Axles, CV transmissions
BRIDGEND
Engines

AMSTERDAM
Truck Assembly
ANTWERP
Tractors
WULFRATH
Components
COLOGNE
Fiestas, Capris, Granadas, engines
DUREN
Axles
GENK
Taunus, Transits
SAARLOUIS
Escorts

ENFIELD
Electrical
DAGENHAM
Sierras, Fiestas, engines
SOUTHAMPTON
Transits
BORDEAUX
Auto transmissions, transaxles
VALENCIA
Fiestas, engines
LISBON
Assembly

Read carefully the article entitled 'Mean street ... easy street'. Then answer the following questions:

(a) Why does the article suggest Workington has become a depressed town?

(b) What is the principal industry in Wokingham? How are schools there helping to provide a 'skilled' workforce?

(c) Describe the communications advantages Wokingham enjoys compared to Workington.

(d) Why are house prices much more expensive in Wokingham compared to Workington? (Use a demand and supply diagram to illustrate your answer.) Why doesn't cheap housing in Workington attract a flood of new industries into the area?

(e) How is the government attempting to solve this problem of the differing standards in Workington and Wokingham?

Fig. 10.15

Mean street, easy street

WORKINGTON, Cumbria

POPULATION: 27,000 and falling
INDUSTRIES: steel, paper, vehicles

UNEMPLOYMENT: 17.8%
DISTANCE FROM LONDON: 326 miles

COMMUNICATIONS: By road – A66, A595, A596. Rail – W Coast main line connection at Carlisle (34 miles); link to Barrow. Nearest major airport – Newcastle (93 miles)

REGIONAL AID: development area status allowing 15% grants on plant and machinery; enterprise zone status allowing business 10-year holiday from rates

WOKINGHAM, Berkshire

POPULATION: 24,000 and rising
INDUSTRIES: services, electronics, software, light engineering
UNEMPLOYMENT: 7.3%
DISTANCE FROM LONDON: 32 miles

COMMUNICATIONS: By road – M4 (five miles), M40, M3, M25. Rail – London-Bristol connection at Reading (eight miles); link to Gatwick Airport. Nearest major airport – Heathrow (22 miles).

REGIONAL AID: none.

by Philip Beresford

In boomtown Wokingham they have a message for firms eager to set up shop in the heart of the M4 computer corridor: please go somewhere else. Pressure on space is such that companies are actually turned away, so that Britain's Silicon Strip can control its headlong development rate.

Just 256 miles north, in work-starved Workington, however, it's the army recruiting office that's turning people away. Even this traditional escape route for youngsters eager to avoid the dole queue has a six-to-12 months waiting list.

Wokingham is in the vanguard of the new information revolution which is changing the face of Britain just as much as the industrial revolution did 150 years ago. Then, Workington prospered mightily as the steel industry mushroomed, while Berkshire was an impoverished agricultural home county.

Today steel making in Workington has been savaged by the recession; coal has come and gone; and the new industries haven't taken their place. Courtaulds paid a fleeting visit to the town which ended abruptly in 1979 with the loss of 450 jobs. The unemployment statistics tell all: Wokingham has 7% on the dole, Workington 17.8%. The contrast among school leavers is even more staggering: only 5% of those who left Wokingham schools this summer are not either in a job or on youth training: the Workington figure is 41.5%.

While the software companies jostle for space in the Thames Valley, the Thatcher government, like its predecessors, is still trying to encourage industry to go to the depressed areas covered by regional aid. But last week's white paper on regional industrial development presented by the industry secretary, Norman Tebbit, seems unlikely to help much.

More aid is to go to service industries, such as computer software, as part of a drive to get value for money out of regional aid, which has cost £20bn over the last 20 years. The white paper doubts the economic case for regional aid, but says: "The government believe that the case for continuing the policy is now principally a social one with the aim of reducing ... regional imbalances in employment opportunities."

But can it work? Fifty years after regional policies were introduced, the gulf between north and south is wider, and growing. At the height of the Great Depression in the 1930s, unemployment in London and the South-East was half the 30% or more prevailing in the North and Scotland. Today that gap has been re-established.

The gap is unlikely to be narrowed by the new technology industries, which show little sign of wanting to go outside the M4 corridor except perhaps to Silicon Glen or other old pleasant market towns.

WORKINGTON is everything that Wokingham isn't – a one-industry town for over a century, miles from major markets and isolated, trapped between the sea and the Lake District. Widespread steel redundancies over the last three years have devastated the town. Some 3,000 steel jobs have gone, leaving British Steel with just 1,350 employees making rails (from Teesside steel) or refurbishing steel plant and machinery.

A century ago there were 54 blast furnaces in the area where Sir Henry

Bessemer first introduced Bessemer steel making. Today there are none.

The take up of small workshops on the old steel works site – now an enterprise zone – is encouraging. These are mainly small local engineering firms which shows solid evidence of Workington picking itself up by its own bootstraps. There is precious little sign of high technology marching into Workington – not a single entry in the local yellow pages for a computer business, nor any sign of a software house or specialist computer shop in the area.

Tony Winterbottom, manager of Mobet – a local non-profit making company piloting the enterprise zone project – is desperately keen to attract the new high-tech industries to the area. But how can a town like Workington compete against the vast infrastructure developing in the Thames Valley?

Wokingham has at least 25 electronics companies, ranging from Hewlett-Packard with over 1,000 employees to small software companies like Control-C-Software, with half a dozen employees.

When a company like Hewlett-Packard considers expansion, it tends to happen along the M4 corridor or in Silicon Glen in Scotland. A new research headquarters is to be built in Bristol, despite the fact that the company's UK boss David Baldwin listened to proposals from 10 enterprise zones. "They gave very good presentations", he says "but in the end the transport connections and the pleasant environment weighted in Bristol's favour."

The whole of Wokingham appears to be switched on to high technology. Over half the jobs advertised in a local employment agency require some computing skills. Schools are busy churning out computer-literate children. Michael Cole, the head of St Crispin's School was amazed when he asked his pupils at assembly to raise their hands if they had access to a home computer. Nearly half did.

As well as its own computers, the school participates in a Computerbus experiment. A mobile classroom with 15 computers on board tours seven local schools providing in-depth computer lessons. Even then the facilities are overwhelmed by the demand.

As the level of computer awareness grows – whether home grown or through the importing of bright and talented graduates – so more firms, not all making computers, are attracted to the area.

IN WORKINGTON, the schools doggedly face up to the fact that the vast majority of the youngsters leave with little prospect of work. One local head reports that morale is surprisingly good, though last year just 6.6% of the school's leavers found jobs. Grades in exams are higher as children try to equip themselves as

well as possible for the bleak world outside. Computing skills are taught, though the head recognises that "there aren't many computing jobs in the area".

On a cold and wet Monday morning, almost the busiest place in town is the local unemployment benefits office, while in the nearby JR's American Pool Parlour, unemployed youngsters pass the time developing formidable skills on the pool table.

Wilson Cowan, the divisional careers officer in Workington, is particularly angry about the prospects for his local school leavers: "It's the 16 to 18 year olds that are in a trap and when YTS finishes next year, I don't know what will happen. All the traditional employers have gone, the steel works, the coal mines and even the shoe industry."

Next year Cowan has 1,365 youngster eligible to leave school, and his officers are already doing the rounds. But cynicism is creeping in, he says, and it is becoming more difficult to persuade teenagers that there is any hope.

The optimism in the south is understandable. "Even if someone lacks any skills needed in Wokingham, they can usually be found a job within a month if they're prepared to travel", says Dick Bushell, the local Job Centre manager. Few of Wokingham's unemployed are long term (57% have been unemployed for less than six months) while the vacancies are spread evenly across the economy, with a strong service sector showing.

One of the by-products of the influx of high growth electronics or software companies has been the increasing affluence of the Wokingham area.

This is most visible in house prices, which are not far off London levels. A three-bedroomed terrace house can go for £35,000 according to one local agent. For a similar property in Workington, £15,000 is judged a fair price.

Derek Lambert, who has lived in the area for 10 years – most of that time with ICL – says that when he came, 'Denmark Street was a slum with one junk shop." Today it's full of expensive shops like Busy Hands Craft or jewellers and designers such as Burnham Fayre. None of these would have been possible without the spending power of the likes of Lambert.

The service sector is the careers officer's trump card in coping with this year's crop of school leavers. Not many will find work in the small electronics companies, but secretaries, office staff and shop assistants are all needed. A new Safeway supermarket, for example, may mean an extra 100 jobs. By this process, nearly 70% of local school leavers are able to find a job without too much trouble.

THE FUTURE doesn't look as bright in Workington, and the same goes for the other one-industry towns in the North, such as Consett, Shildon or Hartlepool. This is not because of a shortage of ideas. The chief executive of Allerdale council, Charles Crane, is banking on a chemical park, hoping that 1,500 jobs may be created from producing low-volume, high-value products such as perfume, where transport costs are not a vital part of the equation.

Ron Graham, local organiser for the Transport Workers union, is pressing for more local workers in any building work at the Sellafield Nuclear Reprocessing Plant. Tourism and textiles are cited as other possibilities.

All these ideas will take time to nurture. In the meantime the gap between North and South will widen, despite the possible revamping of regional policy to concentrate resources on areas of greatest need.

The government is apparently contemplating such a move after consultation and anlaysis of the census returns for 1981. Aid will probably be more selective and some surprises are likely in the regional aid map. Parts of Scotland and Wales, where the micro chip has seeded, may be removed.

This raises a key issue the government has fudged so far: should aid be poured into the near "no-hope" areas, where it might not do much good, or should it go to those parts of the regions which already show some signs of new life, and where state money would reinforce success? The signs are that, despite the arrival of the radical Tebbit at the industry department, this government is going to stick to the traditional yardstick of high unemployment rates in directing its regional aid.

Nor is Tebbit likely to reiterate his famous "on your bike" remark to find a job. Both the chief executive at Wokingham and local employers stress again and again the difficulties that any job seekers from the North have in finding any suitable housing in their price range. Sometimes it's a question of just not being able to sell a home in a depressed housing market in the North. Whatever the reason, Nigel Butler, Wokingham Council's chief executive, writes to any applicants from the North and suggests that they check with local Wokingham agents to see if they can afford to live here.

This may be the salvation of towns like Workington. If employers cannot get key staff in Wokingham they may be forced to move nearer the depressed areas. Even now the M4 corridor is fanning outwards both to the North and South, while mini-silicon valleys are forming in the Wirral and around Cambridge.

The Sunday Times
18.12.1983

149

A CASE STUDY OF AN ENTERPRISE ZONE: THE LONDON DOCKLANDS

The London Docklands Enterprise Zone of 482 acres is less than 3 miles from the Bank of England to the East of the City of London. The Zone lies within the Isle of Dogs (Fig. 10.16) and comprises plots of land in the peninsula which qualify for the special benefits available such as 10-year rate-free allowances.

It is administered by the London Docklands Development Corporation. The LDDC was set up in 1981 to revitalise not just the Isle of Dogs but also the Surrey Docks on the south bank of the Thames and the Royal Docks further downriver. The main job of the LDDC in the Enterprise Zone is to improve the infrastructure of the area. To this end a Light Rapid Transport railway is being developed which will bring passengers from the City to the Enterprise Zone in 10 minutes. A new 'red brick road' has been opened connecting most of the sites in the Zone and a special 'Clipper' bus service runs from Mile End through the Isle of Dogs. Nearby in the Royal Docks a STOL (Short Take Off and Landing) airport has been proposed providing fast access to Heathrow and the continent.

Fig. 10.16a

Fig. 10.16b An aerial view of the Isle of Dogs. Which features of the Enterprise Zone can you identify?

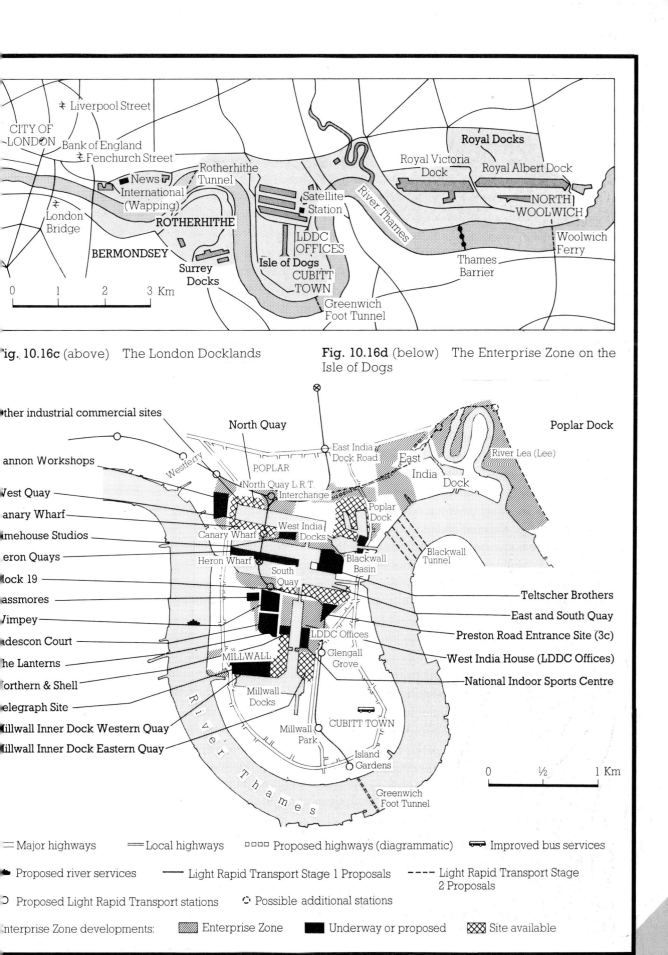

Fig. 10.16c (above)   The London Docklands

Fig. 10.16d (below)   The Enterprise Zone on the Isle of Dogs

Other industrial commercial sites
Cannon Workshops
West Quay
Canary Wharf
Limehouse Studios
Heron Quays
Dock 19
Passmores
Wimpey
Indescon Court
The Lanterns
Northern & Shell
Telegraph Site
Millwall Inner Dock Western Quay
Millwall Inner Dock Eastern Quay

North Quay

Westferry
POPLAR
North Quay L.R.T.
Interchange
Canary Wharf
West India Docks
Heron Wharf
South Quay
LDDC Offices
MILLWALL
Glengall Grove
Millwall Docks
Millwall Park
CUBITT TOWN
Island Gardens
Greenwich Foot Tunnel

River Thames

Poplar Dock

East India Dock Road
East India Dock
River Lea (Lee)

Poplar Dock
Blackwall Basin
Blackwall Tunnel

Teltscher Brothers
East and South Quay
Preston Road Entrance Site (3c)
West India House (LDDC Offices)
National Indoor Sports Centre

0   ½   1 Km

═ Major highways   ═ Local highways   ▫▫▫▫ Proposed highways (diagrammatic)   🚍 Improved bus services

⬤ Proposed river services   — Light Rapid Transport Stage 1 Proposals   ---- Light Rapid Transport Stage 2 Proposals

○ Proposed Light Rapid Transport stations   ○ Possible additional stations

Enterprise Zone developments: ▨ Enterprise Zone   ■ Underway or proposed   ▨ Site available

The London Docklands map labels:

Liverpool Street
CITY OF LONDON
Bank of England
Fenchurch Street
News International (Wapping)
Rotherhithe Tunnel
ROTHERHITHE
Satellite Station
Royal Docks
Royal Victoria Dock
Royal Albert Dock
NORTH WOOLWICH
London Bridge
BERMONDSEY
Surrey Docks
Isle of Dogs
LDDC OFFICES
CUBITT TOWN
River Thames
Greenwich Foot Tunnel
Thames Barrier
Woolwich Ferry

0   1   2   3 Km

The LDDC has also encouraged an intensive private house building programme with more than 4000 units built by the end of 1985. Landscaping and parking is also being provided with all sites being serviced by the main utilities including the best possible telecommunication facilities ranging from electronic mail to video conferencing.

So far, however, although a number of new businesses have taken up sites in the zone (including a large TV studio complex for Channel 4), there is evidence that some companies have merely switched locations from other parts of London. The Daily Telegraph (with a new printing works) and Northern & Shell the publishers, for example, have simply moved into the Zone from other London sites. To the extent that existing workers will be brought in from these former sites, little new employment will be created for people living on the Isle of Dogs itself.

The other questionmark hanging over all Enterprise Zones is, since they have been set up as a 10-year experiment (the Docklands Zone ending in 1991), what happens when all the financial concessions end? Will workers be laid off to pay rates bills? Might firms start to move out? Such questions can only receive speculative answers at this stage.

Rent and Rates Comparison

As no rates are payable in the Enterprise Zone until 1992, offices have a particularly attractive cost. The table below provides comparison with other locations in London and the rest of England.

	Annual rent (sq ft) £	Annual rates (sq ft) £	Total (sq ft) £
City of London	26	15.30	41.30
Westminster	19	10.70	29.70
Reading	12	2.90	14.90
Croydon	11	3.85	14.85
Crawley	8	2.30	10.30
Milton Keynes	7	1.55	8.55
London Docklands Enterprise Zone	6.39	–	6.39

Fig. 10.16e (above)   The cheapness of the rent and rates in the Enterprise Zone
Fig. 10.16f (below)   The Enterprise Business Park on the Isle of Dogs

Fig. 10.16g (above)   Housing development in the London Docklands Enterprise Zone
Fig. 10.16h (below)   Construction of the Docklands' light railway

THE EC AND REGIONAL AID

In 1975 the EC set up a Regional Development Fund to help the less prosperous areas, mainly those a long distance from the 'golden triangle' shown in Fig. 10.2. It was really a way for Britain to get back some money from the Community budget since prior to 1975, most funds went to European farmers of which Britain had relatively few. The allocation of money is shown in the table below and at present the member countries decide how and where the money should be used. In Britain a sizeable amount has been used to finance new industry in former steel towns. Corby, for example, has received considerable aid from the Regional Fund as well as cheap loans from the European Investment Bank. In the future the Commission in Brussels would like much more say in how the money is allocated, but it is proving difficult to get member states to agree to this.

Allocation of regional funds 1982

Country	% of funds
Belgium	1.11
Denmark	1.06
West Germany	4.65
Greece	13.00
France	13.64
Ireland	5.94
Italy	35.49
Luxembourg	0.07
Netherlands	1.24
UK	23.80

THINGS TO DO

1 Find out more about any **Enterprise Zone** near to the area where you live. How does it compare with the activities taking place in the London Docklands?

2 What is meant by the term **infrastructure**? How is the LDDC improving the infrastructure of the London Docklands?

3 In what ways does the London Enterprise Zone have advantages over Zones in other parts of the country?

PART 2

A FURTHER LOOK AT THE PRICE MECHANISM

INTRODUCTION

The basic workings of the price mechanism have already been discussed in Chapter 4 where the concepts of equilibrium price and quantity were examined, together with shifts in the positions of the demand and supply curves. Movements along each curve were caused by price changes. Shifts in the position of each curve were caused by changes in the conditions of demand and supply. The following example summarises what has already been covered.

The coffee crop fails in Brazil due to adverse weather conditions. How will this affect the market for tea?

Figure 11.1 shows the expected supply of coffee Sx, together with the expected price Px. The actual supply is smaller than that expected pushing the market price up to Pa and causing a contraction in quantity demanded. Since tea is a substitute

for coffee, the conditions of demand relating to tea will change.

Figure 11.2 shows what might happen. The demand for tea will rise (the demand curve shifts to the right) affecting the equilibrium price. If tea growers cannot increase supplies immediately then the price will rise to Ps and there will be no extension in supply. Over a longer period more tea may be grown and supply will extend creating an equilibrium of P_2/Q_2.

There is some imprecision in this analysis since it is not clear just how much demand will contract when the price of coffee goes up, nor how much supply will extend when the price of tea goes up. It is here that a new concept becomes useful – price elasticity. **Price elasticity** measures the responsiveness of demand or supply to a change in price. It is this concept which now has to be looked at in some detail both in relation to demand and supply.

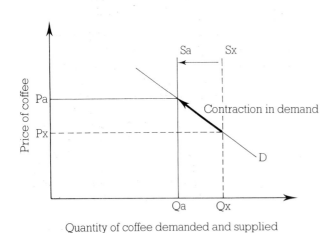

Fig. 11.1 The market for coffee

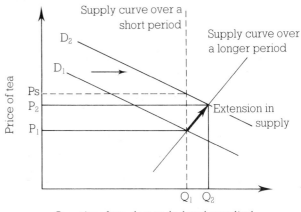

Fig. 11.2 The market for tea

PRICE ELASTICITY OF DEMAND

If demand is very responsive to a price change it is said to be **price elastic**; if it is unresponsive to a price change it is termed **price inelastic**. Graphically the concept of elasticity can be seen by comparing the two demand curves in Fig. 11.3.

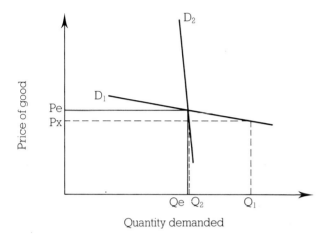

Fig. 11.3 Demand elasticity

If the price of a good falls from Pe to Px then in the case of D_2 the quantity demanded hardly extends at all whereas in the case of D_1 demand extends by a large amount. Thus the steeper curve D_2 can be said to represent a price inelastic demand since it is fairly unresponsive to a price change; D_1 can be said to represent a price elastic demand since it is very responsive to a price change.

More precision can be given to the concept of elasticity when it is represented as follows:

price Elasticity of demand (Ed) =

$$\frac{\% \text{ change in quantity demanded}}{\% \text{ change in price}}$$

If q represents the original quantity demanded and Δq the change in quantity demanded, and p represents the original price with Δp the change in price, then the above formula can be simplified as follows:

$$Ed = \frac{\frac{\Delta q}{q} \times 100\%}{\frac{\Delta p}{p} \times 100\%}$$

Inverting the lower part of the right-hand equation and multiplying gives:

$$Ed = \frac{\Delta q}{q} \times \frac{p}{\Delta p} \quad \text{or} \quad Ed = \frac{\Delta q}{\Delta p} \times \frac{p}{q}$$

This equation can be used to precisely calculate elasticity values. If the value is more than 1 demand is said to be price elastic – the higher the number the greater the elasticity. If the value is less than 1 (but greater than zero) demand is said to be price inelastic – the smaller the fraction the lower the elasticity. This can be made clearer with reference to a demand schedule:

Price of tomatoes/kilo	Quantity demanded (000s)
£1	2
80p	4
60p	6
40p	8
20p	10

If the equilibrium price is originally 80p in the above schedule, then it falls to 60p, elasticity of demand can be calculated as follows:

q (original quantity)	= 4000
Δq (change in quantity)	= 2000
p (original price)	= 80p
Δp (change in price)	= 20p

$$Ed = \frac{\Delta q}{\Delta p} \times \frac{p}{q} = \frac{2000}{20} \times \frac{80}{4000} = 2$$

Thus demand is price elastic when the price of tomatoes falls from 80p to 60p.

ELASTICITY OF DEMAND AND TOTAL REVENUE

The main significance of **elasticity of demand** for producers is the effect it has on total revenue. If lowering the price slightly produces a large increase in the quantity demanded, a producer will find his total revenue increasing. In other words if demand is price elastic a fall in price will boost total revenue. If demand is price inelastic, a fall in price will produce a reduction in total revenue. In the above example where demand was found to be elastic when price is reduced from 80p to 60p, the change in total revenue can be found by multiplying price and quantity demanded together.

Price of tomatoes (p) (pence/kilo)	Quantity demanded (q) (000s)	Total revenue (p × q) (£)
100	2	2000
80	4	3200
60	6	3600
40	8	3200
20	10	2000

Since total revenue increases from £3200 to £3600 in this case, demand is confirmed as being elastic. Notice, however, that demand elasticity does change at different points on the schedule. If the price is lowered from 60p to 40p per kilo, the total revenue falls from £3600 to £3200 showing that demand is inelastic. If when the price changes, the total revenue stays constant, demand is said to have **unit** elasticity: it is neither elastic nor inelastic.

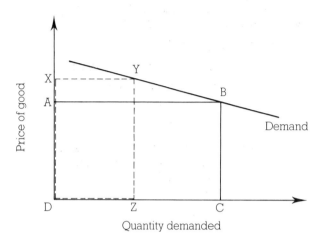

Fig. 11.4 Measuring changes in total revenue

Total revenue changes can also be measured graphically. In Fig. 11.4, if the original price is A then DC will be bought giving a total revenue of ABCD. If the price is raised to X then DZ will be bought reducing total revenue to XYZD.

THE DETERMINANTS OF PRICE ELASTICITY OF DEMAND

What makes demand elastic or inelastic? Several factors are important.

1 The availability of substitutes
If a good or service has a close substitute then demand for it will be elastic. Thus butter and margarine have high elasticities as do wool and acrylic jumpers, and British and Japanese cars. Where there are no close substitutes demand elasticity will be low.

2 The proportion of income spent on a good
If only a very small part of income is spent on a good then changes in its price will not have a dramatic effect on living standards and such goods will have low demand elasticities. Examples of such goods are matches, sweets and newspapers.

3 Habits
Certain people form habits for particular goods which are difficult to break and which will make their demand inelastic. An obvious example relates to cigarettes, and demand for most alcoholic drinks is inelastic. Products which are necessities, such as milk and petrol, also have fairly inelastic demands.

4 Product differentiation
If a manufacturer through advertising can claim unique properties for his product which consumers actually believe, then the demand for his product will be more inelastic. Thus if consumers accept a particular lager as 'probably the best in the world' a higher price could be charged without significantly affecting demand. (**Product differentiation** is the economic term used to describe the creation of real or imaginary differences in essentially the same type of product.)

APPLICATIONS OF DEMAND ELASTICITY

Some knowledge of demand elasticity is extremely important for the government and producers. For the government the concept is particularly useful in both taxation and international trade policy. Producers need to be able to foresee the effects of any price changes on total revenue and governments, in deciding which sales taxes will yield most revenue, have to find goods where demand is inelastic.

Suppose for example trade unionists at the British Leyland Motor Company ask for a large wage rise and the company estimates its demand curve is highly elastic. Clearly a large increase in costs will diminish total revenue as Fig. 11.5 shows. The company will therefore have to try and contain large wage demands if they push the price of BL

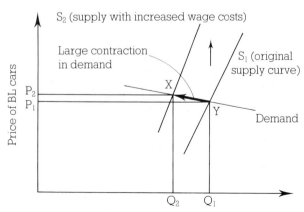

Quantity of BL cars demanded and supplied

Fig. 11.5 The market for British Leyland cars

cars above similar models from Europe and Japan.

In terms of government taxation policy, the most effective sales taxes are those on habit-forming 'luxury' goods. The principal categories of products bearing a high sales tax are tobacco, alcoholic drinks and petrol. As Fig. 11.6 shows, using whisky as an example, even a large tax produces only a small contraction in demand because demand is inelastic. The tax represents the vertical distance between the supply curves and the effect of imposing a tax is to reduce quantity bought only slightly from Q_1 to Qt. Government revenue is equivalent to the tax multiplied by OQt, the quantity bought after the imposition of the tax.

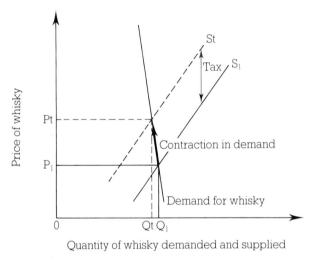

Fig. 11.6 The market for whisky

(PRICE) ELASTICITY OF SUPPLY

Elasticity of supply measures the responsiveness of supply to a change in price. Supply that is very responsive to a price change is called elastic; supply that is unresponsive is called inelastic. Figure 11.7 shows the difference between an elastic and inelastic supply curve.

If the original price of a good is Pe and the price rises to Px then in the case of S_1 supply extends by only a small amount to Q_1, making it inelastic. S_2 is much more responsive extending to Q_2, making it elastic. In general the steeper the supply curve, the less elastic it becomes.

Elasticity of supply can be calculated in a similar way to elasticity of demand but substituting quantity demanded with quantity supplied.

Elasticity of supply (Es) =

$$\frac{\text{\% change in quantity supplied}}{\text{\% change in price}}$$

$$= \frac{\Delta q}{\Delta p} \times \frac{p}{q}$$

where Δq = change in quantity supplied
q = original quantity supplied
p = original price
Δp = change in price

THE DETERMINANTS OF ELASTICITY OF SUPPLY

There are a large number of factors that affect elasticity of supply; some relate closely to the conditions of supply.

1 **The productive capacity of the firm**
If a firm is operating below full capacity it may be possible to easily change supply particularly if there is a significant amount ot local unemployment. In this case supply will be elastic. If the firm is operating at full capacity supply may be very inelastic.

2 **The availability of the factors of production**
The extent to which extra factors can be easily and quickly bought or hired and conversely stopped or laid off will significantly affect supply elasticity. If extra raw materials can be quickly bought in, new machines utilised, and additional labour hired, then supply will be elastic.

3 **The amount of stocks held**
Large factory stocks of a product will ensure that any surges in demand are easily catered for making supply very elastic. Depleted stocks may mean supply is much more inelastic.

4 **The possibility of overtime**
Factory output can be increased significantly if overtime is made available for workers. Its

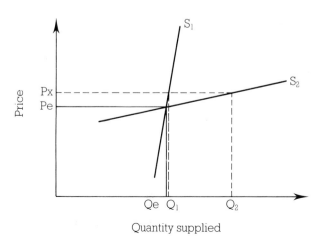

Fig. 11.7 The elasticity of supply

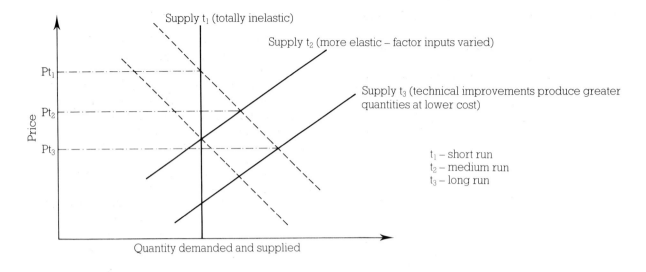

Fig. 11.8 Time variations in the elasticity of supply over different periods

acceptance by them will make supply more elastic.

5 Climatic conditions

For agricultural products, climatic conditions are such that supply must be totally inelastic in the short run because seeds cannot be planted mid-season. It is only at the start of the next growing season that supply can respond to changes in demand.

6 The time factor under consideration

Supply cannot normally respond instantly to a change in demand because changes in production take some time to effect. Therefore in the short run supply will probably be totally inelastic i.e. **fixed**. As the amounts of factor inputs are varied, so supply becomes more responsive and thus more elastic. In the long run technical progress may be such that the conditions of supply change producing a greater output at lower cost. The time variations of supply elasticity are illustrated in Fig. 11.8. The effects on price of these variations are such that it will fall over time from Pt_1 to Pt_3, in response to an initial change in demand.

INCOME ELASTICITY OF DEMAND

In addition to price elasticity of demand, the concept of **income elasticity** is also useful to see how changes in income affect demand. It can be defined as follows:

income elasticity of demand =

$$\frac{\% \text{ change in quantity demanded}}{\% \text{ change in income}}$$

Income elasticity is normally expressed as being positive ($+$), negative ($-$) or zero (0). The above equation shows that if income goes up or down demand can change in the same direction, in the opposite direction, or not at all. If income falls ($-$) and so does demand ($-$), income elasticity will be positive ($+$). Figure 11.9 plots income against demand and illustrates the main types of income elasticity.

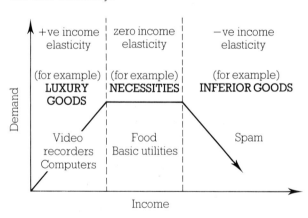

Fig. 11.9 The income elasticity of demand for luxury goods, necessities and inferior goods

Goods with a positive income elasticity can generally be termed 'luxury'. The larger a person's income the more records, fashion clothes, nights out, etc. can be enjoyed. Necessities such as food and basic clothing will have zero income elasticities because they have to be bought regardless of income changes. Goods with a negative income elasticity imply more being bought as income falls, less as income rises. For some people such goods might include spam, sausages and baked beans, since when income rises they might be substituted with steak, ham and sweet corn. They are goods which will only be bought if nothing else can be afforded.

Suppliers of products which have zero income elasticity will be less vulnerable in a recession than suppliers of goods where income elasticity is positive. Supermarket chains such as Sainsbury and Tesco were actually expanding during the early 1980s when companies such as British Leyland and British Steel were making thousands of workers redundant.

CROSS ELASTICITY OF DEMAND

Cross elasticity of demand is a useful concept for identifying whether goods are substitutes for, or complementary to, each other. It can be defined as follows:

Cross elasticity of demand =

$$\frac{\% \text{ change in quantity demanded for good X}}{\% \text{ change in price of good Y}}$$

If the price of good Y goes up (down) and the demand for X goes up (down) then X and Y must be substitutes and cross elasticity is positive. Using the example of cassettes (X) and records (Y), if the price of records goes up, then cassettes being substitutes will be in greater demand.

If the price of good Y goes up (down) and the demand for X goes down (up), then X and Y must be complementary. Taking the example of computers (X) and disc drives (Y), if the price of disc drives goes up sharply, the demand for computers will fall as disc drives are complementary to computers.

Any value of zero for cross elasticity implies the goods are unrelated to each other.

THINGS TO DO

1 Define **price elasticity of demand**.

2 State which of the following goods are likely to have elastic or inelastic demands: apples, salt, sugar, video recorders, telephones, cigarettes, newspapers.

3 Using the following demand schedule for beer, calculate price elasticity of demand if price is reduced from 90 to 80p per pint. What is the effect on total revenue if beer is reduced from 80 to 70p per pint? What does this imply about demand elasticity?

Price (/pint)	Quantity demanded (000s)
120p	50
110p	55
100p	60
90p	65
80p	70
70p	80

4 Why is demand for 'Colgate' toothpaste likely to be elastic, but the demand for toothpaste as a whole inelastic?

5 Show graphically how a large increase in the price of matches will lead to only a small contraction in the quantity demanded.

6 Show graphically how a large tax on blank cassettes might result in a large fall in the quantity of them demanded.

7 In the following supply schedule, what is the elasticity of supply? What type of good might the table be referring to?

Price (£)	Quantity supplied (000s)
10	15
8	15
6	15
4	15
2	15

8 Explain how and why **elasticity of supply** can vary over time.

9 Explain the main uses of the concept of **cross elasticity of demand**.

12

THE ECONOMIC ROLE OF THE GOVERNMENT IN A MIXED ECONOMY

INTRODUCTION: WHY DO WE NEED A GOVERNMENT?

In Chapter 11 it appeared that the solution to the economic problem could come about without a government being involved. Consumers expressed their wants through the demand curve, producers expressed their costs through the supply curve and the equilibrium price where the two curves met ensured that there were no surpluses or shortages. So why do we need to pay taxes, and what does the government spend this revenue on?

There are three main areas where the market economy fails.

1 ALLOCATION

Unfortunately not all the goods and services we require can be provided through the market mechanism. Take defence for example. Will individual consumers demand aircraft carriers or tanks? Probably not, and yet as a country there is a need for a defence system so the government provides it on behalf of the community through taxation. Law and order is another example. Such wants are often called **social wants** because they can only be provided by the government re-allocating factors of production away from other uses. Thus the opportunity cost of providing defence could be fewer manufactured goods.

There are other wants which can be provided through the market but which some consumers would not enjoy because they could not afford the equilibrium price. It would be unfair to exclude some members of the community from having services such as health and education simply because they were on low incomes. Such wants are often called **merit wants** and again the government steps in to satisfy more of them through taxation.

2 DISTRIBUTION

Another problem which arises from the market economy is that wants can be satisfied only if the equilibrium price can be afforded. Many poor people would therefore be excluded from even basic wants, particularly the old and unemployed.

This is clearly unfair so the government adopts a 'Robin Hood' approach and takes from the rich to give to the poor by taking a higher percentage of rich people's income in tax than that taken from low income groups. Such action is called **redistributing income**.

3 STABILISATION

One further problem with the market economy is that left to itself it can get out of control. Economists used to think that *laissez-faire* (leave alone) policies were a good thing, but when the 1930s brought very severe unemployment to Britain it was appreciated that some form of government intervention might be necessary to keep the economy on a steady path. Figure 12.1 shows how activity in the economy tends to fluctuate leading to booms and slumps.

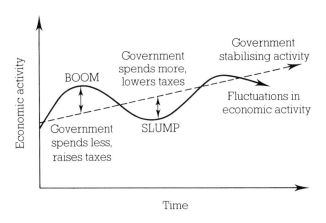

Fig. 12.1 The trade cycle

In a **boom** there is usually too much spending which, especially when there is full employment, cannot be matched by extra supply so that **inflation** (or rising prices) occurs. The government therefore has to try and reduce spending which can be achieved by raising taxes and cutting its own spending. In a **slump** there may be too little spending so in order to create more jobs the government may increase its own spending or lower taxes. Figure 12.1 shows how the government aims, via stabilisation, at steady growth in economic activity.

THE BUDGET

The **Budget** is the name given to the account showing what the government intends to spend and take in taxes during a year. It is normally announced by the Chancellor of the Exchequer in March for the following financial year, 1 April to 31 March. Although the Budget can be used to correct many of the market imperfections discussed above, it has become particularly important since 1945 in its stabilisation role. This has been largely due to the work of an economist called John Maynard Keynes who published *The General Theory of Employment, Interest and Money* in 1936 which made clear that full employment was not a natural phenomenon and could only occur if governments took positive steps to create it. This gave rise to the idea of a **budget deficit** where the government spent more than it took in taxation, borrowing the difference from the public and financial institutions. Similarly in a boom, the government could aim at a **budget surplus** where tax revenue would be greater than spending, to dampen down demand. Finally if the economy was growing steadily without high inflation or unemployment, a **balanced budget** with taxes equal to spending could be appropriate. (See Fig. 12.2.)

There is always a temptation for governments to run budget deficits for as long as possible because it is politically popular to spend money and/or lower taxes. However the consequences of doing this involve increasing the size of the **Public Sector Borrowing Requirement** (PSBR) which in turn means paying out higher interest to the individuals and institutions providing the loans thus necessitating even more borrowing! It is therefore important to monitor the size of the PSBR carefully.

Figure 12.3 (overleaf) shows the government's spending and income for 1984/5. Note that the items refer to *central* government finance which should be distinguished from *local* government finance. The central government in Westminster controls spending on important national items such as defence and the National Health Service, whereas local governments spend money on services affecting the community they administer, such as education, street lighting and refuse collection. It should also be noted that some services are important both nationally and locally, such as the police. Here the cost is shared between central and local governments, in the case of the police each paying half.

It can be seen from Fig. 12.3 that one of the largest items of central government spending comprises the grants that are given to local government and in fact over half of local authority spending is financed through such grants. It is also interesting to note that 6% of government spending has to be used to pay the interest charges arising out of running budget deficits.

THINGS TO DO

1 Explain why the market economy by itself cannot satisfy all of our wants.

2 Distinguish between **social** and **merit** wants. What would be the economic consequences of **privatising** the National Health Service?

3 What problems may arise for a government trying to stabilise economic activity? Can it spend money over and above its tax revenue? How might it do this?

4 Why is the stabilisation role of the Budget important?

5 What makes achieving a budget surplus difficult?

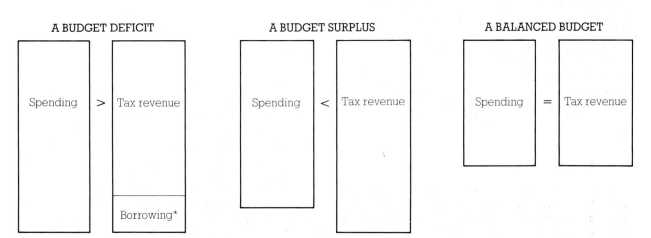

A BUDGET DEFICIT — Spending > Tax revenue / Borrowing*

A BUDGET SURPLUS — Spending < Tax revenue

A BALANCED BUDGET — Spending = Tax revenue

* broadly known as **Public Sector Borrowing Requirement**

Fig. 12.2

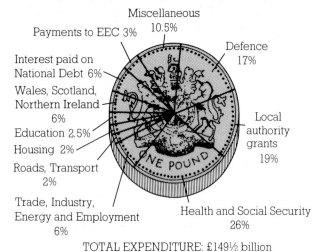

EXPENDITURE
GOVERNMENT EXPENDITURE 1984/85

Miscellaneous 10.5%
Payments to EEC 3%
Defence 17%
Interest paid on National Debt 6%
Wales, Scotland, Northern Ireland 6%
Education 2.5%
Housing 2%
Local authority grants 19%
Roads, Transport 2%
Trade, Industry, Energy and Employment 6%
Health and Social Security 26%

TOTAL EXPENDITURE: £149½ billion

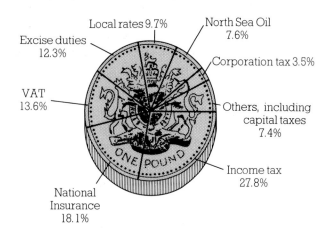

INCOME
GOVERNMENT REVENUE: 1984/85

Local rates 9.7%
North Sea Oil 7.6%
Excise duties 12.3%
Corporation tax 3.5%
VAT 13.6%
Others, including capital taxes 7.4%
Income tax 27.8%
National Insurance 18.1%

TOTAL INCOME: £140 billion

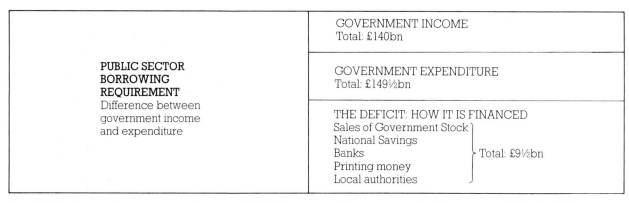

PUBLIC SECTOR BORROWING REQUIREMENT Difference between government income and expenditure	GOVERNMENT INCOME Total: £140bn
	GOVERNMENT EXPENDITURE Total: £149½bn
	THE DEFICIT: HOW IT IS FINANCED Sales of Government Stock National Savings Banks Printing money Local authorities — Total: £9½bn

Fig. 12.3 Central government finance 1984–85 – expenditure exceeded income and the deficit was made up from the PSBR

THE MAIN TAXES

The main taxes we pay can be divided into those paid on income and capital, called **direct** taxes, collected by the Inland Revenue, and those paid when money is spent, called **indirect** taxes, collected by the Customs and Excise Department. Together these two groups make up the **structure of taxation**.

1 DIRECT TAXES

As Fig. 12.3 shows, the most important tax in terms of revenue is **income tax** raising nearly £39 000 000 in 1984/5. It is called a **progressive tax** because as income rises, so a larger % is taken in tax. Figure 12.4 shows for a single person how at first and for low incomes no tax at all is paid until over about £35 000, 60% of every extra £ earned is taken in tax.

Income tax effectively redistributes income away from the rich towards the poor (via welfare benefits); it is fairly inexpensive to collect – many employers pay the tax for their employees through Pay As You Earn schemes; and is fairly

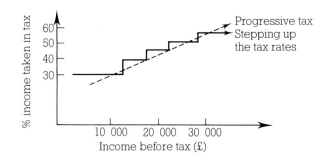

Fig. 12.4 How income tax is progressive

difficult to avoid. However, its main drawback is that high rates of tax are a disincentive to work hard since any extra income earned may attract a higher tax rate. It is also a tax paid twice by many savers. Earned income, which has already been taxed once, might be put into a building society account where any interest earned would be taxed again at the same rates.

Corporation tax is charged on company profits at fixed rates. It is broadly redistributive but could provide a disincentive to investment, with a high tax rate. Other direct taxes include **inheritance tax**, a progressive tax on gifts, etc; **capital gains tax** which is charged on the profit made from selling an asset such as share certificates, a certain amount of profit being tax-free but then being charged at 30%; and **petroleum revenue tax** which is becoming very important.

2 INDIRECT TAXES

Indirect taxes are normally paid on goods and services, the actual tax being paid by shops and manufacturers but passed on 'indirectly' to consumers in the form of higher prices.

Value added tax (VAT) is the most important indirect tax which is placed on the 'value added' in the production and distribution of a product at all stages, being finally passed on to the consumer at a rate of 15%. Its advantages include being zero rated on food and exports and that, since all countries in the EC operate the tax, it helps to unify the tax structure within the Community. In common with all indirect taxes, however, its main disadvantage is that it is **regressive**. This means that the burden of the tax tends to fall on lower income groups rather than on higher incomes. The following example shows why:

Mr Smith buys a Mini Metro car costing £4000 + 600 VAT; yearly income is £8000.
Mr Jones buys a Mini Metro car costing £4000 + 600 VAT; yearly income is £12 000.
For Mr Smith the VAT represents 7.5% of his income

$(\dfrac{600}{8000} \times 100\%)$.

For Mr Jones the VAT represents 5% of his income

$(\dfrac{600}{12000} \times 100\%)$.

Thus a **regressive tax** is one where low income groups pay a higher percentage of their income in tax than people on high incomes. Figure 12.5 illustrates a regressive tax. For comparison a **progressive tax** is also shown as well as a **proportional tax** where the % of income paid in tax remains constant. (Corporation tax, for example, is proportional.)

VAT is sometimes called an *ad valorem* tax because it is added on to the price of the good or service and if the price of the good rises so does the amount collected because it is 15% of the new price. Thus the revenue from this tax automatically rises in line with any inflation. This is not true for the other important indirect tax, **excise duties**, which is known as a **specific tax** because the duty remains fixed even when the price of a good changes. Excise duties are placed largely on

goods with an inelastic demand and principally on cigarettes, petrol and alcohol. These goods also bear VAT so that the total tax charged is very high as Fig. 12.6 shows.

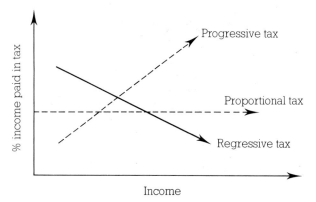

Fig. 12.5

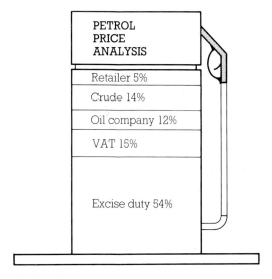

Fig. 12.6 Relative shares of the income from a litre of petrol

Because the duty is fixed, if the government requires more revenue from excise duties it has to raise the duty at the Budget which it usually does each year. Cigarettes have been hit particularly hard in recent years because of the desire to discourage smoking for health reasons.

One further indirect tax worth mentioning is **customs duties** which are charged on foreign imports. The EC has standardised many of the rates which are known as the **Common External Tariff** and much of the revenue from customs duties goes to the Community to help support agriculture. Since Britain is one of the largest Community traders our contributions to the Community budget are very considerable via this tax and many politicians feel that since we are not the richest country in the group that our contributions should be reduced.

THE BALANCE OF TAXATION

How far should the revenue from direct taxes balance that from indirect taxes? This is a difficult question to answer but most governments feel that all citizens should contribute something towards the services they receive so that a wide range of taxes is preferable, covering many different groups of people. It could be said shifting the balance towards sales taxes gives people more of an option about paying the tax but reducing direct taxes and increasing indirect would be very regressive. One problem which does arise regarding the balance of taxation occurs when inflation distorts the revenue received from direct and indirect taxes. If the government does nothing to change the tax structure and inflation becomes significant, income tax revenue will automatically rise as higher earnings drag people into higher tax bands. In particular, people on low incomes previously paying no tax may find themselves worse off if a pay rise drags them into a tax band. This gives rise to the concept of **inflationary fiscal**

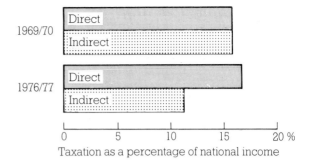

Fig. 12.7 The balance of direct and indirect taxes

drag. In the opposite way excise duty revenue will not catch up with inflation because the duties are a fixed amount so that the balance of taxation becomes distorted in favour of direct taxation. Thus the government may have to alter the tax structure, raising indirect and lowering direct, to restore the balance. Figure 12.7 shows how the high rates of inflation in the 1970s distorted the tax structure.

THINGS TO DO

1 Study Fig. 12.8. Which goods have become relatively cheaper over the time period shown? Can you suggest any reasons for these changes? (Bear in mind the British market for wine and spirits has expanded dramatically over the last 15 years.)

Fig. 12.8 Goods subject to excise duties

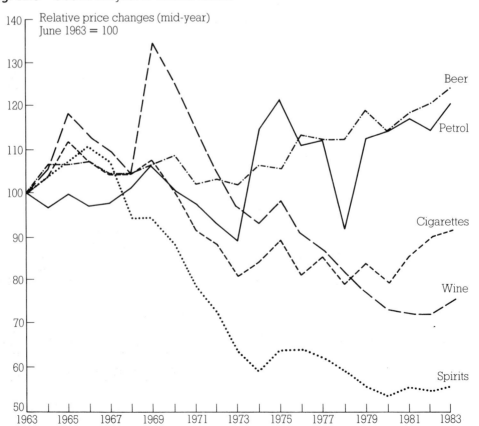

2 Using Fig. 12.3, show how the government uses the Budget to re-allocate resources and re-distribute income.

3 Why is controlling the size of the PSBR difficult?

4 List some of the main advantages and disadvantages of direct and indirect taxes.

5 Explain what is meant by **inflationary fiscal drag** and suggest by what methods you would restore the imbalance in structure for 1976/77 to that shown for 1969/70 (Fig. 12.7).

6 Compare and contrast the following terms: **direct** and **indirect** taxes; **progressive** and **regressive** taxes; *ad valorem* and **specific** duties.

7 If direct taxes (principally income tax) were lowered by £5000m and indirect taxes raised by £5000m, would this have any effect on the economy as a whole?

8 Study Fig. 12.9. How does Britain compare with other nations? Are more or less people paying tax in 1984/5 at basic and higher rates than in previous years?

Fig. 12.9 International comparisons of taxation

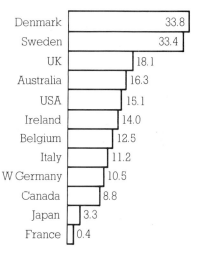

Denmark	33.8
Sweden	33.4
UK	18.1
Australia	16.3
USA	15.1
Ireland	14.0
Belgium	12.5
Italy	11.2
W Germany	10.5
Canada	8.8
Japan	3.3
France	0.4

THE TAX LEAGUE
Income tax as % of earnings (married man, 2 children)

**TAX FREE INCOME:
HOW BRITAIN COMPARES**

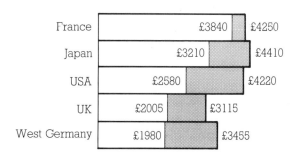

France	£3840	£4250
Japan	£3210	£4410
USA	£2580	£4220
UK	£2005	£3115
West Germany	£1980	£3455

SINGLE ☐ MARRIED ▨

**NUMBER OF TAXPAYERS
& WHAT THEY PAID**

	Basic rate	Higher rate	Total
	(Number of taxpayers)		£m
1938-39	3 800 000	105 000	399
1948-49	14 500 000	218 000	1 460
1958-59	17 700 000	393 000	2 484
1968-69	20 700 000	474 000	4 574
1978-79	21 400 000	763 000	18 763
1984-85	20 400 000	820 000	33 800

Dewhurst – The Master Butcher – is owned by one of Britain's richest families, the Vesteys. In total, the chain of butchers shops made £2.3m in profits in 1984 but the family paid just £10 in income tax. Why? The Vesteys were engaged in a sophisticated tax-avoidance scheme which the House of Lords ruled was legal. The Inland Revenue were claiming that over a four-year period the family owed income tax on £11.6 million, but because of the ruling they were unable to collect the tax revenue.

How did the Vesteys manage to do it? In brief, at one time a UK resident could transfer his earnings abroad and arrange for a nominated trustee to hold onto them. Then, at irregular intervals, the trustee could arrange to pay lump sums back to the UK resident who could legally avoid paying income tax. This loophole was plugged in 1936 with a law which stated that any

receipts from the trustee would be counted as the UK residents' income and taxed accordingly.

What the Vesteys managed to do was to get around that law by arranging for the money to go not to themselves, but their sons and daughters thus avoiding the tax.

THINGS TO DO

1 If tax avoidance is widespread what are the consequences for those people who do pay tax?
2 How does PAYE prevent tax evasion?

Fig. 12.10 Dewhurst the butchers – owned by the Vestey family

TAXATION AND GOVERNMENT POLICY

Any government policy connected with taxation and expenditure is known as **fiscal policy**. Fiscal policy will be directed towards solving the problem of the market failures discussed earlier. **Reallocation** of resources comes in the expenditure on social and merit wants; **redistribution** comes through progressive taxes, and the steeper the higher or marginal tax rates, the greater the redistributive effects. Stabilisation occurs through the overall regulation of the Budget in terms of surpluses and deficits but in addition, certain individual taxes can be used to control spending. Investment, for example, could be encouraged by lowering corporation tax; savings could be encouraged by lowering the income tax charged on many forms of saving; and consumer spending could be encouraged by lowering VAT and excise duties.

The type of fiscal policy pursued by the government will, to a large extent, depend on their political beliefs. A labour government may stress the importance of the redistribution of income and make income tax more progressive. A conservative government, however, may stress the importance of improving incentives to work harder and lower the rates of income tax. It is not for economists to take sides in this debate but rather to understand the consequences to the economy of any fiscal changes.

COULD OUR TAX SYSTEM BE IMPROVED?

Going back as far as 1776 a famous economist, Adam Smith, suggested four attributes of a good tax system. Firstly, people should pay according to their means, suggesting a progressive element in the tax structure; secondly, the cost of collecting the tax should be small in relation to its yield; thirdly, taxes should be easy to pay to minimise avoidance and evasion; fourthly, the revenue from taxes should be easily predictable so that the government can accurately plan the economy.

Not all taxes levied in Britain have conformed to the above principles. A dog licence used to cost more to administer (£4m in 1984/5) than it yielded in revenue (£1m in 1984/5). Perhaps for this reason it was abolished in 1986. Similarly high rates of income tax encourage avoidance (Fig. 12.10), while the yield from indirect taxes is not always predictable because consumer spending varies considerably.

One important reform that has been suggested for improving our tax system is designed to join together the administration of the social security and tax departments. It seems rather wasteful, for example, to charge a married man with a family tax on the one hand only to hand back child benefit on the other. Similarly a person on a low income may be paying some tax but receiving back a greater amount in social security benefit. The reform proposed is called a 'negative income tax system'. It works as follows. Anyone receiving benefit or paying income tax at present would be credited with certain allowances, say £30 per week for a single person, £50 for a married couple and £10 per week for each child. Any income received would be taxed at a constant rate of perhaps 30%. Then to work out the tax bill the credits are subtracted from the tax owed and the balance paid to the Inland Revenue. If the credits are greater than the tax (which could be zero for the unemployed), then negative tax would be paid which in effect would mean the government paying out money to the individual. The examples below make this clearer:

Example 1
A married man with two children earning £85 per week.
CREDITS: £70 per week.
TAX at 30%: £25.50 per week.
TAX BILL: £25.50 − £70 = *−£44.50*.
Net payment by government to family = £44.50/week

Example 2
A single person earning £200 per week.
CREDITS £30 per week. TAX at 30%: £60 per week.
TAX BILL: £60 − £30 = *£30*.
Net payment by single person to government = £30/week

Figure 12.11 shows how below a certain income credits would be greater than tax, but for higher incomes, tax would be much greater than credits. The system seems simple to operate and could save money on the administration side but there would still be special cases requiring some form of extra help outside the normal credits.

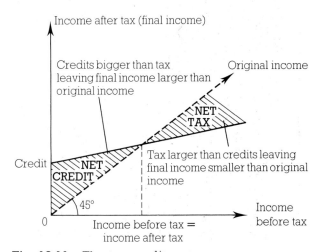

Fig. 12.11   The tax-credit system

Another tax suggested by reformers that could be introduced in Britain to achieve greater redistribution is some form of wealth tax. Britain is one of the few European countries which does not tax wealth as opposed to income, wealth being the total value of a person's assets rather than a flow of money. A suggestion has come from the Labour Party that people with assets worth over £100 000 should pay an annual tax of 1% on the value of these assets, which could rise for assets over £1 million. A wealth tax might enable a reduction in income tax to be possible.

THINGS TO DO

1 Suggest how **fiscal policy** could be used to lift an economy out of a slump. What are the consequences of running large budget deficits?

2 How could a government reduce consumer spending whilst encouraging more private investment?

3 Explain what a **negative tax system** is and how it could simplify the present tax and benefits structure.

4 'A wealth tax would destroy the goose that lays the golden egg.' Explain and discuss.

LOCAL GOVERNMENT FINANCE

Local authorities have their own budgets which, because their ability to borrow is limited, are usually balanced. Figure 12.12 shows how one local authority, Essex raised and spent its money in 1985–6.

For nearly all local authorities, the largest single item of spending is education in schools. Higher education (universities, polytechnics, etc.) is financed by the central government but for primary and secondary education local authorities decide on the organisation, which is why some boroughs have grammar schools, some have middle schools and others comprehensives.

Housing is a very important item of expenditure, principally comprising the building and maintenance of council accommodation, but also including the numerous grants given for home improvements in the private sector. In London alone 800 000 units of accommodation are managed by the borough councils.

Social services spending includes the care of children, the elderly, the blind, the deaf and the physically handicapped in their homes, as well as home helps, day nurseries and a casework service for families in difficulties.

Other important services are civic amenities which comprise items such as parks, refuse collection, street lighting, libraries, swimming pools and recreation centres; and planning, which ensures that building work conforms to certain standards, that factories are not built in residential areas and that historic buildings are preserved (Fig. 12.13).

The revenue side of local authority finance is divided into four important areas.

Fig. 12.12 Essex county finance 1985–6

WHERE DOES THE COUNTY'S MONEY COME FROM?
TOTAL INCOME OF £656M IS PROVIDED AS FOLLOWS:

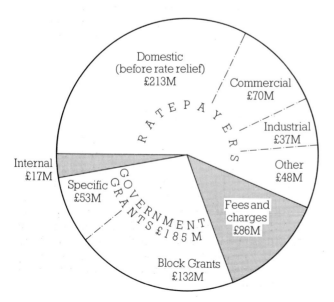

HOW IS THE MONEY SPENT?
ON SERVICES – £656M

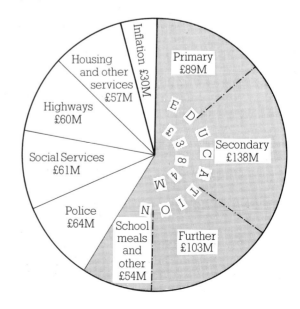

1 RATES

Rates are local taxes charged annually on the value of buildings and land which are beneficially occupied. They are actually based on the annual letting value of a property, which minus insurance and repairs gives the **rateable value**. Since rateable values have not been adjusted for inflation for over 10 years, very few give a realistic idea of just how much rent could be obtained from letting a property. Rateable values do increase as property values increase but not in proportion, so that rates tend to be regressive taking a larger percentage from people's income who live in smaller or newer houses than from those who live in larger or older houses.

The local authority adds together all the rateable values for the borough and compares this figure with the amount it needs to collect from the rates. Supposing the total rateable value comes to £50m and £60m is needed from the rates. The borough can work out that if it charged just 1p in the £ rateable value it could raise £50m divided by 100 or £50 000. To raise £60m therefore the borough would have to divide this figure by £50 000 to find out how many pence in the £ the rates would have to be. In this case the **rate poundage** would be 120p. Each year the rate poundage tends to go up as councils require more money to pay for the increasing cost of services.

Rates do have the advantage of raising a considerable amount of income for local authorities (Fig. 12.12) and the rate poundage is controlled by the borough so that councils elected on a high spending programme can use the rates to finance this. This gives them some measure of independence from the central government. However, there are some major criticisms of rates which have prompted suggestions that rates should be abolished in favour of a fairer system of local taxation. Firstly in many urban boroughs the largest share of rates is not paid by private houseowners who have a vote in the election of a council, but by businesses (sometimes called 'non-domestic rate payers') who do not (Fig. 12.14). Also business rates do not depend on the profitability of a company since they are based on the amount of land and factory buildings a firm owns, so that a firm making little or no profit could be paying higher rates than a highly successful company. Rates are a tax on costs, not profits. Rates also vary widely throughout the country so that a person living outside London (where rates tend to be lower) could work in London where the higher rates could be used to subsidise transport fares, and pay lower fares without contributing to the cost of the subsidy. Rates, as mentioned earlier, are also regressive and it does seem slightly ironic that a person improving their home by fitting double glazing or central heating may end up paying higher rates than the person who does nothing to develop the property.

Several suggestions for an alternative to rates are dealt with towards the end of this section. They include a local income tax and a local sales tax. A local income tax would be fairer than rates because it would probably be progressive, but a local sales tax would put up prices in local shops and mean that big spending boroughs would have the highest shop prices. A poll tax (or 'community charge') is also suggested which would be highly regressive, every voter probably paying a fixed amount in tax regardless of income. Since replacing the rates with one of the above taxes would probably be politically very unpopular, it is likely that rates however unfair, will be around for quite some time!

2 CENTRAL GOVERNMENT GRANTS

These grants form the largest single item of an authority's annual revenue. This is partly because the central government may draw up schemes to improve the care of the elderly, raise the school leaving age or institute nursery education. Having imposed new services upon local authorities, or extended existing ones, and thereby increased local costs it is only fair that the government should give some financial help. Also many local authority services such as education, the police and roads, are a national as well as a local requirement making additional finance important.

The main types of grants given are the **rate support grant** designed to help the less well-off boroughs where rate income may be low because of a lack of industry for example; the **percentage grant** where important services such as the police and roads earn a percentage grant from the central government towards their cost; and **specific grants** given, for example, to buy land which might create public open spaces, or for reclaiming derelict land or for spending necessitated by an increase in the immigrant population. In Fig. 12.12 block grants refer to rate support and percentage, totalling £132m, with specific grants totalling £53m.

3 SALE OF SERVICES

A third source of local authority income comes from charging for services provided. The largest single source of money is from council house rents but a variety of other services bear charges including swimming pools, car parks, and golf courses. In Hull, for example, the council operates its own telephone service; in Birmingham there is a municipal bank; and in holiday resorts the local authority frequently operates many of the catering and entertainment undertakings and even hires out deckchairs.

JUST TO LET YOU KNOW —
LAST YEAR IN HARINGEY...

28,780 children taught in school
(18 pupils per teacher — primary)
(14 pupils per teacher — secondary)
4,613 went on to further education
12,920 attended adult education classes
3,134,144 school meals served

1,555 allotments rented
45 parks and open spaces cultivated
12,000 street trees cared for

586,597 went swimming

514,000 attended sports centres
43,000 went on sports coaching courses
14,111 had a sauna
20,712 used our private baths

1,226 exhibitions and displays put on

2,037 went to celebrity concerts
2,355 children went to Christmas activities
40,000 handicapped, sick or elderly people saw entertainments

11,095 street lamps lit
326 kilometres of roads looked after

46,792 books bought for libraries
1,830,644 books lent
146,829 records or cassettes issued

772 kilometres of sewers maintained

55,699 enquiries dealt with at 4 advice bureaux

41 community centres and tenants rooms used
Grants given to 202 voluntary and community groups

1,786 applications for planning permission dealt with

90,995 tons of refuse collected
3,000 tons of dumped rubbish removed
2,408 abandoned vehicles booked

Fig. 12.13 London Borough of Haringey – services provided

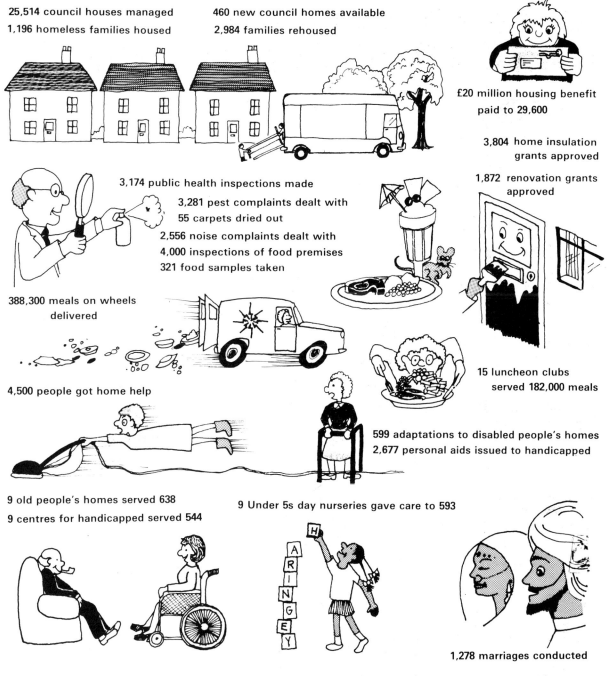

25,514 council houses managed

1,196 homeless families housed

460 new council homes available

2,984 families rehoused

£20 million housing benefit paid to 29,600

3,804 home insulation grants approved

1,872 renovation grants approved

3,174 public health inspections made

3,281 pest complaints dealt with

55 carpets dried out

2,556 noise complaints dealt with

4,000 inspections of food premises

321 food samples taken

388,300 meals on wheels delivered

15 luncheon clubs served 182,000 meals

4,500 people got home help

599 adaptations to disabled people's homes

2,677 personal aids issued to handicapped

9 old people's homes served 638

9 centres for handicapped served 544

9 Under 5s day nurseries gave care to 593

1,278 marriages conducted

All this and much, much more behind the scenes
for less than the price of a pint, per person, per day

HARINGEY COUNCIL PROVIDES
services worth saving

DEFEND
LONDON

Whitehall seeks controls on business rates

by David Lipsey
Economics Editor

BUSINESS rates may in future be payable to the government instead of to local councils. This proposal is a front runner before an internal Department of the Environment inquiry into rates, headed by Kenneth Baker, the new local government minister.

The plan is favoured because of ministerial concern that high-spending councils are milking local businessmen to finance their programmes. Businessmen, unlike domestic ratepayers, have no vote in local elections. Thus, ministers believe, the councils are not properly accountable for the rates they charge.

Under the plan, Whitehall would collect the £6.9 billion at present paid in rates by local businesses. It would then distribute some or all of the cash to local councils, according to an assessment of local needs. Councils which over-spent would be forced to make economies or to raise domestic rates, thus risking the wrath of the local electorate.

The highest-spending authorities reap a disproportionate percentage of their revenue from business rates, ministers point out. For example, the Inner London Education Authority gets 73% of its revenue from non-domestic rates and only 22% from domestic rates. Leicester gets 28% of its revenue from business ratepayers, only 15% from domestic sources (see table).

The government has rejected one alternative way of dealing with the problem: the restoration of a special business vote. It would be impractical because of the difficulty of dealing with a business with several premises in different authorities; and to weight votes according to the wealth of the business would savour too much of plutocracy.

The government is, however, determined to act. The Confederation of British Industry, whose conference opens in Eastbourne tomorrow, charges that "high business-rate increases raise costs, reduce competitiveness, discourage investment and harm job prospects."

Conservative backbenchers have come under mounting pressure from small businessmen, aggrieved at the cost of rates. It has now replaced domestic rates as the number one grievance, many report.

The Baker inquiry was first announced by Patrick Jenkin at the Tory conference in Brighton last month. It will last for 12–18 months – and ministers fervently deny charges that it is a whitewash.

However, the inquiry will studiously avoid considering again the abolition of domestic rates. Mrs Thatcher pledged that in 1974, but it has proved embarassing. Acceptable alternative ways of raising council revenue have failed to materialise.

Major legislation following the inquiry is likely to be delayed until after the next general election. However, minor adjustments to the existing system are not ruled out.

Another concern among ministers is that even domestic ratepayers are insulated from council's spending decisions. Two-thirds of council tenants get all or part of their rates paid through housing benefit, they point out.

The inquiry will range much more widely than business rates:
- New consideration of what percentage of local government spending should be met from central funds and what percentage raised locally.
- A fundamental look at ways to make councils more accountable to local voters.
- A survey of the methods by which local councils raise money, to embrace reforms and possible new sources of revenue.

The rates inquiry is not the only probe mounted by Baker. A separate study is being made of what ministers describe as the "norms of behaviour" of local councils.

Ministers are worried that traditional local government is being undermined by left-wingers, who bend the rules of their councils, insisting, for example, on political vetting of the appointment of officials.

A short-list has been drawn up of senior constitutional figures, including judges, to preside over this inquiry. All-party support for its work is to be solicited.

Many moderate Labour councillors are said to be sickened by the behaviour of what ministers describe as the "new urban left".

The Sunday Times
4.11.1984

Fig. 12.14

Where the rate-capped authorities get their money

	Domestic rates%	Non-domestic rates%	Government grants etc*
Basildon	43	37	20
Brent	29	30	41
Camden	17	60	23
GLC	27	50	22
Greenwich	26	22	52
Hackney	16	17	67
Haringey	28	24	48
ILEA	22	73	5
Islington	22	41	37
Lambeth	18	26	56
Leicester	15	28	57
Lewisham	22	13	65
Merseyside	20	20	60
Portsmouth	15	21	64
Sheffield	22	31	47
South Yorks	21	25	54
Southwark	21	40	39
Thamesdown	29	43	28

*including changes in balances, London rate equilisation

4 BORROWING

Finally many local authorities have to borrow money from the public and financial institutions to pay for large items of capital expenditure. Figure 12.15 shows capital spending in Haringey for 1981–2, housing taking by far the largest slice of the budget in a borough where around 5000 people are on the council house waiting list.

Borrowing is made by issuing local authority bonds at competitive rates of interest to private individuals and financial institutions. They usually run for 2–5 years with a minimum investment of about £200.

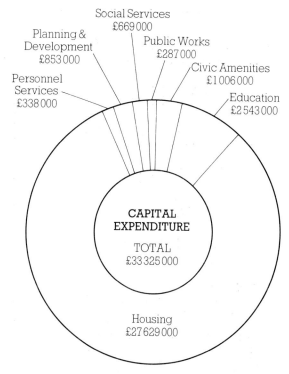

Fig. 12.15 London Borough of Haringey – capital spending 1981–82

THINGS TO DO

Read Fig. 12.16 (on the following pages) carefully then using it and the information in this chapter answer the questions below.

1 What are **rates** and how are they calculated?

2 What does Fig. 12.16 mean when it says that a local income tax would be related more closely to an 'ability to pay'?

3 What problems might arise with a local sales tax?

4 What are the good and bad points of a local poll tax?

5 In the table of local government finance figures for 1981–2, what is meant by 'non-domestic rates'? What is their significance for local authorities? Are they unfair?

6 Why should taxes have predictable yields?

7 Why are central government grants important for local authorities?

8 What other sources of income exist for local authorities besides rates and grants?

9 Why would a local sales tax be **regressive**, but a local income tax probably **progressive**?

10 Do rates tend to be **regressive** or **progressive**?

Fig. 12.16

Alternatives to domestic rates

The Government published a Green Paper on alternatives to domestic rates as a source of revenue for local authorities in Great Britain on 16 December 1981 (HMSO, Cmnd 8449).

The main features of local government finance in Great Britain are shown in the table.

The Green Paper is a response to public criticism about the way in which local people contribute to the cost of local services. It does not set out firm proposals but seeks to identify the range of realistic alternatives on which consultation can now take place.

The main options
The main options identified and discussed in the Green Paper are:

- a local sales tax
- a local income tax
- a poll tax (payable by each resident at a flat rate)
- reforms to domestic rates.

In addition, several other possibilities are rejected:

- local duties on petrol, alcohol or tobacco
- local vehicle excise duty
- charges for licences for the sale of alcohol or petrol
- a local payroll tax (payable by employers on each employee).

Seven criteria
Each potential local tax is assessed against seven criteria:
- is it practicable?
- is it fair?
- does it make councillors who make decisions on local expenditure properly accountable to the local taxpayers?
- are the administrative costs (both for tax gathering and taxpayers) acceptable?
- are the implications for the rest of the tax system acceptable?
- does it encourage proper financial control?
- is it suitable for all tiers of local government?

Separate chapters in the Green Paper consider each of the serious alternatives in turn. Local rates confine the local tax burden to occupiers of property with an unevenly distributed burden across the country; on the other hand, the tax base is relatively easy to identify.

Income and poll taxes
A local income tax would spread the tax burden wider: and an individual's tax liability would be related more closely to his ability to pay; but it would be complex to administer. As with local income tax, local sales taxes would achieve a broader local tax base at the expense of imposing significant costs on traders. Both local income tax and local sales taxes would have unpredictable yields, and, because they could share a tax base with central government, there could be some conflict with the Goverment's fiscal objectives.

A poll tax would spread the local tax burden without the complication of sophisticated measurement of ability to pay, but could be difficult to enforce and would be open to criticism as taxing the right to vote.

Government grants
The Green Paper also considers changes in the system of government grants which could result from a switch to a new local revenue. At the extreme, it might be possible to replace the revenue from domestic rates by extra rate support grant (RSG), but an equivalent amount would have to be realised by the central government in some other way. Moreover, removing the link between local expenditure decisions and local taxation would tend to damage public accountability and local autonomy.

Another section of the paper covers the economic effects of changing the local tax system, including the financial consequences for some typical households in different parts of the country.

THINGS TO DO

Copy out the following information, filling in the blanks to calculate the various rates payable in 'Harldon'.

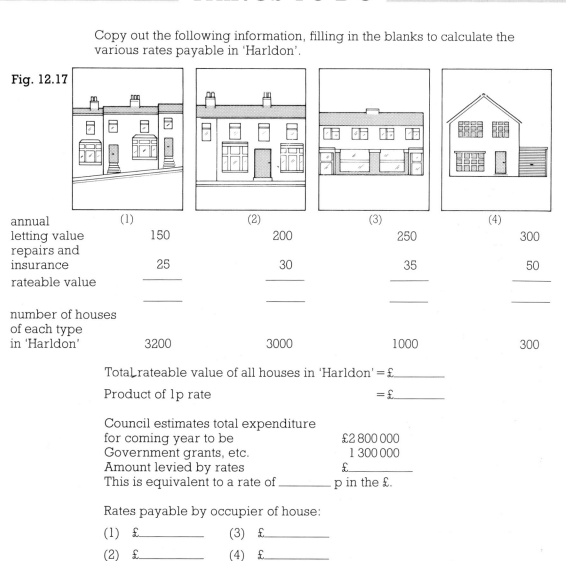

Fig. 12.17

	(1)	(2)	(3)	(4)
annual letting value	150	200	250	300
repairs and insurance	25	30	35	50
rateable value	————	————	————	————
	————	————	————	————
number of houses of each type in 'Harldon'	3200	3000	1000	300

Total rateable value of all houses in 'Harldon' = £————

Product of 1p rate   = £————

Council estimates total expenditure
for coming year to be   £2 800 000
Government grants, etc.   1 300 000
Amount levied by rates   £————
This is equivalent to a rate of ———— p in the £.

Rates payable by occupier of house:

(1) £————   (3) £————

(2) £————   (4) £————

13

AN INTRODUCTION TO NATIONAL INCOME

INTRODUCTION

So far in this book most of the subject matter has dealt with the various components that make up the economy as a whole. In production, for example, the sole trader, partnership, limited company and nationalised industry each form a part of the whole process of production. In the chapters about the price mechanism, *individual* markets for goods and services are important where the prices of individual products and services are determined. **Micro** economics is the term used to describe the components which together make up the whole economy. There is another part of the subject which looks not at the components but at the economy as a whole and this is called **macro** economics. Macro economics is concerned not with the output of a particular firm or industry but with output as a whole – the nation's output. It is concerned with not just the price of video recorders but with prices as a whole. It is also concerned not with an individual's income but with the income of the whole nation – national income.

This chapter provides an introduction to macro economics in showing how the nation's income, output and expenditure are determined.

THE CIRULAR FLOW OF INCOME

The economic problem discussed in Chapter 1 related to the satisfying of material wants. It is the production of goods and services that is designed to solve this problem; these in turn are provided by the factors of production. Two types of good were discussed, consumer and capital, the acquisition of capital goods providing the pointer to economic development. **Investment** is the macro economic term used to describe the process of creating capital so that national output consists of capital or investment goods as well as consumer goods. But what happens to the nation's output once it is produced? The simple answer is that it is purchased by individuals and firms and the prices of the goods and services are the sums of money paid by the purchasers. In other words one way of looking at the value of output is from the side of expenditure.

consumer + investment (capital) goods = national output

national output = national expenditure
(consumer spending + investment spending)

Just as output goes to individuals and firms when they spend money, so output can be seen in terms of the use firms make of the factors of production. The owners of capital receive **interest**, the owners of land receive **rent**, labour receives **wages** or salaries and the entrepreneurs who are the risk takers receive **profits**. In broad terms all of these receipts represent a form of income to the factor owners so that output can be translated into income by adding together all the factor payments (Fig. 13.1).

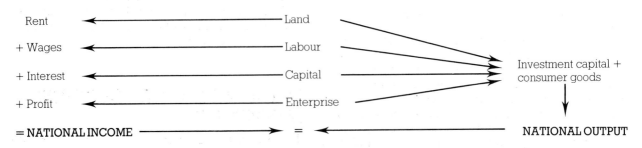

Fig. 13.1   How national income equals national output

Since national output also equals national expenditure, an equation can be formed linking income, output and expenditure.

$$\frac{\text{NATIONAL}}{\text{INCOME}} = \frac{\text{NATIONAL}}{\text{OUTPUT}} = \frac{\text{NATIONAL}}{\text{EXPENDITURE}}$$

This equation should really be seen as a flow of money circulating around the economy which is being measured at different points. The income received by the factor owners will be spent on the nation's output which the firms receive and then pay back to the factor owners.

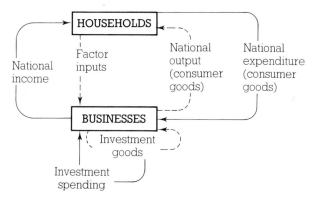

Fig. 13.2   The circular flow of income

Figure 13.2 summarises what is happening in the circular flow system. The 'households' or factor owners supply their services to the businesses where the nation's output is produced. This output is bought by the households mainly in the form of consumer goods. The capital or investment goods are in the main bought and paid for within the business sector. The households receive income from the firms via the various factor payments which can be used to buy business output.

This picture of the circular flow of income (sometimes called a **model**) is of course highly simplified. In particular the role of the government's taxing on spending has been omitted as well as the impact of international trade. The model does nevertheless show how national income can be looked at in terms of output and expenditure, each concept measuring the same money flow at different places. The circular flow diagram will achieve an equilibrium where

income = expenditure = output

but this equilibrium is constantly changing as business and household decisions never remain the same for very long. More importantly there is no guarantee that an equilibrium will occur at a position of full employment. For full employment to be achieved the amount of money in the circular flow has to be adjusted to produce sufficient income, output and expenditure to allow all units of labour to be used. At this point it may be appropriate to add the government sector to the model, since by taking out money with taxes and injecting

money via government spending, it can through fiscal policy adjust the circular flow mechanism. Figure 13.3 summarises the role of the government which might through a budget deficit create a net injection of money into the circular flow, creating a new equilibrium nearer to full employment.

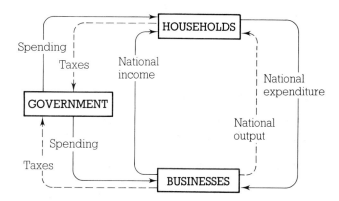

Fig. 13.3   The government's impact on the circular flow

NATIONAL INCOME STATISTICS

The circular flow of income allows the calculation of national income to be carried out in three different ways: by adding up all income received over a year; by adding up total expenditure over a year; and by adding up the value of the nation's output over a year. The three totals should come to the same amount and are often expressed in the form of the **gross domestic product** (GDP). In 1983 for the UK the GDP totalled £257.5 billion. This total can be converted to gross **national** product (GNP) by taking into account income earned and paid abroad. This 'Net property income from abroad' amounted to +£1.9 billion in 1983, making the GNP £259.4 bn. The GNP can be converted into **net national income** by taking into account the amount that capital or investment goods have depreciated in value over a year. This total should more accurately reflect the nation's true worth but unfortunately depreciation can only be roughly estimated since no one quite knows how long machines will last. In 1983 depreciation was estimated at 36.5bn making net national income £222.9bn. Because of the unreliability of depreciation estimates, national income is usually measured in terms of GDP or GNP.

USING NATIONAL INCOME STATISTICS

The process of collecting information to calculate national income is a complex one which is justified by the uses to which the figures can be put. Nevertheless there are certain limitations attached to the conclusions that can be drawn from the statistics which are also discussed below.

1 CALCULATING THE STANDARD OF LIVING OF A COUNTRY

If national income totals are compared over different years they can give an indication of how much better or worse off a country is becoming. The problem is that every year prices rise boosting the *money* totals for national income but without necessarily improving *living standards*. If, for example, money incomes go up by an average of 5% and prices go up by 10%, the nation is actually worse off. (This is discussed in more detail in Chapter 14.) What this means is that national income totals have to be adjusted for inflation. They are then known as *real* figures. Figure 13.4 shows changes in the *real* GDP from 1977 to 1983 in the UK. It indicates that living standards actually fell from 1979 to 1981.

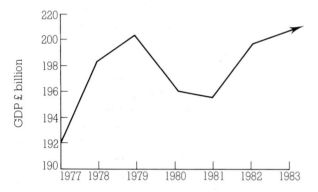

Fig. 13.4 (above)   Changes in real GDP 1977–83

There are other limitations to the conclusion that changes in the real GDP do mean changes in living standards. An increase in GDP may have been the result of longer working hours or a rising population. The totals also do not show how any increase in income is distributed. If the better off in the community are the main recipients of the increase then it is not true that the nation as a whole is experiencing an improvement in its standard of living.

2 COMPARING LIVING STANDARDS IN DIFFERENT COUNTRIES

If all countries prepare national income statistics then comparison figures can identify the richer and poorer nations of the world. The figures might also be used to compare growth rates of competitive countries as a means of evaluating economic performances. Since each country will have a different population size, GDP figures will have to be divided by population to give income per head totals. Thus the **standard of living** is measured as income/head and gives an indication of the well being of a nation in terms of the average amount each person earns and spends. Figure 13.5 shows real GDP/head figures for the major industrial nations from 1965 to 1984 and does reflect the relatively poor performance of the UK compared to its major competitors. In 1965 the UK ranked above France, Italy and Japan with a level of real GDP/head equivalent to 96% of that for West Germany and 68% of that for the USA. By 1977 both France and Japan had overtaken the UK and the

Fig. 13.5 (below)   Standard of living: real GDP per head – constant 1975 $ prices (purchasing power parity basis)

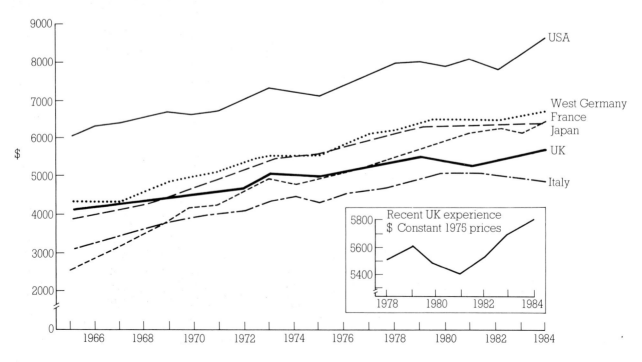

1981 figures show that the ratio of the UK to West Germany had fallen to about 80%, the ratio with the USA being about the same at 67%. The later figures shown on the inset chart up to 1984, however, showed that the UK was making a strong recovery.

Some problems which arise with comparisons of figures from other countries include converting currencies into a common denominator, which is not always easy when exchange rates fluctuate. In addition, working hours between countries vary and some countries have to spend more on necessities than others (e.g. the UK on heating compared to Greece).

3 ASSISTING THE GOVERNMENT PLAN THE ECONOMY

Because national income statistics provide a lot of detail regarding outputs of various industries and a breakdown of the different types of spending and income, they can be used by the government to plan the economy. Information is published annually in the National Income *Blue Book*. The statistics can be used to show which industries are in decline, the rate at which consumer spending is growing and so on, allowing the government to more easily take corrective action where appropriate.

THINGS TO DO

1 Distinguish between **micro** and **macro** economics.

2 Explain why
$$\frac{\text{national}}{\text{income}} = \frac{\text{national}}{\text{output}} = \frac{\text{national}}{\text{expenditure}}$$

3 Why is it unlikely that an equilibrium in the circular flow of national income occurs at a level of full employment? How can the government change the equilibrium if a large amount of unemployment exists?

4 Distinguish between **GDP**, **GNP** and **net national income**. Why are GDP figures preferred to those for net national income?

5 Using Fig. 13.6 answer the following questions.
   (a) How do growth rates for all countries in the 1970s compare with those for the 1960s? Explain possible reasons for the difference.
   (b) How do the UK growth rates compare with the others shown?

6 If UK money GDP figures showed £200bn in 1979 and £100bn in 1974, why is it probably *not* true that living standards doubled between the two years?

Fig. 13.6 Growth: average annual increase in real GDP – constant 1975 prices

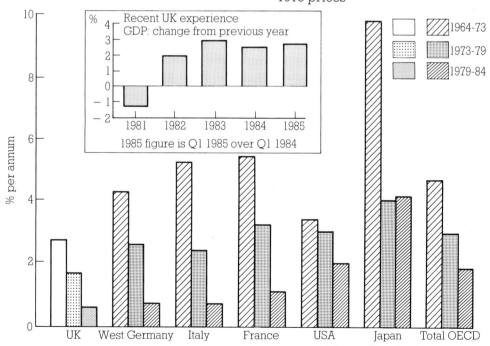

14

THE PROBLEMS OF INFLATION AND UNEMPLOYMENT

INTRODUCTION

In Chapter 12 it was made clear that if the economy is left to its own devices it will tend to become unstable, creating booms and slumps. These fluctuations in activity give rise to the term **trade cycle** (Fig. 14.1). The government does attempt to iron out the booms and slumps by regulating the Budget but it cannot hope to do this in a perfect way, particularly since world conditions outside its control can seriously affect the level of economic activity.

The problems of inflation and unemployment have always been associated with the trade cycle. **Inflation** can be defined as a sustained rise in the general level of prices. A rise in the price of one or two goods may not be sufficient to produce inflation if the prices of some other goods are falling, hence it is the *general* level of prices that is important. Again shortlived price rises are not usually regarded as inflationary, hence the use of the word *sustained*. Inflation tends to become a problem when the economy is booming – too much

spending taking place in relation to the supply of goods – but more recently rising prices have become a problem even when the economy has been stagnating (sometimes called **stagflation**).

High unemployment is traditionally associated with slumps in the trade cycle although even when the UK economy started growing in the early 1980s unemployment remained high and actually increased. It is important to recognise that unemployment caused by a downturn in economic activity is known as **cyclical**. There are other important causes of unemployment such as those caused by the immobility of labour.

Some economists have tried to show a link between inflation and unemployment because there is some evidence that when unemployment is high, inflation tends to be low and vice versa. This relationship, known as the **Phillips Curve** effect (after A W Phillips the economist who first showed the statistical link), poses serious difficulties for governments trying to solve the twin problems of inflation and unemployment at the same time (Fig. 14.2).

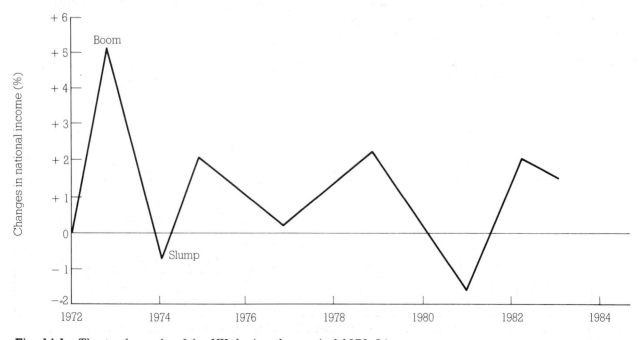

Fig. 14.1   The trade cycle of the UK during the period 1972–84

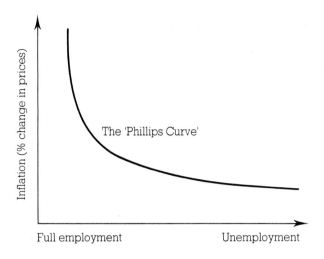

Fig. 14.2 The Phillips Curve

HYPER-INFLATION

If the general level of prices in a country is rising extremely quickly and by a great amount, severe or **hyper-inflation** can occur. In Germany between 1920 and 1923, inflation reached a staggering 24 000% before the currency totally collapsed (Fig. 14.3). It started fairly modestly with 36% in the first year, 63% in the second, then 3 300% in 1922. After that the country went currency mad. In 1923 during September alone, inflation reached an incredible 24 300%. In the end a new currency was introduced (at the end of 1923) with one new mark being worth 100 000 million old marks.

In Israel recently inflation has been over 1000% per annum and in supermarkets there, prices rise so fast that goods are no longer marked in shekels (Israel's currency) but in a code which is translated into the shekel rate of the day by a computer. Clearly hyper-inflation causes great instability in a country and Israelis rarely save money because its value falls so quickly.

Fig. 14.3b (above) Berlin: 1922 – a man being arrested for dealing in foreign money; black market trading in 'hard' currencies (£s, $s etc.) still happens today

Fig. 14.3a German banknotes from 1923; £1 equalled 5 million marks and six old pence equalled 100 000 marks

Fig. 14.3c Hyper-inflation in Germany in 1922 meant that the money wouldn't fit into the cash register and had to be stored in tea chests!

MEASURING INFLATION

Inflation is fairly straightforward to define but not so easy to measure. It is difficult to take account of the price changes affecting all goods in the economy and should price changes be measured at the wholesale or retail stage? Another problem arises because some goods are bought more frequently than others so that any price change in them has a greater impact on consumer spending. To cope with these difficulties, the following principles can be adopted to construct a measure of rising prices, known as a price index:

1 Select a 'basket' of those goods commonly bought by the 'average' family.

2 Measure the price of goods in retail outlets at a base or starting year.

3 Call the base year price index 100.

4 Attach 'weights' to goods in the basket to emphasise their relative importance which should correspond to frequency of purchase.

5 Multiply price and weight together for each good in the basket to find total expenditure.

6 Repeat the exercise for the current year and compare base and current year expenditures.

For a simple index three goods can be selected, for example, milk, butter and bread. The base year calculations might look as follows:

Item	Price	Weight (purchases/week)	Expenditure (£)
milk	20p/pint	14	2.80
butter	50p/250g	4	2.00
bread	35p/loaf	4	1.40
		TOTAL	6.20

For the next or current year, the situation might look as follows:

Item	Price	Weight	Expenditure (£)
milk	25p	14	3.50
butter	55p	4	2.20
bread	40p	4	1.60
		TOTAL	7.30

PRICES

Retail price inflation

Fig. 14.4a (above)   Retail price inflation 1983–85 (with projections). The highest figures were reached in the 1970s with a peak of 23% in 1975.   Fig. 14.4b (below)   Changes in spending patterns – weighting of main groups in RPI 1963 and 1983

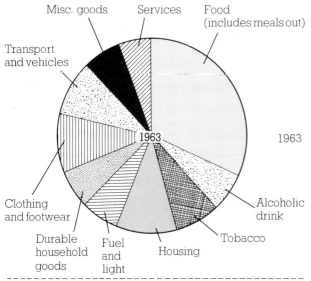

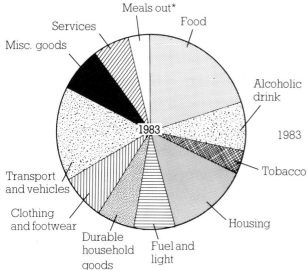

*Note: 'Meals bought and consumed outside the home' were not included as a separate group before 1968.

Comparing current and base years, prices have increased by:

$$\frac{£7.30}{£6.20}.$$

Since the base year index figure is represented by 100, the change in prices can be written as:

$$\frac{7.30}{6.20} \times 100 = 118 \text{ (to nearest whole number).}$$

Thus in this example prices rose 18% between the base and current year for the basket of goods chosen.

In the UK inflation is most commonly measured by the Index of Retail Prices which uses a basket of about 600 goods and services with about 130 000 separate price quote samples being taken. Currently the base year for the Index is 1974 and when it reached 200 in 1978 this showed that the general level of prices had doubled. The weightings are brought up to date each January and Fig. 14.4 shows how the weights have changed. The biggest changes since 1963 have been due to rising living standards, particularly the increase in private motoring expenditure during the 1960s.

THE CAUSES OF INFLATION

There are two principal causes of inflation: firstly when too much spending takes place in relation to the number of goods produced (known as **demand pull**); and secondly when the costs of production increase affecting the selling price of goods (known as **cost push**).

DEMAND PULL

Demand pull inflation is traditionally associated with conditions of full employment and corresponds to the 'boom' in the trade cycle. At this point if consumers spend more money on goods and services with producers being unable to expand supply because there is little spare labour, then inevitably the supply of goods will become scarce in relation to demand and prices will rise. Demand in this sense differs from the notion of 'market' demand because it refers to the spending patterns of the nation as a whole. For this reason it is commonly called **aggregate** demand. Aggregate demand will rise as the nation's income increases (Fig. 14.5 overleaf).

Similarly the total supply of goods and services in the economy is known as **aggregate** supply and it will also tend to increase as national income rises. However, as full employment approaches, aggregate supply will become very inelastic to reflect the scarcity of labour. Any increase in spending where supply is perfectly inelastic will not produce any extra output, only higher prices. Thus in Fig. 14.5 if aggregate demand moves from

185

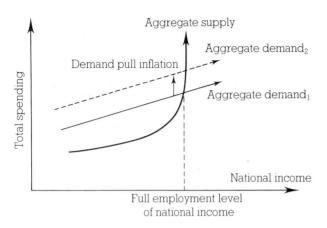

Fig. 14.5 Demand pull inflation

position 1 to 2 to reflect a change in spending habits, no extra goods can be produced so only inflation results, with no increase in output.

The **monetarist** explanation of inflation is essentially the same as the above approach. It emphasises that too much money leads to excess spending which, when the economy is approaching full capacity, results in higher prices. Monetarists would also argue that inflation can still happen below the full employment level of national income because aggregate supply can become 'sticky' even with reserves of labour in the economy. This may be because certain skills are in short supply or employers may be pessimistic about future prospects. In this case more money in the economy could lead to inflation even at quite high levels of unemployment.

Demand pull inflation therefore does not require full employment to be present in order to cause inflationary pressures. If aggregate supply becomes inelastic at any stage for whatever reason then extra spending will cause prices to rise (Fig. 14.7).

THINGS TO DO

1 Inflation means 'rising prices'. Why is this definition inadequate?

2 What is **hyper-inflation**? Why can it seriously disadvantage savers?

3 Figure 14.6 shows the major changes in prices for the main groups of goods and services between July 1963 and July 1983 in *relative* terms. What are the chief implications of these changes for the consumer?

4 Using the following data, calculate the % change in the rate of inflation from the base year to the current year.

Item	Base year price	Current year price	Weight
petrol	180p	200p	4
wine	200p	180p	2
cigarettes	100p	120p	3

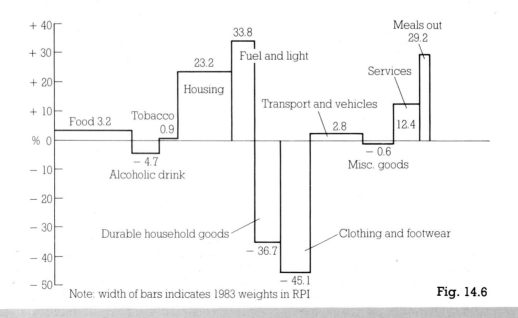

Note: width of bars indicates 1983 weights in RPI

Fig. 14.6

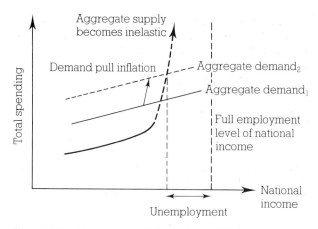

Fig. 14.7 Demand pull inflation with unemployment

Fig. 14.8 The relationship between money and inflation

Figure 14.8 shows the relationship of the money supply to inflation from 1966 to 1980 and at first sight there does not appear to be a strong link. If, however, there is the assumption that changes in the supply of money take about two years to affect inflation, then a fairly close link can be observed. This suggests that demand pull inflation created by an expansion in the money supply, has played a significant part in causing UK inflation which reached over 25% in 1975.

COST PUSH

Industry's costs principally comprise labour and raw materials. If either or both costs increase then they will tend to push up the price of the product, causing inflation. Many raw materials used in manufacturing are imported from abroad and there is little that can be done to prevent foreigners from charging more for what may be an increasingly scarce commodity.

When looking at the impact labour costs have on inflation, it is useful to distinguish between money wages and real wages. **Money wages** represent what people actually earn; **real wages** show the purchasing power of money wages. For example, if money wages go up by 5% from £100 per week

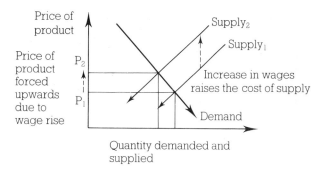

Fig. 14.9 Cost push inflation in a particular product market

to £105 and inflation goes up by 10%, real wages will have fallen because of the reduced purchasing power of the new money wage. Where real wages are rising the inflationary pressures will be greatest since money wages will be increasing faster than the rate of inflation thereby tending to force the future rate upwards. Figure 14.9 shows for an individual product market how this might happen.

Figure 14.10 shows how more recently average earnings have consistently outstripped inflation which can create cost push pressures if the extra earnings are not matched by corresponding increases in productivity.

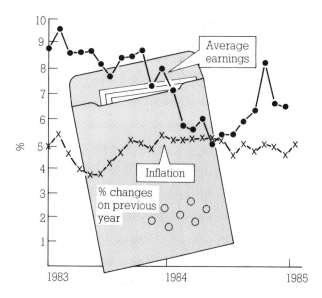

Fig. 14.10 Cost push inflation – wages and average earnings during 1983, 1984 and 1985

Not all real wage increases are inflationary. More overtime may have been worked or productivity may have increased. Figure 14.11 (overleaf) shows when wage push pressures were probably greatest: between 1970 and 1975 real wages rose by 23%, far more than in any other period in recent economic history.

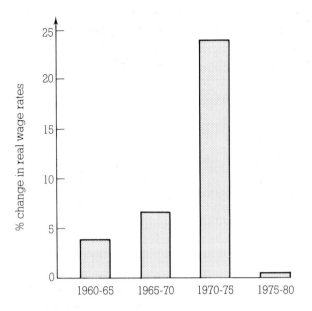

Fig. 14.11 Wage push inflationary pressures

The causes of inflation have created great debate amongst economists. The monetarists, led by Professor Milton Friedman at Chicago University, have always maintained that too much money in the economy has been the dominant cause of inflation. On the other hand Keynsian economists (supporting the teachings of John Maynard Keynes) believe that in many cases more money can lead to extra output and jobs without inflation necessarily occurring and that any inflationary tendencies are caused by cost push pressures. It is probable that in practice both demand pull and cost push factors contribute to the overall level of inflation.

WHY DO WE NEED TO WORRY ABOUT INFLATION?

Keeping down the rate of inflation has been a major objective of all governments in post-war Britain but just why is there so much concern over inflation?

Firstly, and perhaps most importantly for Britain, inflation tends to increase the price of our exports making them less attractive for foreigners to buy. Because imports may become cheaper relative to home-produced goods, people in Britain will tend to buy more of them, creating a trade gap. Britain depends on international trade for survival (half the food we eat is imported) and in broad terms we can only pay for our imports by exporting to the same value. Inflation seriously threatens this equation. In addition, if exports do not sell and British people prefer foreign to home-produced goods, unemployment in the UK is bound to rise.

Inflation also penalises savers and people on fixed incomes. If, for example, the rate of interest is 5% and the rate of inflation is 10% the 'real' value of savings will fall. Similarly with a 10% inflation rate, people on fixed incomes such as pensioners and the unemployed will see the 'real' value of their money fall unless the government increases the benefits to cover the rate of inflation.

For working people, high rates of inflation can create unfairness in wage settlements. Strong unions may be able to secure increases in real wages whilst the weaker and usually the lowest paid may see their living standards fall. High inflation also tends to produce greater trade union 'militancy'. Industrial disputes occur more frequently as unions try to protect themselves against not just present inflation but expected future inflation as well.

Inflation does, however, benefit some sections of the community, particularly borrowers. If money is borrowed over 25 years to buy a house, the money cost of the repayments will vary only with the small changes in interest rates. Because inflation leads to a fall in the value of money, though, the real cost of the repayments will become smaller. Thus if a person's salary keeps up with inflation and their mortgage repayments stay relatively constant, the real burden of the mortgage will quickly fall over time. Similarly for the government, the real burden of repaying the National Debt, created through successive budget deficits, will tend to fall with high inflation.

Overall some mild inflation may be appropriate in an economy and marginally helpful to firms in reducing the real cost of their borrowing. However, levels of more than 5% per annum can be potentially harmful, not least because any further upward movement often becomes cumulative.

CONTROLLING INFLATION

The control of inflation depends on identifying the appropriate cause – demand pull or cost push – since different solutions are applied in each case.

Demand pull inflation occurs through an excess of spending in relation to aggregate supply so a reduction in the level of spending is required. Reducing the level of spending **deflates** the economy. There are two broad methods of reducing aggregate demand: monetary policy and fiscal policy.

Monetary policy concentrates on reducing the amount of money in the economy. Since the bulk of the money supply comprises cheques created by the banking system, the major policy weapons concentrate on limiting the banks' ability to create new deposits. One way of doing this is to raise interest rates. As Fig. 14.12 shows, when people borrow money their demand diminishes if interest

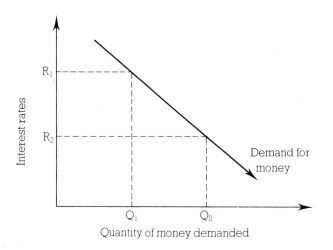

Fig. 14.12

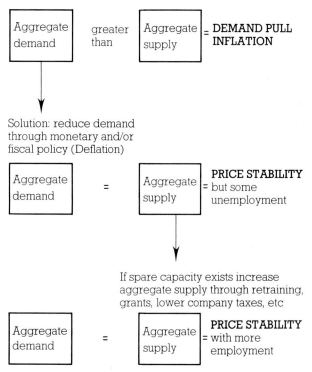

Fig. 14.13   Controlling demand pull inflation

rates go up. If the Bank of England through its intervention rate can raise interest rates from R_2 to R_1 then the quantity of money demanded will contract from Q_2 to Q_1. This is because the intervention rate influences bank base lending rates which rise and fall in line with changes in it. Since the banks need a cash base to lend out money, the Bank of England can also limit their ability to lend by taking away some of this base. It does so by calling for **special deposits** which are obtained from the cash reserves of the clearing banks kept at the Bank of England. People can also be discouraged from spending if the government puts restrictions on hire purchase methods of payments for goods. The minimum deposit required could be raised and the length of time given to pay back the instalments shortened. (Monetary policy is discussed in more detail in Chapter 16.)

Fiscal policy related to inflation is designed to reduce both the government's own spending and private sector spending by raising taxes. Reducing public sector spending is not politically popular since many socially desirable programmes may suffer, such as reducing hospital waiting lists or increasing the housing stocks to reduce the number of homeless families. However, raising taxes may be equally unpopular and the government will have to strike a compromise between the two. Reducing private sector spending may take the form of increasing income tax rates and/or raising VAT and excise duties. Unfortunately, although raising the latter two may reduce spending, inflation will also be affected because inevitably shop prices will rise.

Weighing up the relative merits of monetary and fiscal policy, the evidence suggests that reducing the money supply is difficult to achieve with any precision because, for example, it is difficult to predict how responsive people will be to a change in interest rates. Also there is a time lag of 18 months to 2 years between the introduction of monetary policy and its final impact on the economy. Fiscal policy, on the other hand, is much more instant in its effects since raising taxes will immediately have an impact on spending, but suffers from being rather inflexible since altering taxes creates considerable administrative costs. Thus the annual Budget in April provides the main opportunity for reform with just the possibility of some revision in November.

If demand pull inflation occurs with some unemployment in the economy an alternative to fiscal and monetary policy may be to try and **increase aggregate supply** (Fig. 14.13). This could be done by better retraining facilities, creating more grants and loans for new industries, reducing corporation tax and so on. In this way, if extra spending is matched by greater output rather than rising prices, inflation is avoided. Whilst increasing aggregate supply is obviously preferable to reducing aggregate demand, it is not always easy to encourage firms to expand or new firms to start if they are not wholly optimistic about the future of the economy.

Cost push inflation, where it is caused by high wage settlements, can be controlled by means of **incomes policies**. Such policies have been operated in the past by governments who have tried to limit the general rise in wages by suggesting or imposing 'pay norms'. This might mean an upper limit of perhaps 5% for settlements per annum or a flat rate rise of perhaps £10 a week which would benefit low-paid workers. Incomes policies, however, need to operate by the consent of working people and they have not been wholly successful in the past because unions did not want

THINGS TO DO

1 Explain the meaning of **demand pull** inflation. Why can it occur even with some unemployment in the economy?

2 Explain the difference between **real** and **money** wages.

3 Under what circumstances will an increase in wages *not* lead to cost push inflation?

4 In periods of high inflation why is it often better to be a debtor rather than a lender?

5 In what way does the government benefit from inflation?

6 What is the most important reason for preventing high inflation in the case of Britain?

7 Distinguish between monetary and fiscal policy as methods of controlling inflation.

8 What is a **prices and incomes policy**? What problems exist when trying to introduce such a policy?

9 Why is **indexation** a 'pain killer' for inflation rather than a cure?

10 Using Fig. 14.14:
   (a) comment on the UK's inflation rate relative to our six major competitors between 1980 and 1983;
   (b) suggest reasons for all inflation rates rising during 1979.

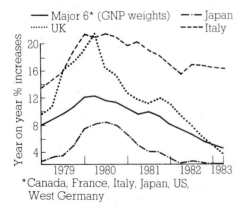

*Canada, France, Italy, Japan, US, West Germany

Fig. 14.14 Consumer price inflation – UK and 6 major overseas economies

to see their bargaining rights removed. Unions are also likely to be unwilling to limit pay rises unless the government make a commitment to similarly restrict price increases: hence the term **prices and incomes policy**. This is not always easy if price rises come from imported goods: governments have little or no control over such movements.

One alternative to an incomes policy is a system of indexing wages and other money variables. This would mean that pay rises could be linked to the existing rate of inflation to ensure 'real' wages did not fall. Indexation has been used in countries which suffer hyper-inflation but it will not on its own cure inflation, merely help to prevent it becoming worse.

THE BACKGROUND TO THE UNEMPLOYMENT PROBLEM

Mass unemployment in Britain is a relatively recent phenomenon as Fig. 14.15 shows. It is only after 1979 that the jobless total began to climb steeply. Prior to that and going back as far as World War 2 unemployment was not a major problem. In fact from 1951 to 1975 male unemployment averaged under 2% of the labour force. Since the 1944 Employment White Paper governments have been committed to try and achieve the target of full employment. Politicians of all parties believed that the theories of John Maynard Keynes had provided the means by which future governments could avoid the kind of economic depression and mass unemployment that had characterised much of the inter-war period. They thought that through changes in the level of public spending or taxation, known as **demand management**, governments could smooth out fluctuations in the trade cycle and control the economy enough to achieve something close to 'full employment'.

In the 20 years after World War 2, the goal of full employment was largely attained. Post-war reconstruction, the release of pent-up demand for consumer durables such as cars and washing machines, and a gradual easing of restrictions on free trade, all helped to make the application of demand management policies easier. The sharp rise in unemployment after 1979 was probably due to a number of factors. A 17% minimum lending rate, a $2.40 pound, dearer energy, pay settlements above 20%, a world recession and the abandonment of the 1944 White Paper commitment to full employment all contributed. In addition, the control of inflation became paramount and to the extent that the 'Phillips Curve' holds true, unemployment could be seen as a way of containing inflationary pay settlements. Keynesian policies were abandoned because they were seen to be creating a large Public Sector Borrowing Requirement which in turn led to high interest rates in

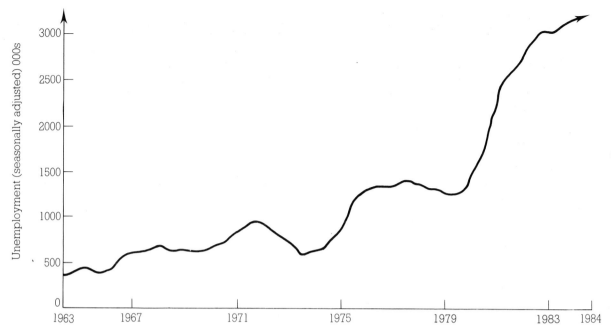

Fig. 14.15 UK unemployment during the years 1963–1984, showing the sharp increase from 1980 onwards

MEASURING UNEMPLOYMENT

In the UK statistics about unemployment are provided in *The Department of Employment Gazette*, published monthly. It is probable that these statistics understate the true extent of unemployment because there will be some people out of work and who would take a suitable job if one became available but who do not place themselves on the unemployment register. A good example of this type of person would be a married woman who does not qualify for unemployment benefit and who may lose her job but does not register as unemployed. The official statistics give information on the numbers unemployed in the different regions, different industries and different occupations. Details are also provided on the duration of unemployment – the length of time various numbers of people have been out of work. *The Department of Employment Gazette* also contains tables showing the numbers employed in the different age groups. This helps to identify where the unemployment problem is most serious: whether, for example, older people experience more difficulty than younger people in finding jobs when they are made redundant. Figure 14.16, shows an increasing proportion of young and middle-aged people joining the longterm unemployed.

order to persuade people to lend to the government. In addition the extra government spending was felt to create demand pull inflationary pressures. It is likely that high levels of unemployment will be an economic feature of the UK for some time to come.

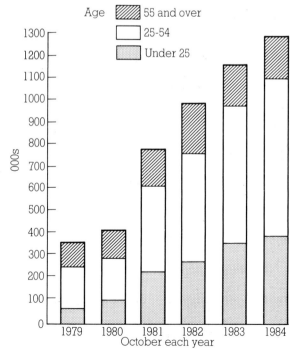

Note: 1983 Budget measures took 125 000 longterm unemployed men of 60 and over out of the official count.

Fig. 14.16 Longterm unemployment – number out of work for a year or more

TYPES OF UNEMPLOYMENT

In order to understand the problems of unemployment it is important to recognise that there are different types of unemployment, each caused by different factors. Policies to deal with unemployment must take account of the fact that there are several types of unemployment, each requiring different solutions.

CYCLICAL UNEMPLOYMENT

Cyclical unemployment is associated with the slump of the trade cycle and is caused by a deficiency in aggregate demand. Because this deficiency extends across all industries in the economy, the unemployment created tends to be widespread involving large numbers of people across the whole country. A world recession could contribute significantly to cyclical unemployment and often its effects are felt most severely in manufacturing industry. The solution to cyclical unemployment lies in **reflating** the economy by fiscal and monetary policies, designed to expand aggregate demand. Thus interest rates may be encouraged to fall, government spending could be increased and taxes allowed to fall. Whilst this seems straightforward enough in reality such policies can create difficulties because reflation may quickly lead to inflation. If, for example, an expansion in the money supply leads to higher wages rather than more jobs then prices will rise (cost push inflation) without a reduction in unemployment. Equally if aggregate supply is sticky, any extra spending may not lead to new jobs and more output, but demand pull inflation. Reflation, therefore, has to be planned carefully and cautiously.

STRUCTURAL UNEMPLOYMENT

Structural unemployment arises when workers have outdated skills no longer required by industry. Structural unemployment is most commonly found in the traditional industries of the UK such as shipbuilding steel and textiles, where demand for the industry's product has fallen dramatically today compared with 30 years ago. This decline has arisen partly because other less developed countries have industrialised and are able to compete more effectively than the UK in world markets with lower labour costs. In addition new technology has meant the replacement of labour with sophisticated capital in many industries, making them more efficient but creating huge job losses. Figure 14.17 shows the net reduction in employees at the British Steel Corporation from 1977 to 1983 and emphasises the large scale redundancies in 1980/81 when nearly 50 000 steel workers lost their jobs. Although some job losses were due to cyclical factors, many reflected the move by BSC towards larger plants and more capital intensive production with the consequent closure of the small inefficient plants.

Many people structurally unemployed are highly skilled and have developed these skills over a large number of years. The only real solution to structural unemployment is to retrain workers in the skills appropriate to the economy at present.

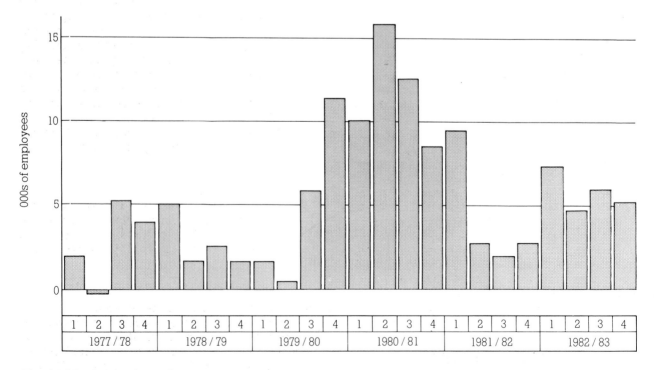

Fig. 14.17 British Steel Corporation – net reduction of employees, by quarter, showing the large number of redundancies in 1980/81

192

This is an expensive process and often difficult too, for some unemployed tend to be resistant to change after a prolonged period using their original skills. Certainly today there is a need for more occupational mobility to cope with the fast changing pattern of demand and improvements in technology.

FRICTIONAL UNEMPLOYMENT

Frictional unemployment is largely connected with geographical and occupational immobility. It is reflected in the unfilled vacancies which are notified to the employment offices (Fig. 14.18). If frictional unemployment did not exist then the majority of vacancies would be filled. However, people may prefer to remain unemployed in the North where their social ties are strong rather than move south where although their skill may be in demand, housing costs will be higher and the adjustment to living in a new area may be difficult. Frictional unemployment can also arise because people may not know vacancies exist in other parts of the country since many jobs are only advertised locally. In addition the process of moving from one job to another including occupational adjustment can take time causing 'frictions' in the working of the labour market.

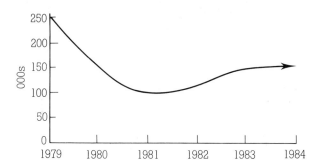

Fig. 14.18 Vacancies notified to the employment offices (000s)

The cure for frictional unemployment probably lies in providing better information about job opportunities in different parts of the country. A scheme to subsidise removal costs could help to improve mobility, as could a contribution towards the cost of board and lodgings for unemployed people looking for work in a new area. Such schemes have been tried by governments in the past but without great success, since for reasons already discussed in Chapter 3, people tend to be both geographically and occupationally immobile.

SEASONAL UNEMPLOYMENT

Some industries have a seasonal pattern of demand for labour which creates variations in employment patterns at certain times of the year. Tourism is a good example of an industry which provides a good deal of employment in the summer months but contracts drastically in the winter. Similarly construction activity tends to fall in the winter months with cold weather and shorter daylight hours. In agriculture, employment demands peak at harvest time in August/September and tail off in the winter months.

GOVERNMENT EMPLOYMENT INITIATIVES

1 The Youth Training Scheme
YTS was started in September 1983 offering work experience for one year to over 400 000 school leavers. It is run by the Manpower Services Commission and is largely employer-based (on the job training) but about 25% of the year is spent on off the job training, usually at a local college. A basic grant is paid to trainees whom, it is hoped, after or during their YTS training, will be better equipped to seek permanent full-time employment. In 1986 YTS was expanded to provide two years of training, adding about 200 000 more trainees to the scheme which cost about £900m to run in 1986.

2 The Temporary Employment Subsidy
Between 1975 and 1979 a subsidy of £20 per week was paid to an employer when without the subsidy they would otherwise have made the employees redundant. It was so successful at exporting unemployment in textiles, clothing and footwear to the EC that the government was forced to withdraw it. Interestingly the Department of Employment calculated that the net cost to the government was zero because fewer unemployment benefits had to be paid out and more tax revenue was collected which together exceeded the subsidy payments made to firms.

3 Job Release Scheme
This scheme pays men aged 62 or over and women aged 59 a tax-free allowance if they retire early, providing their employer agrees to replace him or her from the unemployment register.

4 The Enterprise Allowance Scheme
This government scheme is for anyone who is 18 or over and has been claiming either unemployment benefit or supplementary benefit for 13 weeks or more (Fig. 14.19). It offers £40 per week for up to one year to people who wish to become self employed (Fig. 14.20). No check on

On the one hand you haven't got a job.

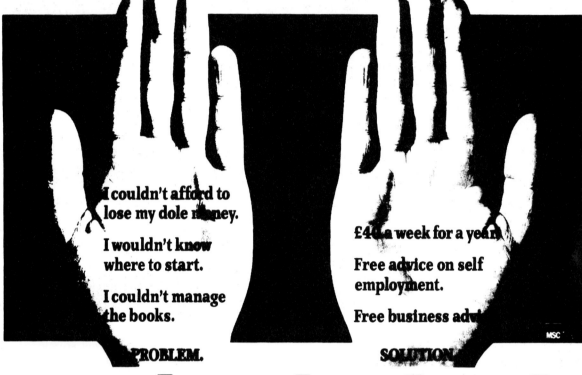

I couldn't afford to lose my dole money.

I wouldn't know where to start.

I couldn't manage the books.

PROBLEM.

£40 a week for a year.

Free advice on self employment.

Free business advice.

MSC

SOLUTION.

On the other hand you could have.

The Enterprise Allowance Scheme is about working for yourself.

What do you get out of it?

- £40 a week for a year. (Plus your earnings.)
- Free advice on starting and running a business.
- Free advice on paperwork and book-keeping.
- Free financial advice.

What do you put into it?

- You must be at least 18 and below state pension age.
- You need to have been out of work for at least 8 weeks.

- You need to be receiving either unemployment or supplementary benefit when you apply.
- You need to be able to put up £1,000. This could be a loan.

Visit your Jobcentre for further details of the scheme. Now you know they've definitely got a job for you.

YOU'VE GOT THE
WE'VE GOT THE
THE ENTERPRISE ALLOWANCE SCHEME

Fig. 14.19 An advertisement for the Enterprise Allowance Scheme – one of the government's measures to combat unemployment

Fig. 14.20 For some the answer to unemployment may be self-employment, perhaps with the help of the Enterprise Allowance Scheme. Craft or small workshop-type businesses frequently start-up in a garage attached to the proprietor's home. Alternatively with a telephone, an answering machine and a home-computer, the spare bedroom or dining room is turned into an office. However, the failure rate of small businesses is high, and in a difficult economic climate very few grow large enough to start employing other people

viability is made but applicants have to be able to put up £1000 towards the capital required. The £1000 does not have to be cash and can be a loan from other sources. The scheme includes practical help and advice from the Small Firms Service, part of the Department of Employment. People who take part in this scheme to set up their own business are not prevented from claiming benefit again if the venture is not successful.

SUMMARY

It is clear that there are a variety of causes contributing to unemployment in Britain but the largest component undoubtedly comprises cyclical unemployment. Tax cuts and extra government spending do provide methods of reducing this type of unemployment but there is no certainty that expanding demand will automatically create a large number of new jobs. Ensuring that extra demand will not just lead to inflation and little extra output implies some form of incomes policy, something that trade unions are very reluctant to accept.

THINGS TO DO

1 How is unemployment measured? Why might official statistics underestimate the true level of unemployment?

2 Under what circumstances can reflating the economy lead to inflation?

3 Distinguish between **structural** and **frictional** unemployment. Why would reflating the economy not by itself cure these two types of unemployment?

4 In Fig. 14.21, which relates to productivity and employment in the British Steel Corporation from 1977 to 1984:
   (a) explain the relationship between productivity and the number of employees;
   (b) suggest the reasons for this relationship;
   (c) what does this relationship imply for other companies wishing to increase efficiency?

5 Evaluate the various government initiatives designed to reduce unemployment. What more could be done to solve the problem?

Fig. 14.21 British Steel Corporation – employees and productivity, 1977/78 to 1983/84

15

WHY WE TRADE WITH OTHER COUNTRIES

INTRODUCTION

Just as in Chapter 3 it was seen that the division of labour helped to increase production through human specialisation so this principle can be extended to whole countries. Each country in the world has differing quantities and qualities of factors of production leading to the production of a wide variety of goods and services when they are combined. Climatically, for example, Spain is very different from Britain so that agricultural products such as grapes are much easier to grow there than here and conversely apples grow rather better in Britain than in Spain. What makes sense is for each country to specialise in what it is best at producing and then exchange goods with countries producing a different range of products. In any case for Britain to try and become self-sufficient in all products would be very difficult since at the moment only about half the food we eat is produced at home. It would be almost impossible to reorganise our factors of production to produce double the quantity of food because for a start land is fixed in quantity.

In this chapter the advantages of international trade will be examined in some detail together with a look at some of the reasons why countries might seek to restrict trade. International trade is more complicated than internal trade because different currencies are used by different countries. Thus keeping account of the payments to and receipts from foreigners is important, as well as an understanding of how exchange rates work. Later in the chapter these concepts will be discussed, together with a look at some of the main organisations connected with international trade, in particular the EC.

THE ADVANTAGES OF INTERNATIONAL TRADE

Because each country has different quantities and qualities of factors of production their optimum combination will result in a different pattern of goods and services (Fig. 15.1). The UK has its strengths in capital, skilled labour and enterprise with a rather limited quantity of land. It makes sense for the UK to broadly specialise in manufactured goods. New Zealand, on the other hand, has large amounts of fertile land, a smaller quantity of labour and more limited capital. It therefore makes sense for New Zealand to specialise in agricultural goods such as lamb and butter.

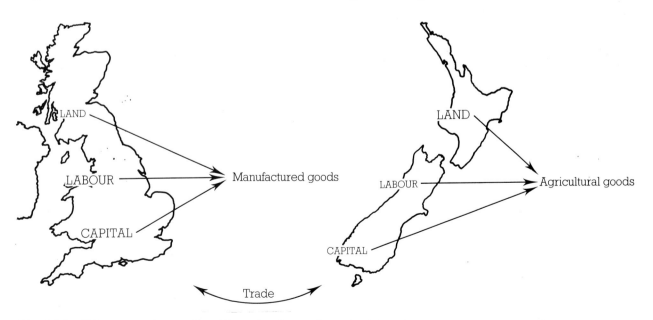

Fig. 15.1 Why countries trade with each other – the principle of comparative advantage

The advantages of specialisation by countries are similar to those gained from the division of labour but with the addition of economies of scale helping to reduce the cost of each product or service. By exchanging goods more wants can be satisfied at a lower cost and thus international trade is an important component in solving the economic problem.

The advantages of specialisation can be easily quantified in a similar way to the division of labour. If the UK and New Zealand each divide their factors in half and produce both cars and butter the hypothetical daily output might be as follows:

	Cars	Butter (tonnes)
UK	500	300
New Zealand	200	600
TOTAL	700	900

It is clear that if each country specialises in what it is best at, using all factors to make one product, a greater total of goods can be produced as shown:

	Cars	Butter (tonnes)
UK	1000	—
New Zealand	—	1200
TOTAL	1000	1200

If the exchange rate is such that 100 cars exchange for 130 tonnes of butter then the UK might swop 400 cars for 520 tons of butter leaving the final position as follows:

	Cars	Butter (tonnes)
UK	600	520
New Zealand	400	680
TOTAL	1000	1200

The exchange rate in this case is negotiable; a wide range of possibilities exist which still allow both countries to be better off. The limits to trade are connected with the concept of opportunity cost. The UK has to give up 500 cars to produce 300 tonnes of butter. Clearly the UK will want at least 3 tonnes of butter for every 5 cars. Similarly New Zealand will want at least 2 cars for 6 tonnes of butter. The opportunity cost ratio of cars to butter for the UK is 5/3 and for New Zealand 2/6 or 1/3. Providing the actual exchange ratio is between these extremes, both countries can benefit from trade. It is in fact 10/13 which is acceptable to both countries.

Whilst the benefits of trade are fairly obvious in the above example, it is not so clear how trade might benefit the UK if in the above example it had an absolute advantage over New Zealand in both cars and butter.

Suppose the following situation existed before specialisation:

	Cars	Butter (tonnes)
UK	600	400
New Zealand	100	350
TOTAL	700	750

It may not be obvious that the UK could benefit from trade with New Zealand. If, however, the UK specialises in the good for which it has the greater **comparative** advantage then both countries can gain from trade. Supposing three-quarters of the factors in the UK are used to make cars and one quarter for butter. New Zealand specialises in butter. The following production would result:

	Cars	Butter (tonnes)
UK	900	200
New Zealand	—	700
TOTAL	900	900

If the exchange rate of 100 cars for 130 tonnes of butter remains the same then the UK may swop 200 cars for 260 tonnes of butter leaving the final trading position as shown:

	Cars	Butter (tonnes)
UK	700	460
New Zealand	200	440
TOTAL	900	900

This principle, sometimes called the **law of comparative advantage** shows above that even when the UK has an *absolute* advantage in the production of both cars and butter, trade can still benefit both the UK and New Zealand if the UK specialises in the good where the *greater* comparative advantage exists. The example above is very similar to the division of labour principle where human specialisation can still result in more output even where one person has an absolute advantage over another in several tasks. The principle of comparative advantage is very important because it provides a strong justification for trade between developed and less developed countries, so that trade with the LDCs should not be seen as simply a form of charity relief.

Of course the example above is very much over-simplified. A complicated network of countries and products exists, and shifting factors from one use to another in order to specialise is not easy. Labour is fairly immobile and changing the use of land may be difficult. Transport costs also have to be taken into consideration when assessing the benefits of trade but all these limitations do not negate the fundamental principle that trade *can* (but not always will) lead to higher living standards.

International trade also has the advantage of promoting more competition between firms; a monopoly in one country will have more limited market power if foreign firms are able to penetrate the home market with a substitute product. International trade also widens consumer choice since a much greater variety of goods will be on sale in shops than would otherwise be the case. Finally, economies of scale will allow the greater use of machinery, the application of the division of labour and a more comprehensive marketing strategy for companies. Although not an economic argument, international trade does help to bring closer ties between countries which, in the case of the EC, has resulted in common political institutions.

BARRIERS TO TRADE

Trade can be restricted in several ways.

1 Tariffs or import duties

By imposing a tax on foreign goods, demand for them will contract (providing demand is not totally inelastic) and the government will in addition earn extra revenue. Whilst this measure is effective in restricting the importation of foreign goods, it has the disadvantage that other countries retaliate by placing similar restrictions on their own imported goods.

2 Quotas

A **quota** is a restriction on the quantity of a foreign good coming into the country. Quotas are often used in addition to tariffs as a means of further reducing the volume of particular imports. In Britain quotas are used on Japanese cars to limit their penetration into the UK market.

3 Subsidies

Rather than tax foreign goods coming into the UK, the government might lower the price of home goods through a **subsidy**, to allow them to compete more effectively. This would benefit the consumer, since lower prices in the shops would result, although the subsidy itself would have to come from taxation. In the past certain food products have been subsidised (such as butter and meats) and certain nationalised industries (such as steel) have been allowed to

produce at a loss to avoid foreign imports creating excessive redundancies at home.

4 Non-tariff barriers

This is a rather broad term covering a variety of initiatives designed to frustrate the importation of foreign goods. In some cases the home country applies rigorous quality standards to imports (e.g. the USA on exhaust emissions from cars); in other cases the documentation required for entry may be prohibitive or customs control slow and bureaucratic. The French, for example, anxious to control the importation of Japanese video recorders, set up a small customs office in a remote part of the country to deal with *all* shipments, causing long delays!

5 Embargo

This represents a total ban on foreign imports and might apply to dangerous products such as drugs or explosives. Equally an embargo may be put on goods coming from a politically hostile country as a means of applying sanctions against it.

It might seem strange that countries want to restrict trade when the principle of comparative advantage suggests living standards can be raised through free trade. Nevertheless there are some good reasons why it may be appropriate to have some form of protection for home industries.

1 Infant industries

New industries with high start-up costs may need protection from foreign competition until they become established. Judging when that moment is can be difficult for a government and the protected industry will prefer to stay sheltered from competition for as long as possible.

2 Unemployment

Where foreign competition is particularly severe from, for example, low wage countries in the Far East, UK industries may suffer a declining market, forcing redundancies. If the industry is a key one for the economy (like steel), it may be appropriate to take some form of action to protect the home industry.

3 Dumping

Dumping arises when foreign firms with excess capacity send products to other countries at uncompetitive prices which the home industry cannot match. They often retail at cost or below cost price. How does 'dumping' arise? Consider the following example:

A Far Eastern radio manufacturer is making 10 000 radios a year selling in the home country for the equivalent of £20 each and costing £15 to make, total profit being £50 000. The manufacturer calculates that if capacity is doubled to 20 000 radios, the economies of scale will be such that the cost of making each radio will fall to £12. If demand is fairly inelastic in the home market the manufacturer may decide to keep the selling price at £20 and will sell 10 000 radios for a total profit of £80 000. There are still 10 000 radios unsold however and these could be 'dumped' in the UK for as little as £12 each without affecting overall profit. Such 'dumping' is unfair for UK radio producers and the government should rightly take measures to outlaw this kind of unfair trade.

4 To correct a trade deficit

Put in simple terms, if a country imports goods or services, it has to export goods and services to pay for them. If imports exceed exports then the country is in deficit to foreigners and unless there are large resources of foreign currency, either exports have to be increased or imports curtailed. Trade barriers provide a means of restricting imports. They are not a satisfactory weapon because retaliation may take place and if the deficit persists the underlying causes have to be traced. As a temporary measure barriers may be appropriate.

THE TERMS OF TRADE

The **terms of trade** compare the prices of a country's exports and imports over time. They can be expressed as follows in index form:

$$\frac{\text{average price of exports}}{\text{average price of imports}} \times 100$$

The terms of trade are useful to measure because changes in them can affect our trading position. The terms of trade are said to 'improve' when the index rises and 'worsen' when the index falls. Whether an improvement/worsening is good/bad for our trading position depends entirely on the price elasticity of demand for exports and imports as the next example shows.

Imagine the terms of trade worsen due to a fall in UK export prices relative to import prices (see Fig. 15.2).

If Fig. 15.2 represents the possible demand elasticities for exports, then a fall in export prices from Pe to Py will cause a large extension in demand from Qe to Qy_2 in the case of an elastic demand (D_2) but only a small extension (Qe to Qy_1) in the case of an inelastic demand (D_1). Where demand is price elastic the worsening of the terms of trade will result in an increase in total revenue for exports. This can be seen by comparing total revenue after the price reduction (Py C Qy_2 O) with the original total revenue (Pe A Qe O). If demand is price inelastic the opposite happens: total revenue falls from (Pe A Qe O) to (Py B Qy_1 O). Thus a worsening of the terms of trade can make a country's trading position better when demand is

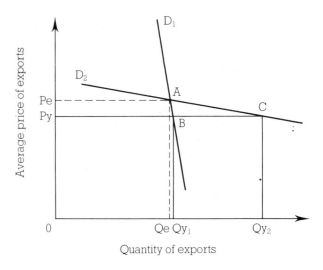

Fig. 15.2 Changes in the terms of trade

price elastic but make it worse when demand is price inelastic. The example relates to exports but the argument also holds true for imports. If their average price rises in relation to exports, the terms of trade *worsen*. If demand for imports is price elastic then it will contract significantly, improving a country's trading position. If demand for imports is price inelastic consumers will continue buying them at the higher price, worsening the trading position.

In practice, for the UK demand for imports tends to be fairly price inelastic in the areas of foodstuffs and raw materials, whereas for exports demand is more price elastic since over wide areas our products have foreign substitutes. Figure 15.3 shows how the terms of trade have moved over the period 1976–82.

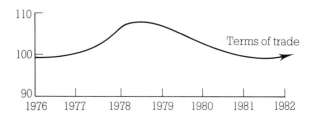

Fig. 15.3 Trends in the terms of trade during the period 1976–82

THE STRUCTURE OF UK TRADE

The tables below show the main changes in the composition of the UK's imports and exports between 1970 and 1983.

The most significant changes for exports have

come in the decline of engineering products from 44% to 33%, in particular a 5% fall in the export of motor vehicles. A big increase comes in the non-manufactures section where oil exports have increased dramatically, and in food, beverages and tobacco where alcoholic drinks such as whisky have shown increased popularity abroad.

On the import side the most significant change has come in the large increase in finished manufactures particularly from the EC. This reflects the increased competition from foreign producers successfully displacing sales away from UK firms making similar products. The increased efficiency in UK agriculture has, however, helped to reduce food imports from 23% to 12%, and North Sea oil has cut fuel imports from a peak of 14% in 1975 to 11% in 1983.

Exports	1970 %	1983
Engineering products	43.6	32.7
machinery	27.4	21.3
road motor vehicles	10.7	5.1
other transport equipment	3.7	3.9
scientific instruments	1.8	2.4
Other manufactures and semi-manufactures	41.1	33.3
Non-manufactures	15.3	34.0
food, beverages and tobacco	6.3	7.0
basic materials	3.0	2.5
fuels	2.6	21.7
others	3.4	2.8
	100	100

Imports	1970 %	1983
food, beverages and tobacco	22.6	11.9
industrial materials and semi-manufactures	42.7	32.8
finished manufactures	22.9	42.4
fuel	10.4	10.7
others	1.4	2.2
	100	100

Source: *Annual Abstract of Statistics*

THE BALANCE OF PAYMENTS

The **balance of payments** is simply an account showing all payments to, and receipts from foreigners. The account is divided into various sections which record the different ways that money flows in and out of the country.

1 THE CURRENT ACCOUNT

The **current account** records all regular transactions that take place in a particular year and is subdivided into **visible** and **invisible** trade. Visible trade represents all physical goods that enter (visible imports) or leave (visible exports) the country and the visible balance or balance of trade is the difference between visible exports and imports. It can be favourable (exports greater than imports) or unfavourable (imports greater than exports).

Invisible items represent services the UK performs for other countries (invisible exports) or services that other countries perform for the UK (invisible imports). An important invisible item is tourism and if, for example, Americans visit London, because Britain is performing a service for foreigners this counts as an invisible export. Similarly when UK residents go abroad for a holiday an invisible import arises. Other services that appear in the invisible section include shipping, aviation, insurance, government spending, and profits, interest and dividends paid to or received from abroad.

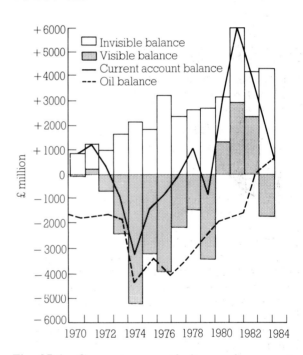

Fig. 15.4 Current account balance of payments 1970–84

Adding the invisible balance to the balance of trade gives the **current account balance**. Figure 15.4 shows the current account balance from 1970–84 with the oil balance also illustrated individually since it has made a significant impact on movements in the current account balance. The deep negative plunge of the current account balance in the early 1970s coincided with the quadrupling of Middle East oil prices, adding

NORTH SEA OIL

North Sea oil now plays an extremely important part in the UK economy and has dramatically improved the country's trading position, helping to reverse a trade deficit of £5000m in 1974 to give a £3000m surplus in 1982. The UK is now the world's second largest producer of oil and is in the world's top ten oil exporting countries (Fig. 15.5). The impact of North Sea oil on the rest of the UK trade, however, has been detrimental. In the early 1980s the value of the £ reached US$2 reflecting the growth of oil exports which meant many of the UK's manufactured goods became over-priced on world markets. This led to widespread redundancies in the manufacturing sector with the result that manufacturing employment went down from 34.1% of the working population in 1954 to 24.9% in 1982. In terms of trade this 'de-industrialisation' is not problematic as long as the oil flows from the North Sea. But, there must be the worry that when the oil runs out (probably in the late 1990s), the UK will be ill equipped to compete again in world markets. This in turn could lead to huge trade deficits as in the mid 1970s. Some economists have suggested that UK firms should be encouraged to invest abroad now so that in the future their profits abroad will bring in valuable foreign exchange to the country. Certainly there is a need to invest some of the oil revenue in the manufacturing industries of the future to ensure that the economy survives after the oil runs out.

It should also be noted that due to the volatility of market forces, the high income from North Sea oil cannot always be guaranteed. The fall in demand throughout 1986 meant lower prices: good for the consumer, but for oil companies and the government this led to declining revenue.

The position of the government, though, is to some extent protected as Fig. 12.6 shows. Because the excise duty is fixed regardless of the pump price, the government only loses some VAT when prices fall. It is more vulnerable when it comes to the petroleum revenue tax which is levied on the oil companies' profits resulting from North Sea exploration. These will sharply decline as the price of crude oil falls.

THINGS TO DO

Why has North Sea oil contributed to the 'de-industrialisation' in the UK?

Fig. 15.5 Advanced technology and skilled labour has been used to extract the reserves of oil in the North Sea – this Shell/Esso Brent C production platform drills, produces oil and gas, meters, stores and pumps. (Shell photographs)

greatly to the visible import bill. The development of North Sea oil in the late 1970s has led to a dramatic improvement in the current account balance, creating a surplus in the early 1980s.

THINGS TO DO

1 For each of the following products, state which country is associated with specialising in its production: watches, video recorders, wine, washing machines, timber, coffee, cotton, iron ore.

2 How is the **principle of comparative advantage** in international trade similar to that in the division of labour?

3 Using the following example, show how international trade can benefit both countries.

	Computers	Textiles (tonnes)
UK	700	900
India	50	850

(Assume each country divides its factors equally between computers and textile manufacture and that one computer exchanges for three tonnes of textiles.)

4 What are **non-tariff barriers**? Why might they be difficult to retaliate against?

5 Which of the arguments for placing restrictions on trade have most economic validity?

6 Under what circumstances will an *improvement* in the terms of trade lead to a *worsening* of a country's trading position? (Use graphs to illustrate your answer.)

7 Outline the main changes in the structure of UK trade between 1970 and 1983.

2 THE CAPITAL ACCOUNT

In addition to the regular transactions in goods and services which take place, longterm investment is carried out by UK firms abroad and by foreign firms in the UK. This investment may also be sponsored by the UK or foreign government agencies. It is listed under a separate section of the balance of payments, UK investment abroad counting as a negative figure, foreign investment in the UK counting as a positive figure. What must be remembered is that although private foreign investment in the UK may bring with it additional employment, any profit will leave the UK to the foreign company's homebase and will count as a negative item in the invisibles section of the current account. Similarly although investment abroad by UK firms will have a negative effect on the balance of payments in the short run, in the long run the profits earned will appear as a positive item in invisibles.

Adding the current and capital account balances together produces what is termed the **total currency flow**. This shows the overall surplus or deficit on the balance of payments account. In the end the accounts must balance and the final item, called **official financing**, shows how the surplus is used or the deficit paid off. A surplus may be paid into gold and foreign currency reserves whilst a deficit may necessitate borrowing from reserves or perhaps the International Monetary Fund. A summary balance of payments account is shown for 1983.

UK Balance of Payments	1983
1 Current account	£m
visible trade	
exports	60 625
imports	61 341
balance of trade	−716
invisible trade	
receipts (exports)	34 975
payments (imports)	31 343
invisible balance	+3 632
CURRENT ACCOUNT BALANCE	+2 916
2 Investment and other capital flows	−3 648
3 Total currency flow	−732
4 Official financing	
borrowing (+increase/repayments−)	+249
charges in reserves (additions to−/drawings+)	+603
balancing item	−120
TOTAL	+732

CORRECTING A BALANCE OF PAYMENTS DEFICIT OR SURPLUS

If the balance of payments account shows a deficit on total currency flow then money is owed to foreigners which has to be paid back. In the short run the gold and foreign currency reserves can be used for small debts but in the long run the deficit has to be corrected or the reserves will run dry. How can a country cure such a deficit? There are several options.

1 Deflation

Deflation involves dampening down demand for imported goods and services. The most direct way to do this is by reducing the amount of money people have to spend on imports which can be achieved by increasing taxes or raising interest rates to reduce borrowing and hence spending. Raising interest rates also helps to make a country more attractive to invest in, thus bringing in foreign capital, further helping to reduce the payments deficit. Deflationary policies, however, also have the effect of dampening down demand in the home market thus creating unwanted unemployment.

2 Floating exchange rates

More will be said about **floating exchange rates** later in this chapter but in simple terms a balance of payments deficit implies a fall in the demand for sterling abroad as fewer exports are sold in relation to imports. If the value of sterling is determined by the market mechanism, the fall in demand will lead to it being worth less in terms of other currencies. This fall in value or **depreciation** will mean cheaper exports, dearer imports and thus the balance of payments deficit can be automatically cured. Similarly a balance of payments surplus causes the value of sterling to **appreciate**. In practice demand elasticities for exports and imports determine the effectiveness of floating exchange rates (see pp. 205–208).

3 Trade restrictions

Applying some or all of the trade restrictions listed on pp. 199–200 can help to reduce imports, although the danger of retaliation means their longterm effectiveness is in doubt.

4 Devaluation

For nearly 30 years after World War 2 the values of foreign currencies were fixed in terms of each other. This helped to stabilise world trade. If, however, a country experienced a serious payments deficit it could be allowed to devalue its currency against others. This had the effect of making exports cheaper and imports dearer, so reducing the deficit.

5 Exchange control

By restricting the amount of foreign currency available to importers, the quantity of imported goods can be controlled. The government through the Bank of England has the authority to impose exchange control limits which could also apply to the amount of foreign currency taken abroad by British tourists.

It might appear at first sight that a balance of payments deficit is more serious than a surplus, but acquiring a surplus can still pose problems. North Sea oil has helped to create a balance of payments surplus for the UK which in turn has increased the value of the pound abroad. This has made manufacturing exports more expensive causing demand for them to fall and leading to a certain amount of de-industrialisation in the British economy. Curing a balance of payments surplus is essentially a reversal of the policies designed to cure a deficit.

EXCHANGE RATES

International trade is made more complex than internal trade because of the existence of a large number of foreign currencies. Historically international trade was less complex than it is today because gold became an international 'medium of exchange', but its current scarcity makes it unsuitable for this role now.

How are exchange rates determined? In simple terms the value of one currency measured in terms of another is found by comparing baskets of similar goods in each country in terms of their total money value. For example if a basket of basic produce came to £10 in value in the UK and a similar basket of goods came to $20 in the USA, then £1 would be equivalent to $2. To be more realistic, the goods should be traded products and the basket as large as possible.

Exchange rates never stand still for very long; they change according to the forces of supply and demand. Suppose the initial equilibrium of the £ against the $ stands at £1 = $2. There are three main areas of influence that could affect this equilibrium: trade, investment and speculation.

Changes in the pattern of trade can be affected by factors such as inflation. If inflation in the UK is much higher than that in the USA the prices of UK goods in the USA will rise causing a contraction in demand for them. Fewer pounds will be required by importers in the USA and, as Fig. 15.6 (overleaf) shows, a fall in demand for sterling due to high inflation in the UK leads to a lowering of the exchange rate. An increase in investment by American firms in the UK will lead to more sterling being demanded, helping to improve the £'s exchange rate against the $. Finally any speculation

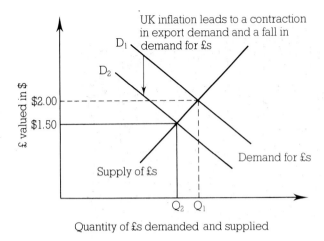

Fig. 15.6

about the future of the UK economy may lead to banks in the USA selling sterling reserves which, as Fig. 15.7 shows, might cause the supply of £s on the foreign exchange market to increase from S_1 to S_2 thus reducing their value.

Since Britain trades with a large number of other countries apart from the USA, similar graphs can be drawn showing movements of the pound against the deutschmark, franc, lire, etc (Fig. 15.9). It is perfectly possible for the value of the £ to be rising against the $, whilst falling against the deutschmark if the conditions of trade, investment and speculation differ between the countries.

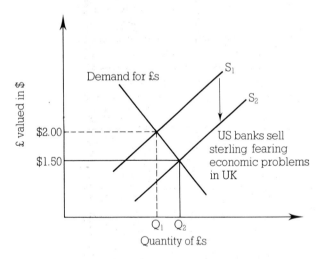

Fig. 15.7

When exchange rates are determined by market forces a system of **floating exchange rates** is said to exist. As stated earlier, the main advantage of having such a system is that in theory any balance of payments problem can be automatically cured by exchange rate movements. This can be illustrated more easily via a graph. If the

balance of payments is in deficit due to a decline in export demand, fewer pounds will be demanded to pay for exports and the value of the pound will fall. This will make exports cheaper and imports dearer. The dearer imports should lead to demand for them contracting thus helping to correct the deficit. This however does not happen in all cases as Fig. 15.8 shows. The key to the effectiveness of floating exchange rates lies in the demand elasticities of imports and exports.

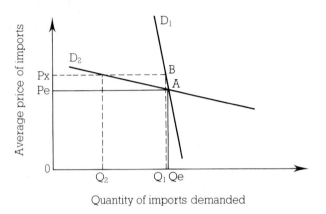

Quantity of imports demanded

Fig. 15.8

If Pe and Qe represent the initial equilibrium price and quantity for the imports then an increase in import prices from Pe to Px due to a fall in the value of the £ will in the case of a very elastic demand D_2, cause a large contraction in demand to Q_2. If, however, demand is very inelastic as in the case of D_1, the quantity bought will hardly contract at all, increasing the amount spent on imports from (Pe A Qe O) to (Px B Q_1 O). A similar position exists for exports. Only if demand is price elastic will a lower sterling exchange rate increase total revenue. Thus floating exchange rates *may* but not necessarily *will* help to cure balance of payments deficits and surpluses. To the extent that they do automatically cure deficits and surpluses, though, governments are free in their economic policy to pursue domestic objectives without having to worry about international payment problems.

Floating exchange rates do have the disadvantage that they increase business uncertainty because of the daily fluctuation in values of currencies. Speculation in particular may distort the true value of a currency. To the extent that demand elasticities for imports and exports may be low they can also actually make the balance of payments surpluses and deficits worse.

Fig. 15.9 Exchange rates against the £ (sterling) of various foreign currencies

Bureau de Change

Rates of Exchange per £

24 SEPTEMBER 1986

		We Sell Notes	We Buy Notes	We Buy Cheques
AUSTRIA		20·20	21·70	21·45
BELGIUM		61·00	65·00	62·10
CANADA		2·00	2·08	2·045
DENMARK		11·00	11·70	11·24
FRANCE		9·53	10·08	9·76
W.GERMANY		2·92	3·10	2·985
GREECE		196·	212·	REFER
HOLLAND		3·28	3·50	3·375
ITALY		2005·	2135·	2069·90
NORWAY		10·53	11·15	10·77
PORTUGAL		209·00	221·00	REFER
SPAIN		190·00	204·00	198·
SWEDEN		9·90	10·50	10·12
SWITZERLAND		2·34	2·54	2·415
U.S.A		1·44	1·51	1·4725
JAPAN		224·	244·	226·50

- Foreign currency notes subject to availability.
- All transactions subject to Commission charges.
- Quoted rates not necessarily applicable to notes of large denomination or transactions of large amounts.

Midland
The Listening Bank

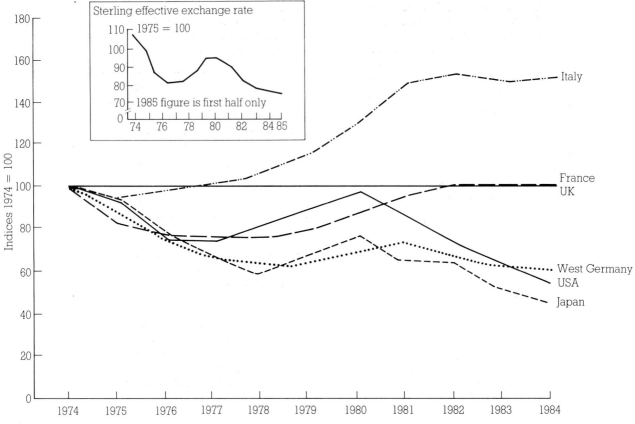

Fig. 15.10 Exchange rates compared to sterling during the period 1974–84

Prior to most of the world's currencies being allowed to float in the 1970s, a system of **managed flexibility** existed where currencies were fixed in terms of each other but allowed to fluctuate within narrow margins. The oil crisis in the 1970s led to widely differing inflation rates in trading countries necessitating large adjustments in the value of their currencies which a basically fixed system could not cope with. Floating exchange rates do more accurately reflect the relative strength of trading countries and allow fast adjustment of values if trading or investment conditions change.

Figure 15.10 shows how the value of the £ has changed in relation to other currencies since 1974. Its effective rate against an average of all major trading currencies is also shown.

THINGS TO DO

1 Distinguish between the **terms of trade** and the **balance of trade**.

2 State whether the following represent visible/invisible exports or visible/invisible imports.
   (a) Ford Fiesta cars come to Britain from Spain.
   (b) A British family visit Greece for their holidays.
   (c) ICI make large profits in their Dutch pharmaceutical factory.
   (d) Amstrad computers are successfully marketed in the USA.
   (e) A Swede wins the UK open golf tournament.
   (f) An American businessman flies Concorde to Heathrow.

3 Fill in the missing figures from the following imaginary balance of payments account.

	£m
visible exports	550
visible imports	490
balance of trade	
shipping	+30
aviation	+10
tourism	−40
profits	−30
current account balance	
investment and other capital flows	−150
total currency flow	
official financing	

4 In what way does investment by UK firms abroad benefit the balance of payments account in the long run?

5 Why is a deficit on the current account more serious than a deficit on the balance of trade?

6 With regard to Fig. 15.11, suggest reasons for some of the main surpluses and deficits on visible and invisible trade.

7 Using the following table, illustrate graphically the principle invisible earners for the UK in 1972 and 1982.

	1972	1982
		(£ billion)
sea transport	1.6	3.6
civil aviation	0.4	2.5
travel	0.6	3.2
financial services	0.5	2.1
other services	1.1	5.7
government	0.1	0.4

8 Distinguish between the terms **deflation**, **depreciation** and **devaluation**.

9 What are the main factors affecting changes in exchange rates? Using a graph show how a sustained fall in the UK's inflation rate might affect the value of sterling abroad.

10 What advantages does a system of **floating exchange rates** offer over a fixed rate system?

Fig. 15.11 Britain's winners and losers, 1984

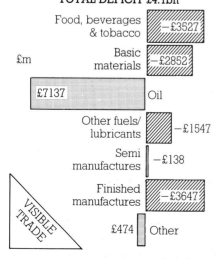

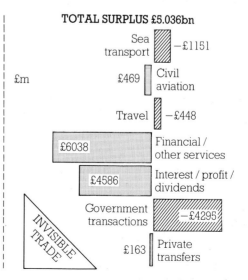

THINGS TO DO

Study Fig. 15.12, then use the data and your Economics knowledge to answer the following questions.

(a) In 1981 which car manufacturer has the largest share of its home market and in which country?

(b) In which country are car imports the smallest % of total sales?

(c) Which country has the world's largest car market?

(d) Where is Japan's largest export market?

(e) In which country have domestic car sales fallen most as a % of the total market between 1980 and 1981? Which foreign manufacturer benefited most from this drop?

(f) Japanese manufacturers in 1980 feared their domestic market would fall the following year. Were their fears grounded?

(g) 'The UK car market has become more competitive over the last 10 years.' Suggest reasons why this might have happened. What have been the consequences for the UK motor industry?

(h) What measures could individual countries take to cut back car imports? Are there any problems connected with such measures?

(i) Using a histogram, show graphically the different shares of the total market individual domestic manufacturers have in the UK car market.

UK	1981	%	1980	%
domestic	568 089	44.33	655 422	43.30
imports†	826 533	55.67	858 319	56.70
total market	1 484 622	100.00	1 513 761	100.00
DOMESTIC				
Ford*	459 365	30.94	464 706	30.70
BL*	285 071	19.20	275 793	18.22
Vauxhall*	107 572	7.24	109 218	7.21
Talbot*	68 048	4.58	90 874	6.00
IMPORTS				
Datsun	88 209	5.94	91 893	6.07
VW-Audi	80 221	5.40	68 285	4.51
Renault	72 041	4.85	88 343	5.84
Fiat	61 977	4.17	51 299	3.39
Volvo	44 558	3.00	38 283	2.53
Citroen	27 395	1.85	27 006	1.82
Toyota	23 405	1.58	34 167	2.26

* includes cars from Continental associates not included in UK figures
† includes imports from all sources including cars from Continental associates of UK companies

Source: *Society of Motor Manufacturers and Traders*

ITALY	1981	%	1980	%
domestic	1 027 452	59.07	1 033 472	60.18
imports	711 830	40.93	683 960	39.82
total market	1 739 282	100.00	1 717 654	100.00
DOMESTIC				
Fiat	779 984	44.85	766 397	44.62
Lancia/ Autobianchi	114 096	6.56	117 335	6.83
Alfa Romeo	112 544	6.47	120 000	6.99
Nuova Innocenti	20 258	1.16	29 150	1.70
IMPORTS				
Renault	176 721	10.16	180 672	10.52
VW/Audi	114 429	6.56	74 060	4.31
Ford	92 638	5.33	78 505	4.57
Citroen	78 340	4.50	84 028	4.89
Opel/GM	60 412	3.47	61 464	3.58
Talbot/Simca	57 266	3.29	75 173	4.38

Fig. 15.12 Car markets of six major countries

USA	1981	%	1980	%
domestic	6 205 000	72.8	6 577 000	73.4
imports	2 328 000	27.2	2 402 000	26.6
total market	8 533 000	100.00	8 979 000	100.00
DOMESTIC				
General Motors	3 796 000	44.5	4 116 000	45.9
Ford	1 380 000	16.2	1 475 000	16.4
Chrysler	730 000	8.6	660 000	7.4
Volkswagen of America	162 000	1.9	177 000	2.0
American Motors	137 000	1.6	149 000	1.7
IMPORTS				
Toyota	576 000	6.7	582 000	6.5
Nissan	465 000	5.5	517 000	5.8
Honda	371 000	4.3	375 000	4.2
Mazda (Toyo Kogyo)	166 000	1.9	162 000	1.8
Subaru	152 000	1.8	143 000	1.6
VW-Audi	133 000	1.5	133 000	1.4
Mitsubishi	111 000	1.3	129 000	1.4
Volvo	64 000	0.75	56 000	0.63
Mercedes	58 000	0.68	50 000	0.55

WEST GERMANY	1981	%	1980	%
domestic	1 697 377	72.8	1 745 875	72.0
imports	632 978	27.2	680 312	28.0
total market	2 330 355	100.00	2 426 187	100.00
DOMESTIC				
Volkswagen/Audi	708 307	30.4	736 109	30.3
Opel	381 193*	16.4	411 076	17.0
Ford	273 174†	11.7	252 044	10.4
Daimler-Benz	245 927	10.6	249 249	10.3
BMW	133 899	5.8	138 927	5.7
IMPORTS				
Renault	100 701	4.3	113 591	4.7
Peugeot	99 964‡	4.3	115 655	4.8
Fiat	94 151	4.0	87 737	3.6
Toyota	47 214	2.0	58 893	2.4
Nissan-Datsun	44 722	1.9	51 503	2.1

* includes 10 908 GM imports † includes 43 890 Ford imports ‡ Peugeot includes 44 594 Citroens, 27 816 Peugeots and 27 544 Talbots

Source: *Federal Motor Vehicle Statistical Office*

JAPAN	1981	%	1980	%
domestic	2 663 046	98.59	2 635 274	98.33
imports	38 110	1.41	44 871	1.67
total market	2 701 156	100.00	2 680 145	100.00
DOMESTIC				
Toyota	1 098 018	40.65	1 064 171	39.7
Nissan	806 878	29.87	828 158	30.89
Mitsubishi	193 571	7.16	208 737	7.78
Toyo Kogyo	220 794	8.17	196 560	7.33
Honda	186 198	6.89	166 975	6.23
Isuzu	64 990	2.40	62 806	2.34
Daihatsu	49 250	1.82	61 420	2.29
Fuji Heavy Industries	43 347	1.60	46 447	1.73
IMPORTS				
VW	12 047	0.44	17 805	0.66

FRANCE	1981	%	1980	%
domestic	1 319 390	71.9	1 444 630	77.1
imports	514 852	28.1	428 516	22.9
total market	1 834 242	100.00	1 873 146	100.00
DOMESTIC				
Renault	712 954	38.9	759 312	40.5
Peugeot	256 195	14	293 461	15.7
Citroen	260 325	14.2	270 983	14.5
Talbot	89 916	4.9	120 874	6.4
Total Peugeot	606 436	33.0	685 318	36.6
IMPORTS				
Volkswagen*	110 500	6.6	83 372	4.8
Ford*	90 821	5.4	59 898	3.5
Fiat*	74 917	4.5	62 416	3.6

* 11 months

Source: *Financial Times*

INTERNATIONAL TRADING ORGANISATIONS

THE EC

Britain joined the European Community (EC) or Common Market on 1 January 1974 together with Eire and Denmark. There are now 12 members of the Community, the latest additions being Spain and Portugal who joined in 1986. The Community has as its foundation the Treaty of Rome, signed in 1956, which set out the main aims of the organisation. The Community is basically a **customs union** where free trade takes place between member countries with a common external tariff being levied on all non-EC goods. In a wider context it aims to unify countries politically through a European Commission, Council of Ministers, Parliament and Court of Justice. The Commission is a body of non-elected administrators who initiate policies which are discussed by the relevant ministers from each country (Figs. 15.13 and 15.14). Agreed policies are further discussed by the European Parliament which, if approved, eventually become law. Alleged law breaking can be brought to the Court of Justice.

The Community also aims to harmonise taxation between member countries, VAT for example, being Community-wide. A common currency unit has been set up (the ECU) as part of a European Monetary system which is managed by the European Monetary Cooperation Fund. There is also a regional fund which provides selective aid to the less developed parts of the Community, managed by the European Investment Bank.

The largest part of the Community budget goes on the Common Agricultural Policy (CAP) which is designed to protect farmers from the wide fluctuations in income which can arise from changes in supply caused by weather conditions. Each year agriculture ministers meet to set a 'target price' for farm produce which they think will approximate to the market price. They then set below the target price an 'intervention price' at which the Commission agrees to buy produce from farmers which can be stockpiled for use, hopefully later. The intervention price acts as a guarantee to farmers that they will receive a minimum amount for their produce without which they could go out of business.

Fig. 15.13 An aerial view of the Berlaymont Building, Brussels, home of the European Community Commission

Fig. 15.14   The members of the European Community Commission in 1986

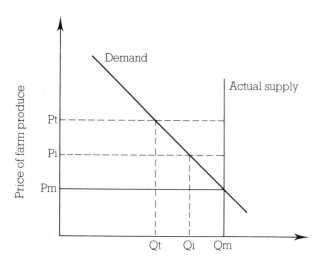

Quantity of farm produce demanded and supplied

Fig. 15.15   How the Common Agricultural Policy works

Figure 15.15 shows how the CAP might work. If Pt is the target price but the actual quantity supplied to the market is Qm then the market price without any support would be Pm. This price might not allow farmers to cover their costs thus forcing them out of business and reducing the Community food supply the following year. By setting an intervention price, Pi, the Community provides support for farmers and since at Pi only Qi will be demanded, a surplus of (Qm − Qi) is created which can be stored in case of shortages the following year or sold off to another country. The acquisition of surpluses, sometimes called 'mountains', has led to criticism, because there is a suggestion of overproduction and wastage which in turn implies factors of production are not being put to their best use. In addition, the intervention subsidy is expensive (£9000m was spent on the CAP in 1980), and it protects the least efficient farmers and allows the most efficient to make sizeable profits. Sometimes surpluses of perishable goods have to be left to rot whilst Eastern Bloc Countries may be offered some 'mountains' at below cost price, something which is not always politically popular!

The economic advantages for the UK of being in the EC stem from the principle of comparative advantage since the free trade between member countries allows specialisation, and provides a huge potential market of over 250m people to sell to. Unfortunately not all goods that member countries produce are complementary to each other so that where two or more countries specialise in the same product over-capacity exists. Nowhere is this more true than for cars where about 20% over-capacity exists as firms like Ford, Peugeot, Renault, Fiat, Volkswagen and General Motors all compete for a limited demand. This leads to unemployment for the workers in the least efficient companies, though for the consumer this intense competition does lead to lower prices.

THE INTERNATIONAL MONETARY FUND (IMF)

The **IMF** was set up in 1944 at the Breton Woods Conference in the USA where plans for post-war trade were put together. The IMF's main role has been to oversee the mechanism of international trade payments and to assist countries that develop balance of payments difficulties. Member countries originally subscribed a quota of money to the Fund which comprised of 75% of their own currency and 25% gold. These quotas have been subsequently topped up and used as the basis of IMF lending. A country with a balance of payments deficit might need to borrow foreign currency from the IMF to clear its debts. The more that is borrowed the bigger the say the IMF has in the measures the country will need to take to repay the loan. Measures usually involve a heavy amount of deflation.

More recently the IMF has become a credit-creating institution in a similar way to domestic banks. It was felt that there was not enough international currency in the world to comfortably finance all of world trade (sometimes called a 'shortage of international liquidity') so a new monetary unit called **Special Drawing Rights** (SDRs) was created which could be used to settle debts between member countries. In this sense the IMF has now become more of a 'bank' rather than a 'fund' although it should be pointed out that SDRs still only form a very small part of total world liquidity.

The IMF also has the aim of eventually returning to a fixed exchange rate system which it believes provides much greater stability for world trade than a floating system. Unless the inflation rates of member countries stabilise to below 5% it is unlikely that such an aim will be achieved in the near future as any par values set would need frequent revision.

The IMF has its headquarters in Washington adjacent to the International Bank for Reconstruction and Development: the 'World Bank' (see Chapter 2).

THE GENERAL AGREEMENT ON TARIFFS AND TRADE (GATT)

GATT came into operation in 1948 with the aim of promoting more widespread free trade through the multilateral reduction of tariffs and other barriers to trade. It works on the 'most favoured nation' principle that any tariff reduction agreed between two member countries should be extended to all GATT signatories. Historically GATT has provided the framework through which successive 'rounds' of tariff reductions have taken place, most notably the 'Kennedy Round' in 1967. More recently it has been active in trying to prevent members from reintroducing protectionist measures as world trade in the early 1980s slumped.

OTHER ORGANISATIONS

1 **The Organisation for Economic Cooperation and Development (OECD)**
The **OECD** came into being in September 1961, formed from 16 European countries plus the USA and Canada. Later Japan and Australia also became members. The OECD aims to encourage economic growth and high employment with financial stability amongst member countries, as well as contributing to the economic development of the world's poorer nations through the expansion of world trade. It functions through various committees and publishes regular statistical bulletins and forecasts.

2 **The Organisation of Petroleum Export Countries (OPEC)**
OPEC was set up in 1960 with a group of 13 major oil-producing countries. It acts as a forum for the discussion and agreement of crude petroleum export prices. In this sense it is a cartel aiming to maximise oil revenue for member countries. It had a powerful effect on the world economy in 1974 when oil prices were quadrupled but more recently the advent of new sources of oil and a slump in world trade have reduced its influence. In addition OPEC production quotas designed to keep the price of oil high have been disregarded by some members anxious to maintain growth in their home economies.

3 **European Free Trade Association (EFTA)**
EFTA was set up in 1959 with seven original members: the UK, Norway, Sweden, Denmark, Austria, Portugal and Switzerland. Subsequently Finland and Iceland have joined but the UK and Denmark left in 1973 to join the EC. The member countries have established a **free trade area** which involves the retention of their own individual tariffs on imports from non-members but the abolition of duties on goods originating in any member country. In this sense EFTA differs from the EC which as a 'customs union' has a common external tariff for all non-member goods.

4 **Council for Mutual Economic Aid (Comecon)**
Comecon was set up in 1949 and now consists of most of the Eastern European Communist countries. Its aim is to develop the member countries' economies by means of central planning to achieve collective self-sufficiency. The individual countries, however, are still seen to pursue their own economic objectives, in particular increasing trade with the West to buy in its technology.

1 What is the **Common Agricultural Policy?** Why is it necessary to have a farm support policy?

2 (a) In Fig. 15.16, state which of the following agricultural supply positions (S_1 S_2 S_3) in the EC would necessitate intervention.
  (b) What would the size of the surplus amount to if intervention buying took place?
  (c) Under which of the above positions might the surplus be released?

3 In what way is the EC more than just a customs union?

4 Why is the IMF now more of a 'bank' than merely a 'fund'?

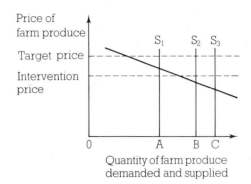

Fig. 15.16

5 What is the 'most favoured nation' principle on which GATT works? Why has the work of GATT become more difficult in the 1980s?

16

FINANCIAL INSTITUTIONS AND MONETARY POLICY

INTRODUCTION

In Chapter 5 the importance of money was discussed together with how banks create their own money in the form of cheques. Banks form only a part of the network of financial institutions which accept and use deposits in a wide variety of ways. Monitoring the activities of all English financial institutions is the Bank of England, which, through monetary policy, can significantly affect the activities of institutions by both direct and indirect methods. This chapter looks at the two principal financial markets – the money and capital markets – together with the main institutions involved. It then focuses on the lending activities of the commercial banks and discusses the main activities of the Bank of England, particularly in relation to monetary policy – controlling the supply of money.

THE MONEY MARKET

The **money market** is the term used to describe the demand for and supply of money for use over short periods of time, typically around three months. Activities centre around institutions in the City of London called **discount houses** which deal principally in securities called bills of exchange. A **bill of exchange** is simply an international IOU used by exporting firms to invoice the foreign importers buying the goods. International trade convention allows the importers up to three months to pay the amount on the bill and this time gives them a chance to sell the goods they have bought thereby providing the money for the bill. The problem for the exporting firm is that it has to wait three months for its money which may cause a cashflow problem. If, for example, the goods in question are Jaguar cars, the workforce at the company will not want to wait three months for their wages so Jaguar may want to find a means of recovering their income more quickly. It is at this point that the discount houses can help. They will offer to buy the bill of exchange for its face value less a 'discount' of X% which varies according to market rates. They then recover the full value of the bill three months later, thus earning a profit equal to the discounted amount.

The discount market therefore is a useful way for companies to obtain short-term credit avoiding the cashflow problems that might otherwise arise from delayed payment for imports. But how do discount houses get their capital in the first place to buy the bills of exchange? The answer lies with the commercial banks which provide short-term loans known as 'money at call and short notice'. **Call money** can be taken back by the banks any day before noon; money borrowed at short notice has to be repaid within two weeks to a month. Money is offered at preferential interest rates because of the short recall time period. If the banks do take back their money (because perhaps customers are making heavy cash withdrawals) the discount houses can turn to the Bank of England for help in its capacity of 'Lender of Last Resort'. The Bank of England sets its interest charges above market rates to discourage borrowing unless it is essential. It does not want to see the money market collapse, however, and so is always ready to step in and help when required.

It should also be noted that in a small number of cases the discount houses may feel that some risk may be attached to discounting a bill. If the foreign importer is in a country experiencing some political instability then defaulting on the payment of the bill is a possibility. In such cases an exporter may need to turn to an **acceptance house** or **merchant bank** which may have more expertise in international trade finance, but which will charge a higher discount rate to cover the increased risk of non-payment.

Commercial banks also play another role in the money market: buying bills off the discount houses before they mature for amounts below their full value, which vary according to the maturity date. They do this so that they can be sure of converting some of their assets into cash within a short space of time to guard against possible heavy customer withdrawals.

The money market is also characterised by another bill issued by the government and called the **Treasury bill**. This represents a form of borrowing by the government for 91 days and Treasury bills are really just postdated cheques which the discount houses bid for as a consortium. Their **tender** or bid price will be below the face value of the bill, the difference being their profit over the three months. It may be that for every £100 bill, the

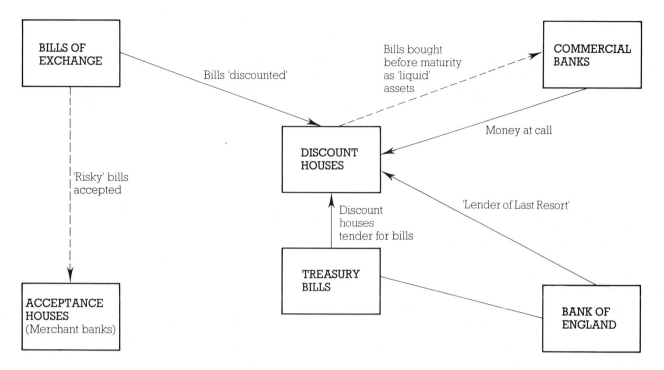

Fig. 16.1 The main institutions of the UK money market

tender price is £98, representing a 2% return over three months. The government through the Bank of England issues Treasury bills primarily because its spending and tax receipts do not always match time-wise. Perhaps a motorway is completed in October but tax revenue to pay the contractors will not arrive until January. Treasury bills provide a means of tiding over this gap. Treasury bills are also bought by banks and often from discount houses some time before maturity.

The institutions involved in the money market together with their interconnections are summarised in Fig. 16.1.

THE CAPITAL MARKET

The **capital market** is the term used to describe the demand for and supply of money for long periods of time, often over 20 years. There are a large number of institutions operating in the capital market, principally the Stock Exchange, building societies, insurance companies, investment/unit trusts and pension funds.

THE STOCK EXCHANGE

The **Stock Exchange** is a market where largely secondhand securities are bought and sold. There are in fact several exchanges in the major cities of the UK but the centre for most activity is in Throgmorton Street in the City of London (Fig. 16.4 overleaf).

Securities is the general term used to describe stocks and shares. A **stock** represents a loan to a company or the government; a **share** gives an entitlement to ownership. Loans to companies normally take the form of **debentures** whilst a loan to the government involves buying 'gilt edged' securities. **Gilts** are issued in denominations of £100 at interest rates which reflect those prevailing in the market at the time. The life of a gilt is usually over 40 years and some have undated repayment times. Since interest will always be paid and they can be sold at any time on the Stock Exchange, there is a ready market for them. The price offered for a gilt, however, will vary according to the original interest offer and its relation to current market rates. Suppose a £100 gilt was originally bought with a 5% annual interest payment but current market rates are 10%; no one will want to buy the gilt at its original price. Since the government will only pay £5 interest, to receive a yield equivalent to 10% an offer price of £50 would be more appropriate, since £5 represents 10% of £50. Thus the market price of a gilt varies according to demand and supply which in turn are determined by interest rates. Some gilts bought originally with high interest payments will have market prices higher than the original if market interest rates are low, for example,

original interest rate $12\frac{1}{2}\%$
current market rate 10%

$$\text{market price of gilt} = \frac{12\%}{10\%} \times 100$$
$$= £125$$

Security prices in general move up and down according to changes in supply and demand. Suppose ICI shares have a current market price of 350p. What factors might lead to their price rising?

Figure 16.2 shows that the conditions of demand could change to create the price increase and might be caused by increased profit expectations, a new product innovation, or a new raw material discovery. Often rumoured takeover bids increase the attractiveness of shares – a new management style perhaps meaning improved efficiency. Equally, poor profits, lost tenders, strikes, etc. can lead to a fall in share prices. To give an indication of share price movements in general the *Financial Times* has constructed a share index representing the average share price of 30 leading public companies. Since 1975, 11 of the top companies have been removed, mainly in manufacturing reflecting the relative decline in this sector. New entrants into the index include Thorn-EMI, the National Westminster Bank and Trusthouse Forte. Figure 16.3 shows how the FT index changed over 10 years from a low of 146 in January 1975 to over 1000 in June 1985. It gives an indication of just how successful the market has been for investors who if investing £100 in 1975 would have assets worth £680 in 1985 if the securities bought had kept pace with the 30 share index.

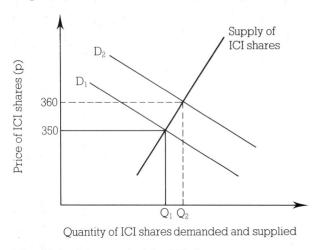

Fig. 16.2 The market for ICI shares

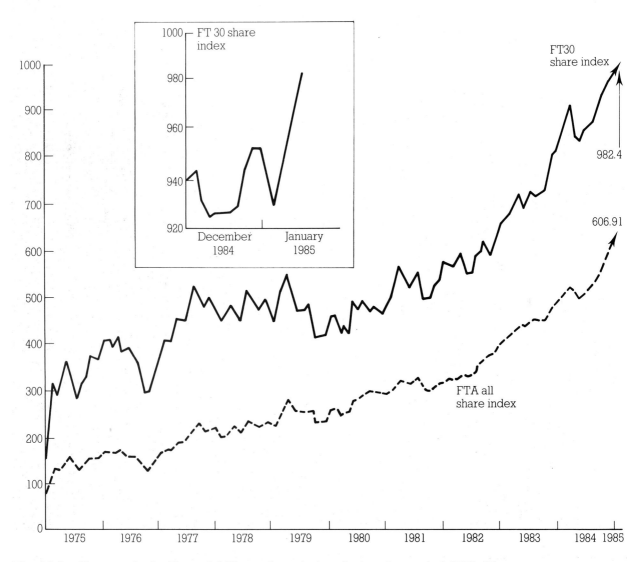

Fig. 16.3 Changes in the Financial Times share index during the period 1975–85

Fig. 16.4   The London Stock Exchange at Throgmorton Street. In October 1986 the reforms of the 'Big Bang' made this traditional institution more competitive in the international financial arena

Traditionally the Stock Exchange was operated by two groups of people, the brokers and the jobbers (Fig. 16.6). **Stock brokers** were the 'retailers' of securities dealing directly with the public and charging a fixed commission for their services. **Jobbers**, on the other hand, were effectively 'wholesalers' buying and selling through brokers, operating on the floor of the Exchange and holding considerable quantities of securities. They earnt their living by purchasing securities at a lower price than they sold them for. Their mark-up was known as the 'jobber's turn'.

The organisation of the Stock Exchange underwent major change in 1986 – the 'Big Bang' – partly in response to the criticism that there has been a lack of competition in the market in the past. Figure 16.5 shows how the number of jobbing firms shrank drastically in the 1960s and 1970s, resulting in several large cartels dominating the market.

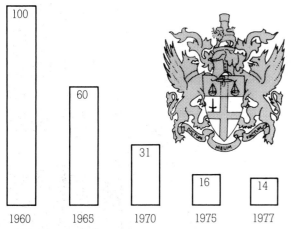

Fig. 16.5 How the London jobbing system shrank between 1960 and 1977

Part of the reason for forming the cartels stemmed from the change in the types of investor using the Stock Exchange. The dominant investors today are the large pension funds and insurance companies; the small individual investor has become relatively insignificant. Since these large 'institutional investors' deal in amounts of hundreds of millions of pounds at a time, jobbers needed to possess the capital to trade with them. By merging together they were able to combine resources to buy and sell in large denominations. The Monopolies Commission, however, established that jobbers dealing in the same share were agreeing to quote the same difference between their buying and selling price and this practice together with the fixed commission percentage all brokers charge prompted reforms which were designed to create more competition, increase efficiency and generally modernise trading practices.

In the first place the 'Big Bang' allowed the practice of fixed commissions to be abolished in both the broking and jobbing areas. This was fol-

lowed up by a policy of allowing outside institutions to own up to 100% of a broking or jobbing firm. This move allowed extra capital to be injected into the running of the market, giving economies of scale to transactions and enabling lower commissions to be charged. Finally the distinction between brokers and jobbers was abolished (in fact the UK Stock Exchange was the only one in the world to create the distinction anyway). This abolition allowed the middleman's profit to be cut out creating increased efficiency.

The injection of new capital into the Stock Exchange has helped modernisation to take place. Technology has opened up new methods of trading and new habits which the London market in its previous form could not have hoped to live with. In New York for example, the world's largest stock-broking firm, Merrill Lynch, now runs a 24-hour book in stocks by dealing in London, then New York then Tokyo using satellite communications. It is this kind of international competition that the Stock Exchange needs to contend with.

The fact that considerable sums of money can be made from the buying and selling of securities on the Stock Exchange has given rise to considerable speculative activity. A speculator who buys a security at a low price expecting to sell at a higher price is known as a **bull**. A bull is also labelled an optimist since he has to hope a company's performance will improve, to allow a profit to be made. A **bear**, on the other hand, is a pessimist who expects a company's market value to deteriorate. He sells stocks or shares that he may or may not possess hoping to buy them back at a later date at a lower price to make a profit. Since three weeks may elapse between the selling transaction and the settlement day when the share certificates have to be presented, providing the 'bear' buys back the same shares he sells, he doesn't need to own the shares in the first place! A speculator who specialises in buying new issues hoping to sell them at a later date for a profit is known as a **stag**.

Although the Stock Exchange has come under criticism for the lack of competition in the securities market, it does provide some important economic functions. Firstly and most important it allows stocks and shares to be **liquid**. A liquid asset is one which can easily be converted into cash. Thus anyone buying a share in a public company can convert their asset into cash by disposing of it at the prevailing market price on the Stock Exchange. Because shares are liquid, companies find it much easier to raise capital in the first place, investors knowing that should the need arise the asset can easily be disposed of. In this sense the Stock Exchange is also useful for the government, allowing gilt-edged securities to become liquid assets.

Secondly, the Stock Exchange can act as a kind of barometer of economic performance since changes in the profitability of British industry will be reflected in share price movements. The ac-

Fig. 16.6 The traditional method of share dealing of the Stock Exchange floor – now most shares are traded via computers and telephones from office desks and the floor is deserted

curacy of this function is rather questionable when looking at the FT index over the last 10 years. Its steady rise does not take account of the early 1980s recession and it perhaps reflects the economic *potential* of the country rather than economic *performance*. The development of North Sea oil has certainly helped to ensure that the UK has lasting economic potential.

Finally by providing accurate market prices of securities, the Stock Exchange facilitates the valuation of wealth in the hands of securities owners. This is useful not least for tax purposes, in particular assessing capital gains.

Perhaps the main criticism of the Stock Exchange is that it is now very much a secondhand marketplace with only about 3% of new capital being raised there. In this sense industry gains very little directly from the Exchange and there has been the charge that the market has been left open to speculators – parasites who gamble and distort market prices for their own personal gain. This is something of an exaggeration since the main investors today are the institutions which in the main are looking for a good return on their assets in order to pay people their pensions when they retire.

THINGS TO DO

1 Read carefully the passage on 'The Big Bang', then answer the following questions:

(a) What does the term 'Big Bang' refer to?

(b) Why was the Stock Exchange opened to more competition?

(c) Why did the abolition of fixed commission charges on security deals lead to the merging of broking and jobbing functions?

(d) How have improvements in information technology affected the scale of organisation in security dealings?

Fig. 16.7

The Big Bang is part of a world-wide revolution which is rapidly transforming the way everyone's money is managed everywhere. Any substantial accumulation of cash is likely to be in almost constant, round-the-clock orbit as its owners seek the safest, most remunerative home for it. Instant electronic communication, with prices of securities, currency values and interest rates altering in seconds, means that the most secure and profitable haven for money can change half-a-dozen times in just one day. When office lights go out in London, trading continues full belt as New York, Sydney, Tokyo, Hong Kong, Singapore, Frankfurt and Paris come progressively to life.

Conventionally, the countdown to the 'Big Bang' started on July 19, 1983. That was when Sir Nicholas Goodison, the Stock Exchange's suave and long-serving chairman, shook hands with Cecil Parkinson, then Secretary for Trade and Industry, and agreed to abandon the charging of fixed commissions on stock and share deals. This was the cosy arrangement which, throughout this century, had financed all those beautiful houses in the stockbroker belt and paid for the Rolls-Royces and Mercedes parked in their drives. Its abolition, which is one of the two key changes that comes into effect on Big Bang day, was the price the government demanded for not subjecting the Exchange's 200-year rule book to the unsympathetic scrutiny of the Office of Fair Trading, and Goodison paid it without much argument. But as things turned out, it was rather like taking a brick out of a wall and starting a landslide.

Next to go had to be the rigidly maintained distinction between the commission-collecting brokers, merely carrying out their clients' buying and selling orders, and the jobbers, who act as pure wholesalers, making their money on the difference between buying and selling prices which they have to quote for each stock or share in which they trade. Once fixed commissions disappeared, neither group would be able to make a living without taking over a large part of the other's job. Once the Exchange authorities accepted the logic of that there was a hectic flurry of mergers, so that there is now virtually no firm of any significance not equipped to act as both "salesman" and "market-maker". After Big Bang, the jobber will go the way of such defunct trades as the falconer and the cordwainer.

With the prospect of Big Bang, people finally woke up and started scrambling to recover lost ground. But the landscape had dramatically changed. Computers and advanced telecommunications had created a five-continent market that never slept, and to take full advantage of it, massive resources were required. For the new broker-jobber groupings this meant massive injections of new capital, virtually impossible to find while Stock Exchange membership was restricted to individuals acting in partnership, as they always had in the past.

So in June 1984 that rule was scrapped, allowing brokers to incorporate themselves as limited companies; and even more important, letting outsiders, including banks, and even foreigners, buy their way in and start building up their infantry and their specialised assault units. At first they were limited to 29.9 per cent, but from March 1 this year ("Little Bang") that was raised to full 100 per cent.

The effect was electric. Six months later every single stockbroker of note (barring Cazenove) had become part of some larger financial conglomerate. The sums involved, on a conservative estimate, ran close to £2 billion, and made a small army of senior partners into overnight millionaires. Those excluded from the bonanza, or dissatisfied with their share, promptly voted with their feet and sought greener pastures elsewhere. A whole new vocabulary of "golden hellos", "golden shackles" and "golden goodbyes" had to be developed to describe the incentives devised to hold them, or to get them on the move. Anyone with senior staff experience or a half-decent specialist reputation—let alone an ability to install and tune-up a computer-dealing room—was more or less guaranteed a six-figure offer, as demand far outstripped supply.

The next question, though, is can it stand the strain? For as long as most people can remember, London's gilt-edged market, which handles the buying and selling of all the government's massive debt, has been serviced by just two jobbing firms, Wedd Durlacher and Ackroyd & Smithers (now part of Warburg's merchant banking empire). From October 27 the Bank of England accepted applications from 29 separate organisations—all of them highly competitive and backed by huge capital resources—to act as primary gilts dealers. Two, including the vast but troubled Bank of America, have already dropped out. The rest can do little more at this stage than slug it out and hope to be still on their feet at the end of what can only be a bitter and costly fight. But sheer prestige and machismo will demand that most of them make the effort.

The Sunday Times 3.10.1986

(e) Why may competition in the security market mean job vulnerability?

2 Distinguish between the **money** market and the **capital** market. Why is the money market sometimes called the **discount market**?

3 What is a **bill of exchange**? Why do bills provide a useful mechanism of payment for an importer?

4 Why is it important that the Bank of England acts as 'lender of last resort' in the money market?

5 If the annual market rate of interest averaged 12% and a £10 000 bill of exchange was presented to a discount house, what would be the likely profit margin assuming the bill was accepted?

6 Read Fig. 16.8.
Explain why jobbers felt it necessary to merge in the light of the 'large institutional deals which now dominate the market'.

Fig. 16.8

Commission nods in a third force jobbing merger

THE Monopolies Commission last week cleared the way for the formation of a third major jobbing force in the London Stock Market. The would-be partners, Smith Brothers and Bisgood Bishop, have so far remained tight-lipped on whether they will go through with the marriage. But the logic of the arguments put forward and accepted by the Commission were so compelling that it is probably now just a matter of agreeing a price.

Judged by the number of firms involved, the jobbing system, which acts as wholesaler of shares buying and selling to brokers, has shrunk almost to the point of vanishing. But the central and much misunderstood argument endorsed by the Commission is that the effectiveness of competition depends more on the strength of the firms than on their number. The ability of jobbing firms to carry stocks on their books and to compete in the large institutional deals which now dominate the market, hinges largely on the capital resources which they can muster.

The Commission's decision will no doubt have surprised the critics of the present dealing systems, who tend to equate fewer jobbers with less competition. But the report published last week noted the disappearance of the small firms dealing only in a handful of companies and the wider spreads (trading margins) quoted today. But it also commented "gross jobbing profits do not appear to have increased correspondingly."

As an outsiders view of the workings at the heart of all stock exchange dealings, the report was a welcome exercise which laid to rest a few ghosts and also raised a skeleton or two.

On the central issue of competition the Commission recognised that only 48 stocks overlap on the Smith and Bisgood books and that there are 2 700 securities in which they also deal where competition is unchanged. The expansion of the international business made possible by the merger was also hailed as in the public interest.

The sour notes came in the form of critical comments on the effect on small investors and the price spread arrangements whereby the jobbers dealing in a particular stock agree to quote the same differences between their buying and selling prices.

The report clearly indicated that there is little in the creation of a third major jobbing firm for the small investor. But the interests of the small man, where they have been damaged, have been more affected by the increasing importance of institutional business than by the decline in the number of jobbers.

The increasing importance attached to large deals by both brokers and jobbers would not be materially affected, said the report. It concluded that the price spread agreements were having an anti-competitive effect.

Overall the report depicts a system struggling with the enormous rise in costs and increased scale of money resources needed to perform its function. It leaves aside the question of whether a better system is possible. But the message emerges quite clearly that jobbing *has* become less competitive and that the Commission would take a keen interest in any future mergers involving the takeover of a large jobbing firm.

John Bell

The Sunday Times 16.5.1979

BUILDING SOCIETIES

Building societies form part of the capital market by virtue of the fact that they lend money for house purchases in the form of a **mortgage**. The repayments for the mortgage are usually spread over 25 years.

Around 40% of the adult population has a building society account and total deposits have risen from £10 000m in 1970 to £80 000m in 1983. The societies have been taking an ever increasing share of the savings market with the result that they are now more popular than the commercial banks, accounting for about 47% of total savings compared to 32% for the banks. They have achieved this astonishing success by offering security, competitive rates of interest, flexible saving schemes and convenient opening hours including Saturday morning. Relaxations in banking regulations have also allowed the societies to virtually take on the role of banks with a number offering chequebooks, cashcards and travellers' cheques. It is likely that in the future the distinction between their activities and those of the banks will be further eroded, increasing competition in the financial services market (Fig. 16.9).

PENSION FUNDS

Pension funds receive their income from the 'Superannuation' contributions employees and employers make, which are designed to provide future incomes for people retiring from work. Pension funds are exempt from any tax on their earnings and they are of major significance to the UK capital market.

INSURANCE COMPANIES

The principle of insurance is based on the pooling of risks – **premiums** are paid to insurance companies in return for which compensation is paid when certain eventualities occur (e.g. a theft or motor accident). The traditional forms of insurance are **general** (i.e. marine, fire and accident) and **life** which should strictly be called **assurance** because cover is provided against the occurrence of an event which is inevitable.

Since premiums are paid which will not be redeemed for a considerable period of time (particularly with life assurance), insurance companies are interested in longterm investments. The capital market is the ideal place for their money and it is a measure of the importance of insurance companies that at the end of 1982 their investments totalled £96 000m.

INVESTMENT AND UNIT TRUSTS

Investment and **unit trusts** use the funds subscribed to them to invest in a wide range of securities, often in different countries. In this sense they act as 'managers' of money using their expertise to get the best returns for savers. Inevitably some are more successful than others: the best achieving growth rates of over 100% per annum, but the worst actually losing money through poor investing. Savers can sell their unit holdings at any time, enjoying any capital gains arising from the investments. In 1982 the market value of investment and unit trusts was around £15 000m of which about £7 000m was invested overseas.

Fig. 16.9 The Halifax Building Society – the largest in the world. Building societies now offer cashpoint machines, chequebook facilities and a whole range of banking services. Many banks have reintroduced Saturday morning banking in order to stave off the increasing competition from building societies

THE COMMERCIAL BANKS – RECONCILING LIQUIDITY AND PROFITABILITY

So far the commercial banks have been seen to be active in the money market by lending funds to the discount houses. They are also present in the capital market buying a range of securities as a means of profitably investing depositors' money. In fact their lending activities are fairly diverse and this is because they have to satisfy two different groups of people connected with the bank, each with different interests. On the one hand the **customers** who deposit their money with the bank want to be sure that it is available to be withdrawn at any time as and when necessary. On the other hand the **shareholders** who own the bank want to see money loaned out as profitably as possible to ensure the highest possible dividend.

This poses the banks something of a dilemma. The most profitable form of lending is also the least liquid. This means that the highest interest is usually charged on loans taken out for the longest time period. Thus if customers do for some reason demand heavy cash withdrawals and the banks commit all their lending to longterm advances, they could risk a situation where they actually run out of cash. The answer therefore is to spread lending over different time periods so that some loans such as 'money at call' can be recalled on a daily basis and others such as longterm advances can be the profit earners.

Figure 16.10 summarises the main assets of the commercial banks.

Since banks are in business to make a profit the main part of their lending comes in the form of advances. Investing in securities (gilts and companies) is also regarded as profitable. At the other end of the scale notes and coins obviously possess maximum liquidity with some short-term loans able to be turned into cash with three hour's notice. Most short-term loans do not exceed one year. By maintaining a balance between liquidity and profitability the banks are able to satisfy both customers and shareholders. The Bank of England will also want to monitor this balance to ensure that the amount of credit the banks create (mainly in the form of advances) is appropriate for the economy. Too much money could lead to inflation; too little to stagnation.

THE BANK OF ENGLAND

The Bank of England was founded in 1694 as a private company formed by a group of London merchants to lend money to the government and deal with the National Debt (Fig. 16.11). It was only recently nationalised in 1946 though it obviously has always maintained close links with the government. It is the central bank of the British monetary system and in this respect performs several important functions:

1 It issues bank notes

The 1844 Bank Charter Act gave the Bank the exclusive right to issue notes as a means of regulating the amount of legal tender so that the commercial banks now only *distribute* notes and coins.

2 It acts as banker to the government

The Bank of England performs two important areas of work for the government. Firstly it manages the National Debt, issuing Treasury bills and gilts and paying interest on the latter half yearly to stockholders. Secondly it manages the gold and foreign currency reserves through the **Exchange Equilisation Account**. In this account reserves are topped up using sterling to buy foreign currencies. Equally to stabilise the value of sterling, reserves may be sold and sterling bought to prevent the value of the pound falling.

3 It acts as banker to the commercial banks

The commercial banks hold their accounts at the Bank of England, usually keeping about a third of their cash there. At the end of a day's cheque clearing they can adjust their accounts through the Bank of England settling inter-bank debits and credits.

4 It carries out monetary policy on behalf of the government

Controlling the amount of money in an economy is essential for economic stability and growth. Since the commercial banks 'create' deposits which form part of the money stock, it is the Bank of England's responsibility to ensure that appro-

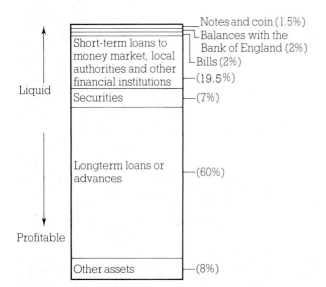

Fig. 16.10 The assets structure of a commercial bank

priate measures are available to limit or, if necessary, encourage credit creation. Essentially the demand for money in the form of credit is like the demand for a good or service: the cheaper the price the greater the quantity demanded. In this case the 'price' of money is the interest charged to borrow it; the lower the interest, the greater the demand and vice versa. Thus the demand curve for money might look like that shown in Fig. 16.12.

If the government decides it needs to reduce the amount of money in the economy then one strand of monetary policy could be to raise interest rates. The Bank of England can influence market rates as 'lender of last resort' and adjusting this intervention rate has a knock on effect for all other market rates. Using the weapon of changing interest rates has not been very successful in the past, however, probably because the demand for money is fairly price inelastic. Figure 16.12 shows that in the case of an inelastic demand curve for money even a large increase in interest rates from r_1 to r_2 produces only a small contraction in demand from Q_1 to Q_2. If changing the price of money is not a very effective way of pursuing monetary control, the other option is to try and control the quantity of money itself and leave price to be determined by market forces.

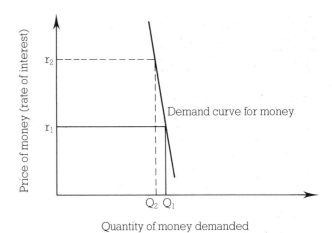

Fig. 16.12

Fig. 16.11　The Bank of England – the 'Old Lady of Threadneedle Street'

In the UK the quantity of money supplied has enjoyed several definitions, but a commonly used aggregate is sterling M3 (£M3). This includes notes + coins and public + private sector current and deposit accounts. It is obviously from the bank accounts that credit is created and cheques drawn. Figure 16.13 shows movements in £M3 from 1982 to 1985.

MONEY SUPPLY

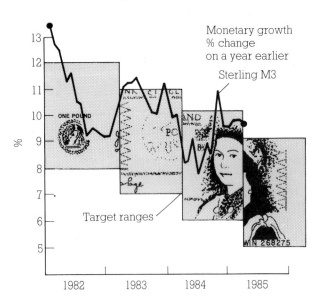

Fig. 16.13 Changes in the UK money supply 1982–85

There are several ways of controlling the supply of £M3:

1 Monetary 'base' control
In simple terms monetary base control means adjusting the supply of cash, the 'base' on which credit is created. A smaller amount of legal tender would allow less credit to be created.

2 Open market operations
Another way of influencing the cash reserves of banks is to encourage customers to withdraw or add cash to accounts. The Bank of England does this by either selling gilts on the market at prices which may encourage bank customers to buy them or offering to buy back gilts at favourable prices providing cash for bank customers.

3 Special deposits
Since the commercial banks deposit part of their cash reserves at the Bank of England, the Bank is able to 'freeze' part of these reserves if the requirement is to reduce the money supply. This frozen cash is placed in 'special deposits' which can be released when monetary controls are relaxed.

4 Ceilings on lending
Under the 1946 Act the Bank of England can 'request' or 'direct' banks to limit the quantity of advances they create. This may take the form of a fixed ceiling per month or allowing special preference to be given to exporters or labour intensive companies.

5 Limiting the size of the PSBR
To the extent that some government borrowing is financed by the banks creating credit, limiting the borrowing requirement will help to contain the growth in the quantity of money. The Bank is, of course, not directly responsible for the size of the PSBR. This is controlled by the Treasury.

6 Making government savings schemes more attractive
Another way of inducing bank customers to take cash out of their accounts is to make government savings schemes attractive. These include the National Savings Bank which offers favourable and tax-free interest, and premium bonds which offer an extensive range of prizes including a large monthly jackpot.

Taken together these controls allow considerable influence to be exerted over the quantity of money supplied to the economy though it must be added that accurate monetary control is difficult partly because of time lags in the system and also because the commercial banks as profit maximising institutions will, if possible, find ways round restrictive monetary controls. Using interest rates as a monetary weapon is also unreliable because in practice the demand for money seems to be very interest inelastic.

THINGS TO DO

1 Why have building societies become the fastest growing savings institution?

2 Explain the role insurance companies, investment and unit trusts companies and pension funds have in the capital market.

3 Explain the connection between bank customer and liquidity, and between bank shareholder and profitability.

4 What is the **Exchange Equalisation Account**? How is it used to prevent a run on the £?

5 Explain the difference between monetary policy being carried by *price* controls and *quantity* controls. Why have price controls been abandoned? (Explain using a graph.)

6 In Fig. 16.14 estimate the likely effects on interest rates if the Bank of England used monetary policy to expand the quantity of money supplied.

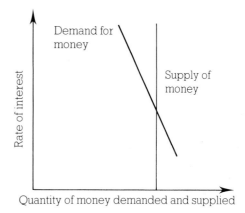

Fig. 16.14

EXAMINATION
QUESTIONS

KEY TO EXAMINATION
QUESTIONS

N   Northern Group GCSE sample paper
L – London/East Anglia GCSE sample paper
M – Midland Group GCSE sample paper
S – Southern Group GCSE sample paper
W – Welsh Group GCSE sample paper

CHAPTER 1

1 Describe the main factors of production.   (London CSE paper 1980)

2 (a) What is meant by saying that Britain is a mixed economy?
  (b) In what ways is our economy similar to and different from a state planned economy?   (London CSE paper 1983)

3 (a) Distinguish between capital and consumer goods giving one example of each type of good.
  (b) Why does an economy seek to acquire capital goods?   (L)

4 The problem of what to produce in a command economy is mainly solved by
  A consumer preferences
  B government directives
  C the profit motive
  D market forces
  (S – multiple choice)

5 A mixed economy is defined as having
  A agricultural and industrial sectors
  B large and small firms
  C external and internal trade
  D private and public enterprise
  (S – multiple choice)

6 Before the airport was built at Gatwick, the land was used for farming. More land has been taken over as the airport has expanded. How does this example illustrate the idea of 'opportunity cost'?   (M)

7 A mixed economy is defined as having
  A agricultural and industrial sectors
  B large and small firms
  C external and internal trade
  D private and public enterprise
  (S – multiple choice)

8 In a free market economy the price mechanism
  A measures national wealth
  B reduces unfair competition
  C aids government control
  D allocates resources
  (S – multiple choice)

9 Which of the following is normally classified as a consumer good?
  A an office typewriter
  B a delivery van
  C a factory
  D a child's bicycle
  (S – multiple choice)

CHAPTER 2

1

Data 1: Newspaper Article

THE WORLD SEES MILLIONS RACE AGAINST TIME

At 4pm, London time, yesterday an estimated 30 million people in 286 cities in 75 countries simultaneously began running to raise funds for famine relief in what was the biggest athletic event ever to be staged in the world.

Billed as the Race Against Time by the organisers, Sport Aid and the United Nations Children's Fund, the global event is expected to produce millions of pounds for the famine-stricken regions of Africa.

A thread of criticism of politicians ran through the proceedings. A large banner trailing over part of the Hyde Park run read: "Stars and public £100 million; British Government £1 million".

The World Development Movement said that figures from the Overseas Development Agency showed that the level of foreign aid in 1985 had in real terms, sunk to the lowest point ever.

(Adapted from "The Guardian" May 26th 1986)

Study Data 1 carefully.
(a) State **one** thing being done by individual people and groups of people to help people in Africa as part of the race against time.
(b) What is meant by the term 'foreign aid'?
(c) Why is the World Development Movement worried about foreign aid?
(d)

"The price of wheat is right"
... *Food buyer from a rich country*

"The price of wheat is too low"
... *Farmer from a poor country*

Explain the thinking behind each of these two views.

(e)

In the world food market there are surpluses of food in Europe and starvation in Africa. More could be done to bring surpluses and starving together.

  (i) What do economists mean by the term "surpluses" as used above?
  (ii) What problems might there be in bringing surpluses and starvation together?
 (f) Describe up to **four** ways in which the UK government could best help people in Africa. In each case say why you think it would help. (N Section B)

2 (a) Distinguish between (i) capital goods and (ii) consumer goods. Give one example of each type of good.
 (b) Why does an economy seek to acquire capital goods?
 (c) Examine the difficulties which developing countries face in acquiring capital goods. (L)

3 Why are some countries which have many natural resources still poor? How can such countries be helped by the richer nations? (London CSE paper 1982)

4 Give reasons why people of the underdeveloped (developing) countries have a low standard of living. (London CSE paper 1979)

5 'The average national income per head of people living in the UK is higher than that of people living in India.' 'The rate of growth of national income is higher in India than in the UK.' Explain carefully the meaning of these two statements. How can both be correct? (London CSE paper 1978)

6 (a) From the following list give examples of (i) *two* capital goods and (ii) *two* consumer goods.
   a blast furnace;
   a fishing trawler;
   a packet of cigarettes;
   a railway engine;
   a household washing machine;
   a delivery van.
 (b) Distinguish between capital goods and consumer goods.
 (c) Mules and tractors are examples of capital goods for Botswana farmers. What economic advantages do tractors have over mules?

An OXFAM publicity leaflet stated that:
'Developing countries want capital goods'.
 (d) Why do developing countries want capital goods?
 (e) Examine the difficulties which face developing countries which want capital goods.

CHAPTER 3

1 Give three advantages of the use of the division of labour. (M Section A)

2 (a) Explain carefully what is meant by.
   (i) 'internal economies of scale'.
   (ii) 'external economies of scale'.
  Give *one* example of each.
 (b) State *two* diseconomies of scale. (S)

3 (a) Describe **two** advantages of the division of labour.
 (b) Giving examples, explain the difference between *internal* and *external* economies of scale.
 (c) Assess the advantages for a manufacturing company of:
   (i) vertical integration;
   (ii) ploughing back retained profits;
   (iii) worker participation in ownership.
   (W)

4 What advantages does the division of labour bring to
 (a) the worker
 (b) the business owner?
  (London CSE paper 1982)

5 (a) What is 'mobility of labour'?
 (b) With the use of examples show the connections between the mobility of labour and economic development.
  (London 'O' 1980)

6 A shoe manufacturer buys a chain of shoe shops.
 (a) Give **one** advantage this might bring the shoe manufacturer.
 (b) Give **one** benefit this might bring the consumer of shoes.
 (c) Give **one** reason why this action might be to the disadvantage of the consumers. (N Section A)

CHAPTER 4

1 Study the three drawings given below and the
  table and the graph on the following page.

(Adapted from: W.B. Davies & D.C. Hender,
Production and Trade, Longman.)

An unemployed school-leaver who lives opposite the station has noticed the behaviour by customers at the flower stall. Over some days she observes that customers want to buy more roses when the price falls, but the stall holder wants to sell more roses when the price is high. The school-leaver has drawn up a table to show this kind of behaviour.

Prices of roses (pence per bunch)	Number of roses demanded (bunches)	Number of roses supplied (bunches)
150	10	120
50	30	70
30	50	50
10	150	20

The school-leaver uses the above figures to draw a graph which shows the supply of roses (S) and the demand for roses (D). She puts the above figures on the axes of her graph, which is show below.

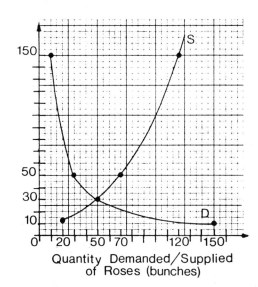

Price of Roses (pence per bunch)

Quantity Demanded/Supplied of Roses (bunches)

Use the information in the drawings, the table and the graph to answer questions (a), (b) and (c).

(a) Explain why more customers are buying flowers at 5.15 p.m. than at 8.55 a.m. In your answer refer to: price, the amount of roses for sale; the number of customers buying roses.

(b) (i) What is the price at which the amount of roses demanded matches the amount of roses supplied?

(ii) What do economists call this price?

(c) (i) What happens to the customers' total spending on roses if the price changes from 50p to 30p?   (L Section C)

2 In the UK when Value Added Tax (VAT) was first put on take-away food, it was estimated that demand fell by 25%.

(a) Draw diagrams to show the equilibrium price of take-away meals before and after the introduction of VAT.

(b) Explain, or show by diagrams, the effect on the price and output of take-away meals of

(i) a fall in the price of potatoes and rice

(ii) advertising which leads consumers to believe that take-away food is unhealthy.   S)

3 (a) Explain **clearly** the difference between *wants* and *demand*.

(b) **With the aid of diagrams** distinguish between:

(i) an increase in the quantity of tape cassettes demanded, and

(ii) an increase in demand for tape cassettes.

(c) Assess the influence on the price of tape cassettes of **each** of the following circumstances:

(i) an increase in unemployment amongst young workers;

(ii) a major cut in the cost of electronic components used to manufacture tape recorders;

(iii) a successful advertising campaign for compact discs.   (W)

4 State two possible reasons why the supply curve for bread might shift from S_1 to S_2.   (M)

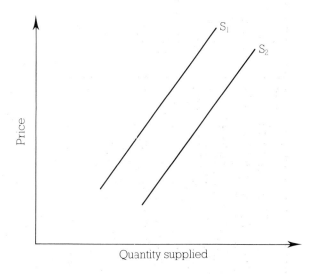

Price

Quantity supplied

CHAPTER 5

1 Explain clearly the difference between each of the following:
 (a) current account and deposit account
 (b) bank giro and standing order
 (c) loan and overdraft.
  (London CSE paper 1984)

2 (a) What are credit cards and cheques?
 (b) Account for the use of these methods of payment. (London 'O' 1980)

3 List *four* functions of money. (L Section A)

4 As usual, your dad got more pairs of socks for Christmas than he wanted. He managed to swap some of them with his brother for after-shave.
 (a) What do economists call this system of exchange, where no money is involved?
 (b) Give **one** reason why your dad might have preferred money rather than socks for Christmas. (N Section A)

5 (a) Describe the functions of money.
 (b) State *two* characteristics of money.
 (c) What are the main types of money in use in the UK? (S)

6 (a) **Briefly** explain to a friend, who is opening a bank account, the differences between:
  (i) a current and a deposit account;
  (ii) a bank loan and an overdraft.

 (b) *Cheque; credit card; direct debit.*
  Select **one** of the above methods of payments for use in **each** of the following circumstances, explaining your choice:
   (i) making a single payment to a mail order firm;
   (ii) paying your quarterly telephone bill conveniently;
   (iii) paying conveniently for a pair of jeans bought in a chain store.
 (c) Explain why economists say that the banking system *creates* the money supply. (W)

7 (a) Study the names of various banks given below. Give the names of *two* commercial (clearing) banks.
 (b) With specific reference to banking:
  (i) What are cleared?
  (ii) How are they cleared?
 (c) How are commercial banks able to arrange and manage business transactions by using very little cash?
 (d) (i) When banks use the term 'liquid assets', what does the word 'liquid' mean?
   (ii) Why do commercial banks have some of their assets in liquid form?
   (iii) Explain fully why commercial banks try to satisfy their need to be both liquid and profitable. (L Section B)

(*Reproduced by permission of the various banks.*)

CHAPTER 6

1 (a) A consumer buys a record in a shop, paying for it with cash. In what ways is this consumer protected by law?
  (b) What are the economic reasons for consumer protection laws?
  (c) What factors, other than price, might a consumer take into account before buying an expensive household item?
  (d) Explain how the degree of competition faced by a firm affects the price of its product.   (S)

2 (a) What are the characteristic features of a multiple chain of retailers?
  (b) How do small retailers try to compete against large retail organisations? (London 'O' 1983)

3 (a) What are the functions of a wholesaler?
  (b) How can he help the retailer to reduce his costs?
  (c) The number of wholesalers has been declining in recent years: what are the reasons for this? (London CSE paper 1984)

4 What are the differences between
  (a) a retail cooperative society
  (b) a department store?   (London CSE paper 1982)

5 Only about 10% of advertising in Britain is informative. How can the other 90% be described? (M Paper 1 Section B Short Answers)

6 State *two* reasons why a supermarket can sell food relatively cheaply. (M Paper 1 Section B Short Answers)

CHAPTER 7

1 (a) Distinguish between (i) primary (ii) secondary and (iii) tertiary occupations.
  (b) What changes have taken place in the UK during the last 20 years in the distribution of the working population between these main classes of employment?
  (c) Examine the reasons for these changes and outline their likely economic effects.   (L)

2 (a) What is meant by the term 'birth rate'?
  (b) Briefly explain the following heading in a newspaper 'Population is outstripping resources'.
  (c) Outline the economic consequences of a high birth rate and a declining death rate in an underdeveloped economy.   (M)

3 (a) What are the main changes that have occurred in the size and age structure of the UK's population since 1945?
  (b) What have been the economic effects of these changes? (London 'O' 1984)

4 For what reasons may the size of a country's population change?   (London CSE paper 1984)

5 Suppose the following data were collected for a year:
  Total population: 56 000 000
  Live births: 700 000
  Registered deaths: 560 000
  Calculate:
  (a) the death rate
  (b) the natural increase in population.
  (W Section A)

6 Besides changes in the birth rate, what can account for changes in the size of world population?   (M paper 1 Section B)

7 Study the various illustrations overleaf which are labelled A to J and then answer questions (a) and (b).
  (a) Make two lists to classify each illustration as either a good or a service by using the appropriate letters.
  (b) Classify into the appropriate occupational group (primary, secondary or tertiary) the person(s) mainly involved in producing or working at:
      (i) illustration B;
      (ii) illustration D;
      (iii) illustration J.   (L Section C)

8 The number of old age pensioners in Britain is increasing. State **two** economic effects this might have on the rest of the population. (N Section A)

RITZ
★ NOW ★
SHOWING
7 DAYS A WEEK

A

B

C

ROVERS
versus
UNITED

D

Haircuts

E

F

G

LONDON
TOURS

H

I

J

CHAPTER 8

1 (a) Give four main advantages of the sole trader as a form of business organisation.
  (b) Fully explain the main advantages gained by a sole trader in becoming a private limited company.
  (c) 'Although public corporations may incur losses, they operate in the public interest.'
    (i) What are the main features of a public corporation?
    (ii) State, with reasons, whether you agree or disagree with the above statement. (M)

2 (a) Give one economic reason for the nationalisation of British Rail.
  (b) Give one economic reason for the privatisation of British Telecom.

3 (a) Write in full the names of (i) *two* public limited companies and (ii) *two* public corporations.
  (b) What are the differences between a public limited company and a public corporation from the point of view of (i) aims (ii) ownership (iii) management (iv) finance? (L)

4 (a) Outline the main arguments which can be used in favour of the public ownership of industry.
  (b) What disadvantages may be associated with the public ownership of industry? (London 'O' 1984)

5 There may be a conflict of interest between privately owned firms and consumers because
  1 Firms want to increase sales, while consumers want to raise living standards
  2 By competitive advertising, firms promote their own products while consumers seek perfect knowledge of all competing products
  3 Firms want to maximise profits, while consumers want to maximise satisfaction.
  (DIRECTIONS:
  A 1 and 2 only correct
  B 2 and 3 only correct
  C 1 only correct
  D 3 only correct)
  (S – multiple choice)

CHAPTER 9

1 Name two functions of a trade union. (L Section A)

2 When you begin work you may join a trade union.
  (a) In what ways might you expect it to help you?
  (b) How could you influence its decisions?
  (c) Are there any disadvantages in joining? Explain your views. (London CSE paper 1983)

3 Explain the meaning of FOUR of the following terms relating to the trade unions:
  (a) closed shop
  (b) conciliation
  (c) picketing
  (d) work to rule
  (e) demarcation disputes. (London CSE paper 1984)

4 Why do doctors usually earn more than bus conductors? (London CSE paper 1982)

5

Year	1967	1977
Number of Trade Unions	606	480
Number of Union members (millions)	10.2	12.7
% of female workers in Unions	26%	41%
% of male workers in Unions	54%	68%

  (a) What happened to the average size of trade unions between 1967 and 1977 as shown in the table above?
  (b) Describe the trends in trade union membership shown in the table.
  (c) Why do you think a smaller percentage of female workers were in trade unions than male workers? (N Section A)

6 (a) A teacher earns £800 per month (gross) but receives £670 per month (net). Why is there a difference between gross pay and net pay?
  (b) Some workers are paid according to time rates and others are paid according to piece rates. If you were a builder employing people to build an estate of 20 houses, by what method would you pay the following? Give a reason in each case.
    (i) a bricklayer;
    (ii) a foreman of the bricklayers;
    (iii) a clerk working in the site office. (M)

CHAPTER 10

1 Read the newspaper report and the figures for unemployment given below and answer the questions which follow.

END OF THE LINE FOR NORTHERN SHIPBUILDERS

Percentage of workers unemployed by region in England and Wales:

	1977 %	1984 %
North	8	18
Yorkshire/Humberside	6	14
North West	8	16
East Midlands	5	12
West Midlands	6	15
Wales	8	16
East Anglia	5	10
South East	5	9
South West	7	11

Source: Dept of Employment (adapted)

For a long time the shipyards of the North have sent new ships to all parts of the world. All this could soon be over, writes Sue Jones.

Overseas orders have been lost to countries like Sweden and Japan. In these countries new machinery and good labour relations have kept costs down and delivery times short.

Orders from British Shipowners have also been lost because of foreign competition. The decline in Britain's own shipping fleet has made things even worse.

The industry has introduced new ways of working and up-to-date machines and the work force has been cut. This has helped to keep parts of the industry going. However, other countries are also keeping up with the times. The future looks gloomy.

The North is not the only region that has problems. In many regions unemployment doubled between 1977 and 1984 (see percentage unemployed). In the West Midlands, for example, changes in the motor vehicle industry have led to a sharp fall in the numbers employed.

Everyone knows that the loss of jobs, not only in shipbuilding, but also in coal-mining and iron and steel, makes the problems in the North particularly bad.

(a) What reasons does the reporter give for the decline in shipbuilding in the North?

(b) What does the reporter think about the future of Britain's shipbuilding industry? Why does she think this?

(c) How might cutting the workforce have helped to keep parts of the shipbuilding industry going in the North?

(d) The decline in shipbuilding is one reason for the high percentage of unemployment in the North. State **one** other reason the reporter gives.

(e) Look at the figures for unemployment. What happened to the percentage of workers unemployed in England and Wales as a whole between 1977 and 1984?

(f)

_____

In the West Midlands changes in the motor vehicle industry have led to a sharp fall in the numbers employed.

_____

Suggest possible reasons why this happened.

(g)

_____

Governments have tried to give people in regions with a high percentage of unemployment more chance of finding jobs by trying to attract new firms to those regions.

_____

Look at the unemployment figures for the North, the North West and Wales given in the newspaper report.
   (i) Explain whether you think this policy has succeeded.
   (ii) Give **one** reason to say why you think it has succeeded or failed.

(h)

Until recently Jim Smith was a welder in a northern shipyard. His wife and two young children were born and bred in the town. He had worked there for 15 years until the yard closed. Local jobs are hard to find with one in five workers looking for a job. With the decline in mining and iron and steel, Jim's chances of a welding job locally are almost nil.

The Smiths have an important choice to make:

1. They can stay where they are and take their chances, **or**

2. They can move to the south east where they know welding jobs are easier to find.

Outline the kinds of things the Smith family would have to consider before reaching a decision that is best for them. (N Section B)

2 Name *four* factors which affect the location of firms in the UK. (L)

3 (a) State the main factors which affect the location of industry.
   (b) How have changes in these factors affected the location of industry since 1945? (London 'O' 1981)

4 Explain the importance of the following factors in the location of industry in Britain.
   (a) raw materials
   (b) markets
   (c) development areas (London CSE paper 1984)

5 Outline the main factors which a new electronics company should consider when deciding the location of its first factory. (London 'O' 1983)

6 (a) Explain briefly how the development of a motorway network affects the location of industry.
   (b) Why is it that 90% of the UK's internal freight is carried by road when rail transport can accommodate much larger loads? (London 'O' Section A 1984)

7 What are the main factors which determine the location of industry in Britain today? Why does the government closely control location? (London CSE paper 1979)

CHAPTER 11

1 Study the table below which gives information about the demand for and the supply of grommets, and then answer questions (a) to (c).

Price of grommets (pence)	Quantity of grommets demanded/week	Quantity of grommets supplied/week
15	1	12
5	3	7
3	5	5
1	15	2

   (a) On graph paper plot and draw the demand and supply curves. Label each axis clearly.
   (b) State the equilibrium price.
   (c) Calculate the elasticity of demand when price increases from 3p to 5p per unit. (L)

2 Original price = £10,
new price = £9,
original quantity bought = 1000,
new quantity bought = 1200.
From the above data, calculate the coefficient of elasticity. (W)

3 State one reason why the demand for matches is likely to be relatively price inelastic. (M)

	Butter		Margarine	
	Price (p/kilo)	Quantity demanded (per week/ kilo)	Price	Quantity demanded
Week 1	50	500	25	400
Week 2	45	600	25	300

4 (a) Calculate the price elasticity of demand for butter from the above table.
   (b) Calculate the cross elasticity of demand between butter and margarine. (L)

5 (a) In a wholesale market the price of apples during October was 10 p per pound and during November it rose to 12 p per pound.
     (i) Suggest why the wholesale price may have changed from October to November.
     (ii) What does 'wholesale market' mean in Economics and how does it operate?
   (b) The relationship of change in demand/ supply and change in price may be measured through price-elasticity.
     (i) How do you measure price-elasticity of demand and price-elasticity of supply?
     (ii) Explain, with the help of diagrams, the following statements.

(1) The demand for matches is inelastic.
(2) The supply of FA Cup Final tickets is absolutely inelastic.
(iii) Explain, with examples, why price elasticity is a useful measurement for the Chancellor of the Exchequer to consider in deciding on taxation policies in the Budget.

6 Study the following demand and supply schedule for cocoa.
(a) On your answer paper accurately draw the demand and supply curves. Correctly label each axis.
(b) State the equilibrium price.

(c) Give the numerical value for price-elasticity of supply. What is the name given to describe this value?
(d) Calculate the price-elasticity of demand when price increases from 20p to 30p. Show all your workings.   (M)

Price (pence)	Quantity demanded	Quantity supplied
10	250	100
20	200	100
30	150	100
40	100	100
50	50	100

CHAPTER 12

1 State **two** reasons why the Government might wish to reduce income tax.

2 Study the brief extracts below from different newspapers published on Wednesday 19 March 1986, the day after Budget Day, and then answer the questions which follow.

3 Amy earns £8000 per year and pays £2000 per year in income tax. Clare earns £16000 per year and pays £5000 per year in income tax. This income tax system is therefore
A flat rate
B progressive
C proportional
D regressive
(S – multiple choice)

LAWSON CUTS INCOME TAX

THE standard rate of income tax was cut by 1p to 29p, and 550,000 people were taken out of the income tax system

A CUT of one per cent. in the basic rate of income tax is the big surprise in this year's Budget.

It comes down from 30 per cent. to 29 per cent.

BUDGET HIGHLIGHTS

Rate of income tax cut to 29%

The Chancellor cut the basic rate of income tax from 30 to 29 per cent, the first reduction since 1979

(a) (i) State whether income tax is a direct or an indirect tax.
(ii) Distinguish between direct and indirect taxes.
(b) What is meant by the statement '550 000 people were taken out of the income tax system'?
(c) With reference to the table below, state for each of the columns X, Y and Z whether it illustrates (i) a progressive tax, (ii) a proportional tax or (iii) a regressive tax in relation to Gross Income.

Gross Income (£)	Tax paid (£)		
	X	Y	Z
20 000	200	2 000	5 000
10 000	200	1 000	1 000
5 000	200	500	100

(d) Give reasons for each of your answers to part (c).
(e) Examine the likely economic effects of increasing the tax on tobacco by 100%. (L Section B)

4 How do local authorities raise money to finance local services?   (London CSE paper 1982)

5 (*a*) What are the main objectives of taxation?
   (*b*) Describe the UK system of taxation in relation to these objectives.   (London 'O' 1984)

6 (*a*) What are local rates?
   (*b*) How are they calculated?   (London CSE paper 1984)

7 (*a*) Describe the main differences between income tax and VAT.
   (*b*) If the Chancellor of the Exchequer *reduced* the various rates of income tax by 5% and also *raised* the rate of VAT by 5% what would be the economic effect on:
      (i) the desire to work
      (ii) the distribution of household incomes
      (iii) the finance of public expenditure? (W)

8 (*a*) What is a 'progressive' tax?
   (*b*) To what extent may each of the following taxes be describes as 'progressive'?
      (i) income tax
      (ii) value added tax
      (iii) local authority rates
   (*c*) Discuss the view that 'everyone should receive exactly the same income'.   (S)

9 The use of taxation and government expenditure to influence the overall level of economic activity is known as
   A   monetary policy
   B   regional policy
   C   fiscal policy
   D   incomes policy (S – multiple choice)

CHAPTER 13

1 What is meant by the term 'standard of living'? What difficulties are there in making comparisons of living standards between (*a*) two different years (*b*) two different countries?   (London CSE paper 1982)

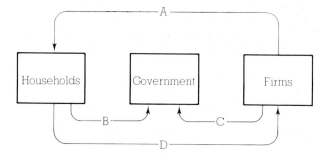

2 In a model of an economy showing its circular flow of income and expenditure, which of the flows marked A to D represents:
   (i) private consumption?
   (ii) taxes?
   (iii) households' income?   (N)

CHAPTER 14

1 (*a*) Explain the meaning of the terms (i) unemployment (ii) inflation.
   (*b*) What are the main causes of the current high rate of unemployment in the UK?
   (*c*) Why might government policies to reduce unemployment cause an increase in the rate of inflation?   (M)

2 Changes in the cost of living are measured by the Index of Retail Prices.
   (*a*) Explain how the Index is constructed.
   (*b*) Describe carefully how changes in prices from one year to the next are measured by the Index.
   (*c*) Comment on some of the difficulties in its use.   (London CSE paper 1984)

3 Identify by names *two* types of unemployment. Explain briefly how each of these types develops.   (London 'O' Section A 1984)

4 The table below represents earnings in the period 1972–80.

	1972	1976	1980
Average weekly earnings (£)	35	50	100
Adjusted for inflation to 1980 prices (£)	60	100	75

Illustrate the figures on a graph and explain the differences.   (London CSE paper 1983)

5 Study carefully the graph below then answer the questions which follow.

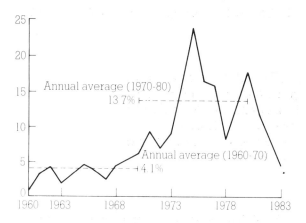

(*a*) Explain the meaning of the term 'retail price inflation'.
(*b*) From the graph, estimate the rate of inflation in 1978.
(*c*) Describe the trends in inflation since 1960, as shown by the graph.
(*d*) Explain the causes of the trends in inflation since 1980.
(*e*) Outline the effects on the UK economy of the fall in the rate of inflation after 1980.   (S)

6 Study the extracts below which were taken from the front pages of different newspapers on the same day in 1986, and then answer the questions which follow.

Each of the extracts refers to inflation.

(a) What do you understand by the term 'inflation'.
(b) During a period of inflation which group of people may:
  (i) benefit;
  (ii) suffer?
(c) Give reasons why 'Jobs boost as inflation drops'.
(d) Comment on the accuracy of measuring inflation as a percentage.
(e) (i) Give *two* methods by which a Government might attempt to control inflation.
  (ii) Examine both the advantages and the disadvantages of using *one* of these methods.

INFLATION EASES TO 5.5p.c.

CHEAPER petrol is helping the Government win its battle against inflation, official figures out yesterday show.

According to the Department of Employment, the annual inflation rate fell to 5.5 per cent in January after touching 5.7 per cent in December. Rail fares, bread, vegetables and alcoholic drinks all went up in price during the month, but this was offset by a fall in petrol prices and a large number of bargains in the shops for household goods and clothing.

Inflation set to hit 3% by summer

The rate of inflation fell to 5.1 per cent last month, its lowest level for over a year, from 5.5 per cent in January. A sharp fall to 3 per cent is expected by the summer.

Jobs boost as inflation drops

A FALL in price inflation from 5·7 to 5·5 per cent, last month was acclaimed by the Government yesterday as 'good news for everyone.'

7 Domestic inflation is most likely to benefit
  A debtors
  B exporters
  C tax-payers
  D creditors
  (S – multiple choice)

8 Changes in the value of money are measured by the
  A level of interest rates
  B Retail Price Index
  C Financial Times Share Index
  D level of wage rates
  (S – multiple choice)

CHAPTER 15

1 (a) Explain carefully the difference between a visible export and an invisible export. Give one example of each.

(b) Describe two ways in which the UK could reduce its visible imports from other countries.

(c) Using demand and supply analysis, explain the likely effect of a large balance of payments deficit on the exchange rate. (S)

2 (a) State **briefly** the broad categories of *imports* of goods into the United Kingdom, indicating recent trends.

(b) Examine the Balance of Payments accounts of the United Kingdom, using the following headings:
   (i) the balance of trade;
   (ii) the current account balance;
   (iii) the balance for official financing.

(c) Assess the effects on the Balance of Payments of **each** of the following trends:
   (i) the rapid contraction of the Welsh coal industry;
   (ii) a major expansion of the tourist industry in Wales;
   (iii) a continuing trend for multinational firms to close branch manufacturing plants in Wales. (W)

3 Study carefully the table below which appeared in a newspaper in 1984. It gives information on what it will cost British holidaymakers in various countries.

(a) Why are certain prices marked with a star?

(b) What does 'current inflation rate 6.5% in France' mean?

(c) Which country has the highest rate of inflation?

(d) Which country appears to have experienced the greatest inflation since 1979? Explain your reasoning.

(e) What does 'current exchange rate 11.60 Francs' mean?

(f) Against which currency has the £ improved most since 1979?

(g) To describe the movement of the escudo (Portugal) against the £ since 1979 you would say that the escudo has . . .

(h) What is the dollar price of petrol in the USA?

(i) What is the price, in pesetas, of wine in Spain?

(j) Name two currencies against which the value of the £ has fallen since 1979.

Complete the following sentences:

(k) If more people from the rest of Europe go to Spain on holiday then that will increase Spain's invisible . . .

(l) If more people go from the UK to holiday on the continent then that will increase the UK's . . . imports.

(m) Name two currencies against which the £ has become worth less since 1979.

(n) Explain why this change is likely to have occurred. (M)

	FRANCE	SPAIN	ITALY	GREECE	USA	W GERMANY	NETHERLANDS	PORTUGAL	SWITZERLAND	AUSTRIA
½ litre of wine in a typical restaurant	£2.24	70p	**40p**	64p	£2.80	£1.20	£1.93	72p	£3.20	£1.50
½ litre of beer, local if available	81p	41p	40p	88p	£1.10	69p	70p	**37p**	96p	£1.75
A cup of coffee	22p	21p	**20p**	42p	40p	48p	35p	21p	57p	£1
A fizzy soft drink	94p	30p	38p	34p	40p	41p	45p	**25p**	70p	85p
A postcard and stamp to send it home	23p	22p	60p	19p	**37p**	35p	46p	23p	35p	20p
Car hire, per week for the cheapest model	£133	£139	£121	£152	£100	£132.82	£68	**£59.37**	£104	£129.50
A gallon of petrol - three-star quality	£1.94	£1.96	£2.40	£1.69	£1.18	**£1.48**	£1.76	£2.31	£1.70	£1.85
A decent cheese roll or sandwich	56p	**37p**	38p	£1.04	£2	89p	50p	65p	£1	85p
An ice cream - street or beach price	34p	**14p**	40p	25p	60p	30p	25p	15p	32p	20p
Current inflation rate	6.5%	12%	12.5%	20%+	3.8%	3%	3.5%	30%	**2.5%**	5.7%
Current exchange rate	11.60 Francs	213 Pesetas	2,305 Lire	147.48 Drachmas	1.41 Dollars	3.90 Marks	4.40 Guilders	191 Escudos	3.12 SW Francs	26.30 Schillings
Rate of exchange five years ago	9	142	1,776	79	2.12	3.88	5	103	3.45	29.90

4 Study the tables below and then answer all the questions which follow.

	1970 (£ million)	1980 (£ million)
visible exports	8 150	47 389
visible imports	8 184	46 211
invisible exports	5 082	25 167
invisible imports	4 269	23 581
investment and other capital flows (net)	+ 545	− 1 418

Table I United Kingdom Balance of Payments, 1970 and 1980

Commodity	1970	1980
manufactured goods	50	44
semi-manufactured goods	34	30
fuels and lubricants	3	14
others	13	12
Destination		
European Community	30	44
other West European countries	16	14
North America	15	11
other developed countries	11	6
oil exporting countries	6	10
rest of world	22	15

Table II Structure of United Kingdom visible exports, 1970 and 1980 (percentages)

(Source: *United Kingdom Balance of Payments*, 1981, HMSO)

(a) What was the current account balance in 1970?

(b) To which of the categories given in Table I would the following transactions belong?
  (i) An American on holiday in Europe pays for his stay at a London hotel.
  (ii) J Brown, a British resident, purchases shares on the New York Stock Exchange.

(c) What major economic development led to the change in the visible balance between 1970 and 1980?

(d) What was the value of UK exports of manufactured goods in 1970?

(e) The section called 'Total Official Financing' has been omitted from Table I.
  (i) Why is this section necessary?
  (ii) Name *two* items that would normally appear in this section.

(f) With reference to Table II:
  (i) Describe the changes in the structure of the UK's visible exports between 1970 and 1980.
  (ii) Explain the causes of these changes.   (London 'O' 1984)

5

Balance of Payments Accounts				
Year	1980	1982	1984	1986
Export of Goods (£)	1000	1200	1300	1300
Imports of Goods (£)	900	1100	1200	1300
Invisible Balance (£)	400	500	600	700

(a) Explain what is meant in the table by the term 'Invisible Balance'.

(b) Give **one** example of an 'Invisible' item.

(c) Describe the trend in earnings from the export of goods over the years 1980 to 1986.

(d) What was the size of the Current Account surplus in 1980?   (N Section A)

6 (a) Explain carefully the differences between a tariff and a quota in international trade.

(b) Apart from tariffs and quotas, describe **two** other ways in which the United Kingdom could reduce its imports from other countries.

(c) Explain **two** reasons why the United Kingdom government may wish to reduce the level of imports.

(d) (i) Draw a graph showing a normal demand curve and a normal supply curve. Label the curves.
  (ii) On your graph, label the axes so that the graph shows the market for pounds sterling (the United Kingdom currency).
  (iii) On your graph, draw the likely effect of a rise in the level of United Kingdom exports on the market. Show clearly how it will affect the market.
  (iv) State the effect that this rise in United Kingdom exports is likely to have on the United Kingdom exchange rate.

7 Free trade occurs when
A countries send food aid to drought areas abroad
B exports are subsidised by governments
C governments do not intervene in trade
D trade takes place without money
(S – multiple choice)

CHAPTER 16

1 (a) Name *three* clearing banks.
  (b) How do banks attempt to reconcile profitability with liquidity? (L)

2 (a) What is meant by the phrase 'the supply of money'?
  (b) By what methods could a central bank limit the growth of the money supply? (London 'O' 1984)

3 In what ways are the functions of a central bank different from those of a commercial bank? (London 'O' 1981)

4 What are some of the factors which cause the Stock Exchange price of a share to change? (London CSE paper 1984)

5 Read the following passage carefully, and then insert a *suitable word or words* in each space:

A stockbroker buys securities on behalf of an investors in a marketplace called the ......
The investor may become a creditor of a company by purchasing a ...... or an owner by buying a share.

If dividends vary with declared profits, the investor has bought an ...... If the investor paid a market price of £5 for shares with a nominal value of £1, and receives a dividend of 50p per share, the percentage yield of the investment is ...... (W)

6 (a) Describe the functions of money.
  (b) State two characteristics of money.
  (c) What are the main types of money in use in the UK?
  (d) Explain the likely effects of a fall in the supply of money on interest rates. (S)

GLOSSARY OF TERMS

ARBITRATION the process of referring a dispute to an independent third party for judgement

BALANCE OF TRADE the difference between the value of visible exports and visible imports

BARTER the direct exchange of goods and services requiring a 'double coincidence of wants'

BILL OF EXCHANGE an international IOU issued by an exporter to the organisation receiving the traded goods or services

BIRTH RATE an indicator of the size of births expressed as the number of 'live' births ($\times 1000$) divided by the total population

CAPITAL GOODS those goods which make the production of consumer (and other capital) goods easier

CAPITAL MARKET a market where finance is raised for long time periods e.g. the Stock Exchange

CENSUS a detailed count of the UK's population taken every 10 years

CHEQUE an IOU signed by the 'drawer' and written to the 'payee'

CLOSED SHOP a situation where obtaining union membership is a condition of working for an organisation

COLLECTIVE BARGAINING the process whereby employers and unions negotiate pay and working conditions

COMMAND ECONOMY an economic system where a central authority 'commands' the use of the factors of production

COMMON AGRICULTURAL POLICY the system of farm support operating in the European Community offering a subsidy to farmers if market prices fall below an agreed level

COMPARATIVE ADVANTAGE a situation in international trade where one country is not only better than another at producing certain goods, but has a much greater advantage in some of those goods rather than the others

CONGLOMERATE MERGER a joining together of two companies where the products or services of each are only indirectly related

CONSUMER GOODS those goods which give pleasure or directly satisfy wants

CURRENT BALANCE used in connection with the Balance of Payments account, it measures the difference between visible and invisible exports and visible and invisible imports

CYCLICAL UNEMPLOYMENT unemployment which arises as economic activity over the whole country declines

DEATH RATE an indicator of the size of deaths measured as the number of deaths ($\times 1000$) divided by total population

DEBENTURE the term used to describe a loan to a limited company

DEFLATION a condition where the government attempts to reduce spending in the economy usually via fiscal or monetary policy

DEPENDENCY RATIO the proportion of dependents (pensioners, children, etc.) in a country relative to the working population

DEVALUATION where exchange rates are fixed between countries a government may decide to lower the value of its own currency against others to boost exports and reduce imports

DISINTEGRATION arises when a company specialises in one part of the production process

DIVISION OF LABOUR arises when production is broken down into a series of simple tasks performed by the workforce

DUMPING occurs when foreign foods are sold in a country, at near or below cost price

ECONOMIES OF SCALE refer to the advantages gained from large-scale production

ENTERPRISE ZONE (largely inner city) areas given special assistance by the government in order to regenerate employment

EQUITIES a Stock Exchange term for ordinary shares

EXCHANGE EQUALISATION ACCOUNT the term used to describe the account at the Bank of England where UK gold and foreign currency reserves are kept

FACTORS OF PRODUCTION the essential resources (land, labour, capital and enterprise) required for production to take place

FISCAL POLICY government policy directed towards changing taxation and expenditure

FRICTIONAL UNEMPLOYMENT unemployment arising through imperfections in the job vacancy market so that people with skills the economy needs may be unaware of appropriate vacancies in other areas

GENERAL AGREEMENT ON TARIFFS AND TRADE (GATT) an international organisation set up in 1948 with the aim of encouraging countries worldwide to reduce their trade barriers

GILT EDGED SECURITY a longterm loan to the government receiving a fixed rate of interest

GROSS DOMESTIC PRODUCT (GDP) a measure of the total goods and services produced within a country over a given time period

HORIZONTAL INTEGRATION the merging together of two firms producing the same or similar products/services at the same stage of production

INDUSTRIAL INERTIA a situation where a firm or industry stays in an area even after the best location position has moved elsewhere

INFANT MORTALITY RATE measures the number of infants who die before reaching the age of 1 (per 1000 live births)

INFLATION the general term for rising prices, more accurately defined as a 'sustained rise in the general level of prices'

INFRASTRUCTURE a term used to describe the capital goods of an area which may (or may not) attract industrial development, such as roads, housing, education, and amenities

INTERDEPENDENCE a word used in connection with large-scale production where one group of workers depend on another for the finished article to be completed

INTERMEDIATE TECHNOLOGY easy to construct capital goods which make production more efficient in less developed countries whilst not putting people out of work

INTERNATIONAL MONETARY FUND came into operation in 1947 to encourage international monetary cooperation and stabilise exchange rates. Its headquarters are based in Washington

INVESTMENT spending on capital goods

INVISIBLE TRADE services provided by the UK for foreigners (invisible exports) or services provided by foreigners for UK residents (invisible imports)

LEGAL TENDER MONEY notes and coins issued by the Bank of England which have to be accepted by law in exchange for goods or services

LIMITED LIABILITY applies to companies with shareholders where their liability (financial risk) is limited to the amount of capital they have invested in the company

LOCALISATION when an industry is substantially located in one specific area it is said to be localised

MACRO ECONOMICS the study of the economy as a whole

MARKET ECONOMY an economic system where wants are expressed by consumers in the form of demand and are satisfied by producers in the form of supply

MERGER the joining together of two producers

MICRO ECONOMICS the study of the individual components of an economic system

MIXED ECONOMY an economic system where some wants are satisfied through the forces of demand and supply and others through the state allocating certain resources to the public provision of goods and services

MONETARY POLICY government policy directed towards changing the amount of money available in the economy

MONEY MARKET the market where finance is raised for short periods of time, usually around 3 months

MONOPOLY where a single firm is the sole supplier of a particular good or service, a monopoly is said to exist

NEGATIVE INCOME TAX a tax system where people are awarded credits for benefits which may exceed their tax bill resulting in a negative amount of tax owed giving entitlement to a positive sum of money from the government

OLIGOPOLY a market where only a small number of sellers exists

OPEN MARKET OPERATIONS a form of monetary policy where the Bank of England can affect the size of bank deposits by selling or buying gilt edged securities on the open market

OPPORTUNITY COST the cost of the foregone alternative, which illustrates the basic economic problem that all wants cannot be satisfied, forcing a choice of alternatives to be made

OPTIMUM POPULATION the appropriate size population which produces the highest income per head

ORDINARY SHARE an entitlement to a full share in the ownership of a company with a variable dividend providing a share of profits

PERFECT COMPETITION a market with a large number of buyers and sellers where an individual firm is unable to influence the market price of the product

PHILLIPS CURVE a curve showing the relationship between unemployment and inflation, implying that the higher the unemployment level, the lower the rate of inflation

PRICES AND INCOMES POLICY a means whereby the government can attempt to control inflation by directly limiting pay rises and the extent to which certain product prices are allowed to rise

PRIMARY PRODUCTION the first stage of production involving the extractive industries

PRODUCTION POSSIBILITY CURVE a curve showing the possible combinations of goods that could be produced with a given amount of factors of production

PUBLIC SECTOR BORROWING REQUIREMENT the amount the government needs to borrow each year to cover the difference between its spending and tax receipts

QUOTA a restriction on the quantity of a good imported from abroad

SECONDARY PRODUCTION the manufacturing stage of the production process

SPECIAL DEPOSITS a form of monetary control where some of the commercial banks' cash deposits at the Bank of England are 'frozen'

STRUCTURAL UNEMPLOYMENT a situation where people possess outdated skills inappropriate to the current needs of the economy

SUBSIDY a means of lowering the cost of production through a government grant to the producer

TARIFF a duty or tax placed on a good coming from abroad

TERMS OF TRADE an index showing the average price of exports ($\times 100$) divided by the average price of imports

TERTIARY PRODUCTION the distributive stage of production also involving other service industries

TOTAL REVENUE the total amount of money received from the sale of a good or service. It can be calculated by multiplying the price or the good or service by the quantity sold

TREASURY BILL a form of short term borrowing by the government for 91 days

UNIT COST the cost of making or providing a single item or unit. Unit costs can be calculated by dividing the number of units supplied into total costs

UNIT TRUSTS a form of saving where a management company buys securities on the savers' behalf with a view to maximising returns on capital outlay

VERTICAL INTEGRATION the merging of two companies making the same or similar products but at different stages in production

VISIBLE TRADE physical goods exported from or imported to the UK

WEALTH TAX a tax on the physical and monetary assets of a person, rather than the income earned

WORLD BANK (International Bank for Reconstruction & Development) a bank sharing the same premises as the International Monetary Fund and providing low interest loans for less developed countries

INDEX